Professional Ethics
and
Social Responsibility

Professional Ethics and Social Responsibility

Edited by
Daniel E. Wueste

ROWMAN AND LITTLEFIELD PUBLISHERS, INC.

ROWMAN & LITTLEFIELD PUBLISHERS, INC.

Published in the United States of America
by Rowman & Littlefield Publishers, Inc.
4720 Boston Way, Lanham, Maryland 20706

3 Henrietta Street
London WC2E 8LU, England

Copyright © 1994 by Rowman & Littlefield Publishers, Inc.

British Cataloging-in-Publication Information Available

Library of Congress Cataloging-in-Publication Data

Professional ethics and social responsibility / edited by Daniel E. Wueste.
p. cm.
Outgrowth of a conference held at Clemson University in Nov. 1991.
Includes bibliographical references and index.
1. Social ethics. 2. Professional ethics. I. Wueste, Daniel E.
HM216.P687 1994 174—dc20 93-48401 CIP

ISBN 0-8476-7815-6 (cloth: alk. paper)
ISBN 0-8476-7816-4 (pbk.: alk. paper)

Printed in the United States of America

 ^{TM} The paper used in this publication meets the minimum requirements of
American National Standard for Information Sciences—Permanence of
Paper for Printed Library Materials, ANSI Z39.48—1984.

Contents

v

Preface

Charges of unethical conduct by professionals are not new. Indeed, in some quarters, they are something of a commonplace. Cases abound: the forced resignation of House Speaker Jim Wright; the savings and loan scandal; the so-called Keating Five of the U.S. Senate, and, in particular, charges of whitewash in the handling of these cases by the Senate Ethics Committee; the BCCI scandal and the indictments of Clark Clifford and Robert Altman; the Iran-contra affair; sadly, this list could be much longer.

Yet, some professionals, for example those involved in scientific research, have seemed to be beyond reproach. Lately, however, such charges have received a great deal of attention, most of it unwelcome. Indeed, in an editorial of March 26, 1991, discussing the "David Baltimore Case," *The New York Times* employed the now-standard linguistic emblem of perfidy when it spoke of a "Scientific Watergate." The halo of science does not glow as brightly as it once did.

Interest in professional ethics and social responsibility is both more intense and widespread than in the past. This is partially explained by the attention allegations of wrongdoing by professionals have received in the media and from lawmakers. But other factors enter into the explanation as well: the large number of "emerging professions"; the increasing and, it seems, unavoidable reliance on professionals—experts—by individuals, the general public, governments, and professionals themselves; the fact that the milieu of professional practice has changed as more and more professional activity is housed and supported by institutions (e.g., hospitals, universities, corporations, government agencies).

Although the high level of interest is new, there is a received view in the area that, among other things, holds that all conflicts of interest are morally problematic and hence to be avoided; that conduct such as that which has brought unwelcome attention to the scientific community is properly attributed to aberrant individuals—bad apples—rather than institutional arrangements—bad barrels; and that scientific autonomy is an unmitigated social good. The papers in this volume challenge these and other elements of the received view. Directing attention to five increasingly interrelated spheres of professional activity—namely, politics, law, engineering, medicine, and science—they probe issues that are properly the concern of professionals and nonprofessionals alike.

This book is the upshot of a conference on professional ethics and social responsibility at Clemson University in November 1991. The conference was supported by a Clemson University Innovation Fund Grant. I am grateful to the university for the support it provided for the conference and the preparation of this volume. I speak for myself and the Department of Philosophy and Religion at Clemson University in expressing gratitude to Mrs. Kathryn C. Lemon. The generosity of Mrs. Lemon and her late husband, C. Calhoun Lemon, has made it possible for the department to sponsor the C. Calhoun Lemon Lecture in Philosophy. The first of these lectures, given by Professor Joel Feinberg, was the keynote address of the conference. I am indebted to several people for suggestions, comments, criticism, and the willingness to lend a hand when it was needed. In particular, I want to thank Joan Callahan, Joy Kroeger-Mappes, Larry May, Bruce Russell, Stephen Satris, Stuart Silvers, J-C. Smith, and Harry van der Linden. Finally, I want to thank my wife, Kathleen, for her support, encouragement, advice, and tolerance. Without her I would be lost.

1

Introduction

Daniel E. Wueste

A person's conduct is guided by and evaluated on the basis of various norms. The most obvious examples are legal and moral norms. There is considerable overlap here but the overlap is not complete. Some acts are legally but not morally required (or permitted) and vice versa. Thus, we speak of legality and morality, of legal obligations and moral obligations. This manner of speaking is appropriate because law and morality are distinct sources of obligation. It also helps to frame the issue in cases of conflicting obligations. Within the moral arena itself we confront a similar situation—some cases of conflicting obligations are intramural—and it is handled in much the same way by, for example, speaking in terms of professional ethics and social responsibility, or private morality and public morality. As we shall see, particularly with cases of conflicting obligations, some of the problems are much the same as well.

Professional Ethics

Talk of professional ethics presupposes a distinction between ethics writ large and the norms of ethical conduct peculiar to a profession. Put another way, it presupposes a distinction between constraints arising "from what it means to be a decent human being"[1] and constraints arising from the enterprise in which one is engaged. The former constitute what Paul Camenisch calls "ethics plain and simple," while the latter constitute an occupational or role morality. Like the law, a professional ethic is not a mere restatement of the norms of ordinary morality (i.e., norms governing human conduct generally); the norms of a professional ethic are tied to an occupation or role. Durkheim put the point and its upshot this way: "The ethics of each

1

profession are localized. . . . Thus centres of a moral life are formed
which, although bound up together, are distinct, and the differentiation
in function amounts to a kind of moral polymorphism."² So, for
example, a physician is permitted to do things that are proscribed by
the standards of ordinary morality (e.g., cut into a person's body and
remove and discard something found there); indeed, in some cases a
physician has an obligation to do such things. And, in general, doing
their work—attending to, representing, or looking after the interests of
a patient or client, for example—professionals are allowed to put to
one side considerations that would be relevant and perhaps decisive in
the ethical deliberations of a nonprofessional. Thus, attorneys are free
to plead the statute of limitations as a bar to a just claim; block the
introduction of illegally seized evidence, thereby undermining the
prosecution's case against a party who is, as a matter of fact, guilty of
a heinous crime; or, as in the celebrated case of Oliver North, convince
a court to overturn a conviction on the basis of a technicality.³
Similarly, scientists may put to one side social, political, and moral
concerns about the uses to which their discoveries may be put. Indeed,
it has been claimed that, as professionals committed to the expansion
of human knowledge, scientists have a moral responsibility not to
forgo inquiry even if the fruits of that inquiry can be put to immoral or
horrendous uses. With this last, especially, what Durkheim called "the
peculiar characteristic of this kind of morals [emerges]: we see in it a
real decentralization of the moral life."⁴ In any case, at this juncture
professional ethics appears to be anything but innocuous.

Social Responsibility

When we speak of social responsibility we direct attention to or invoke
norms that express legitimate and stable expectations respecting the
conduct of persons in positions of public trust or power within a
social practice or institution. Like a professional, an officeholder or
functionary in government (e.g., in the executive, legislative, and
judicial branches of government, agencies such as the Food and Drug
Administration, National Institutes of Health, and Equal Employment
Opportunity Commission, or a local zoning commission) as well as an
officer or functionary in business (including the media), education, or
health care is bound by norms attached to an occupation or role. Here
too, the norms in question are not simply restatements of the norms of
ordinary morality. They constitute distinct norm sets—institutional

role moralities. Thomas Nagel captures the point in a discussion of the apparent discontinuity between private morality and public morality: "[W]hat is morally special about public roles and public action . . . [is that] they alter the demands on the individual."[5] Indeed, as he goes on to say, "the *content* of public obligations differs systematically from that of private ones."[6] Public institutions—Nagel's examples are the state and its agencies, universities, political parties, charitable organizations, and revolutionary movements—"come under a kind of public morality" that accords greater weight to consequences and allows greater latitude respecting means than private morality. These institutions "create the roles to which public obligations are tied."[7] The roles are designed to advance certain interests (e.g., health, safety, justice) and those who occupy them are obligated to serve those interests in ways that are more or less well defined. In accepting these obligations the occupants of such roles "correlatively reduce their right to consider other factors, both their personal interests and more general ones not related to the institution or their role in it."[8]

They may also thereby be licensed to employ means (e.g., coercive, manipulative, or obstructive means) that are otherwise morally disallowed. Thus, an individual acting in an official capacity might be permitted or even required to do things that would be impermissible if judged by the criteria of ordinary morality.[9] For example, as Stuart Hampshire notes in a discussion of moral conflict, the "Chancellor of the Exchequer is not required to respond honestly to questions about a future devaluation of the currency."[10] Other cases are equally straightforward but less agreeable. Consider the case of the public prosecutor. Public prosecutors are permitted to engage in plea bargaining; indeed it has been argued that more often than not circumstances are such that they must. Yet, as Kenneth Kipnis points out, plea bargaining is quite like the gunman situation:

> Both the gunman and the prosecutor require persons to make hard choices between a very certain smaller imposition and an uncertain greater imposition. In the gunman situation I must choose between the very certain loss of my money and the difficult-to-assess probability that my assailant is willing and able to kill me if I resist. As a defendant I am forced to choose between a very certain smaller punishment and a substantially greater punishment with a difficult-to-assess probability. . . . Of course the gunman's victim can try to overpower his assailant and the defendant can attempt to clear himself at trial. But the same considerations that will drive reasonable people to give in to the gunman compel one to accept the prosecutor's offer. . . . In both cases reasonable persons

might well conclude (after considering the gunman's lethal weapon or the gas chamber) "I can't take the chance."[11]

In such cases, the moral principles governing official action are different from those governing private action. This is more than a little troubling. There will be questions respecting the propriety of action sanctioned by principles of institutional morality, of course. But not only that. Because a person who accepts a public role runs the risk that fulfilling her role responsibilities will require actions on her part that fly in the face of other obligations she has or principles that she accepts,[12] there will be questions respecting the role that makes such acts obligatory as well as concern that in accepting the role one puts one's personal integrity in jeopardy. Here, then, as in the case of professional ethics, there is what Durkheim called "a kind of moral polymorphism" and "a real decentralization of the moral life." Durkheim would certainly agree; however, on his view, there would be no reason to say "as in the case of professional ethics," for at this level of generality there is one case rather than two.

Professions—Salient Features and Characteristic Claims

When Durkheim spoke of professions and professional ethics, no occupation was excluded.[13] Contemporary usage of the terms "profession" and "professional" is less generous. However, the criteria for the application of the term "profession" are not fixed. Both the definitional literature on professions and the critical literature about it are extensive. Thus, it has frequently been noted that there is no generally accepted definition of the term "profession."[14] Some writers suggest that although there is no set of necessary and sufficient conditions for the application of the term, among the characteristics common to recognized professions some are necessary or essential. The idea is that with these in mind it will be possible to mark a serviceable distinction between professional and nonprofessional occupations. Of course, disagreement respecting a characteristic claimed to be essential is possible and, in fact, such disagreements do exist among writers who take this tack. Still, one thing is clear: contemporary usage of the term is honorific.[15] This fact largely explains the movement to professionalize that is prominent in many occupations. It also suggests that there is a normative dimension to the notion of a profession.

Michael Bayles identifies three necessary features of a profession: (i) extensive training that (ii) involves a significant intellectual component and (iii) puts one in a position to provide an important service to society. According to Bayles, other features are common but not essential; for example, the existence of a process of certification or licensing, an organization of members of the profession, monopoly control of tasks, self-regulation, and autonomy in work. Several of these, in particular the last three, cannot properly be regarded as essential because so many professionals work in bureaucratic organizations where tasks are shared (often grudgingly) and activities are directed and controlled by superiors.[16] On this view, an occupation may be a profession even though it lacks certain features common to most professions. Although sociologists are divided on the question whether normative features are among the defining features of a profession (a question Bayles answers emphatically in the negative[17]), few, if any, would disagree with this last point.

From the sociological perspective, there is "no absolute difference" that distinguishes professional from other occupational behavior; different forms of occupational behavior manifest varying degrees of professionalism. As Bernard Barber puts it, some occupational behavior is "fully professional," some is "partly professional," and some is properly regarded as "barely or not at all professional." Barber identifies "four essential attributes [that] define a scale of professionalism, a way of measuring the extent to which it is present in different forms of occupational performance." The first of these attributes, "a high degree of generalized and systematic knowledge," is also an element of Bayles's characterization. From this point on, however, their lists of necessary or essential features differ.

Barber argues for the other attributes on his list on the basis of functional assumptions common to the Parsons tradition in the sociological study of professions. Again, professional behavior involves generalized and systematic knowledge. Because such knowledge is a source of power and control over nature and society, where it exists, the "orientation [of those who possess it] is primarily to community rather than individual interest." In professional behavior, the latter "is subserved *indirectly*." The third attribute is connected to the first two. Social control, which, among other things, imposes constraints on the pursuit of self-interest, can be enlightened and effective only if the behavior to be controlled is understood. If the behavior in question involves a high degree of knowledge, only those who have been "trained in and apply that knowledge" will have the requisite understanding. Thus, Barber concludes, in the case of professional behavior, "some kind of self-control . . . is necessary." And, he says, as a matter of fact, professional behavior is subject to a kind of self-control; it is governed by normative standards of community orientation (e.g., codes of ethics) that are "internalized in the process of work socialization" and voluntary associations organized and operated by those who possess the generalized and specialized knowledge. The fourth attribute is linked to the second and third. Because professional behavior is oriented primarily to community interest, and because prestige and honors rather than money are the forms of social reward appropriate to behavior with this orientation, the "actual reward system in the professions tends to consist . . . in a combination of prestige and titles, medals, prizes, offices in professional societies, and so forth, together with a sufficient monetary income for the style of life appropriate to the honor bestowed." On the whole, Barber says, professionals are not paid as well as persons in "equal-ranking business roles in American society." Yet studies show that the professions are consistently at the top of the occupational prestige hierarchy and that professionals themselves are more satisfied with their work-rewards than members of other occupational groups.[18]

Another sociologist, Everett C. Hughes, identifies what he calls characteristics and collective claims of the professions. Like Barber, Hughes thinks that professions evolve. But Hughes and his followers— who work in what has come to be called the Hughes tradition—tend to concentrate on workplace studies and eschew functionalist logic. For the Hughes tradition, professions evolve and this evolution is interactional; it is the product of negotiation in an environment. Professional evolution is influenced by functional nature and environmental nurture.

According to Hughes, professions provide esoteric services. These services are provided to individuals, organizations, governments, or the general public in the form of advice or action or both. Actions taken by professionals, some of which may be manual, are accompanied by an assumption or claim to the effect that they are determined by "esoteric knowledge systematically formulated and applied" to the problem at hand. Thus it appears that professional services always include advice. Either the advice itself constitutes the service or, at a minimum, the person upon whom or for whom the service is performed (or another person thought to have a right or duty to act *in hoc*) is advised that the action of the professional is necessary. The crucial point for Hughes is that professionals "profess to know better than others the nature of certain matters, and to know better than their clients what ails them or their affairs." Indeed, according to Hughes, that "is the essence of the professional idea and the professional claim." Its consequences are many. It reaches to matters of jurisdiction: "professionals claim the exclusive right to practice, as a vocation, the arts which they profess to know." This claim is the basis of the "license" a professional has to deviate from lay conduct in action and in her mode of thought with respect to matters within her area of expertise. The license and the "institutionalized deviation" it allows may be understood in the narrow sense of legal privilege, though it need not be understood in this way. Professionals have a license in a broad sense as well: the public allows them a certain leeway in their practice and expects that their thinking and judgment will differ from that of laypersons because expertise blunts the normally substantial influence of orthodoxy and sentiment.

The exclusive right to practice is not the only jurisdictional upshot of the claim to esoteric knowledge: "Every profession considers itself the proper body to set the terms in which some aspect of society, life or nature is to be thought of and to define the general lines or even the details of public policy with respect to it." The character of the professional relation and the notion of self-regulation are implicated as well. Because they profess, professionals ask that they be trusted. Hughes says that in the arena of professional activity the rule is *credat emptor*. That the "buyer" in the professional relation is to give credence or to trust is significant; it distinguishes the professional relation from the relation that obtains in markets where the rule is *caveat emptor*. In general, nonprofessionals are not in a position to evaluate the judgments, advice, and performance of professionals because they lack the expertise professionals possess—professionals claim and are thought to know better than others the nature of the matters that fall within the province of their profession. Consequently, only professionals judge professionals. At any rate, as Hughes notes, professionals "make it very difficult for any one outside—even civil courts—to pass judgement upon one of their number."[19]

Professionalization

A common theme in the sociological literature on the professions is that there is a pattern or trend in the development of professions.

This notion of professionalization arose as successive answers to the definitional question proved inadequate in the face of the diversity of professional life. The idea of a common pattern in the development of professions makes it somewhat easier to handle troublesome cases of classification. The question whether a particular occupation, say, social work, is a profession can be answered—parsimoniously—in terms of its present position on the ladder of professionalization. Taking this approach, one tends to the view that professional status is an end state that few have reached.

Andrew Abbott is a critic of the notion and theory of professionalization. Although there are several theories of professionalization (e.g., functional, structural, monopolist, and cultural), Abbott argues that the various views can be synthesized into a general concept of professionalization. Abbott points to some grave difficulties with this concept and the synthetic theory of professionalization. Most troubling of all is that "its basic assumptions have all been overthrown by recent empirical work."[20] Professionalization theorists assume, wrongly, that the evolution of professions is unidirectional; that the development of individual professions does not depend on that of others; that what professions do—the work as well as the requisite expertise—is less important than how they are organized to do it; that professions are homogeneous units; and that the process of professionalization does not change over time.

Abbott maintains that "profession is not 'objectively' definable precisely because of its power and importance in our culture." Moreover, he argues that "a firm definition of profession is both unnecessary and dangerous."[21] Definitions, he says, "must follow from theoretical questions"—a definition is a means rather than an end. What one needs is a working concept adequate for the purpose at hand. Abbott sets out to develop a theory of professional development that, unlike the synthetic account of professionalization, is both *historically* and sociologically sound. Thus, he defines the term "profession" loosely—"professions are exclusive occupational groups applying somewhat abstract knowledge to particular cases"[22]—arguing that abstract knowledge is the basis of an effective definition of professions. The crucial point here is that while many occupations battle over turf, "only professions expand their cognitive dominion by using abstract knowledge to annex new areas, to define them as their own proper work."[23] Abbott also "reverses" the assumptions of professionalization theories.

Unlike earlier studies of professions, which were based on an individualistic view of professions and focused on parallels in organizational development—national association, governmental licensing, professional examinations, professional journal, ethics code, etc.—Abbott's historical sociology of the professions focuses on the contents of professional activity and the larger social setting in which that activity takes place. From the perspective of historical sociology, the central phenomenon of professional life is jurisdiction—control over a set of tasks—and jurisdiction is the upshot of competition. Each profession is bound to a set of tasks by ties of jurisdiction that turn on expertise *and* the success of jurisdictional claims made in the legal system, the workplace (typically an organization or institution), or the arena of public opinion. (Whether a claim succeeds is largely a matter of fit with legitimizing social values.) Because professions often seek new turf and technological developments and organizational or political changes create, subdivide, or eliminate tasks, jurisdictional stability is merely temporary. "Vacancies" and "bumps" that create movement are inevitable. And, because jurisdiction is more or less exclusive, "every move in one profession's jurisdictions affects those of others."[24] Thus, the central claim of Abbott's historical sociology of the professions is that professions constitute an interdependent and interacting system, "an ecology."[25] The pace of developments outside the system that create and subdivide tasks requiring expertise is rapid. As a consequence, reliance on professionals (experts) by individuals, the general public, governments—the very "audiences" that hear and adjudicate jurisdictional claims—and professionals themselves is increasing. Thus, it seems clear that here, as in the more familiar context of environmental concerns, it is important to recognize an ecological system for what it is, if it is seen as valuable and worth preserving.

Professionalism and the Institutionalization of Expertise

In industrialized countries, professionalism has been the main way of institutionalizing expertise. But, as Abbott points out, it is not the only way. Expertise can be institutionalized in people, things—many "forms of esoteric expertise can easily be reduced to a series of keystrokes"—or rules.[26] Thus, professionalism competes with alternative means of institutionalizing expertise; in particular, commodification and bureaucratic organization. This competition can have a profound effect on the milieu of professional activity.

According to Abbott, professionalism exists because (i) a market-based occupational structure favors employment based on personally held resources and one such resource is knowledge; (ii) nearly every kind of knowledge can be organized as a common resource for a group of individuals—there are few limits to professionalization "in the sense of creating a coherent occupational group with some control of an abstract expertise"; and (iii) competing forms of institutionalization have not yet overwhelmed it.[27] Not yet. As it happens, commodification has not made substantial gains on the professions in the past century. Moreover, it seems that this process opens the door to new professions devoted to the development, maintenance, and support of things that embody expertise. Yet, because ownership and operation of "professional commodities" by nonprofessionals is increasing, some believe that the very idea of professionalism is in danger.

On Abbott's view, however, the threat here is not great. Noting that organization destroyed craft labor—highly skilled tasks can be accomplished by unskilled persons when the division of labor is machine based—Abbott contends that commodification is much less menacing to professionalism than organization. As he sees it, professionalism is likely to continue to hold its own against commodification, but organization (bureaucratized organizations) may well win the contest with professionalism. In any case, the existence of multiprofessional firms in accounting and architecture, the team concept in social services and medicine, and elaborate bureaucracies in engineering and law show that professional work has already been significantly restructured. Moreover, most of these organizations "are either overtly heteronomous or governed by professionals more or less openly identified as professional administrators . . . [and they] clearly seek to maximize both the quantity of expertise institutionalized in their arrangements and the economic returns to that quantity."[28]

For most of the twentieth century and certainly since World War II, this last statement would be an apt description of the work environment of professional scientists. It can scarcely be doubted that the description is apt in the case of scientists in academe. And, in any case, a professional scientist is more likely to be a researcher with an industrial laboratory or a government agency than a professor at a university.[29] Moreover, although the public continues to think of professional life in terms of solo, independent practice, today "only about 50 percent of even doctors and lawyers are in independent practice."[30] Indeed, recent census data reveal that professionals who work alone are in the minority.[31] Our image of the professional does not match the reality of professional life. Modern professionals characteristically work in an institutional setting.[32]

Professions and Institutions

Although Bayles, Barber, Hughes, and Abbott do not agree on every particular, they do agree on several points that, taken together, provide a helpful picture of professions and professional activity. The picture we get is rather like a sketch made by a police artist who works with descriptions provided by various witnesses. (1) One distinguishing feature of professions is the centrality of abstract knowledge in the performance of occupational tasks. (2) A second distinguishing feature is the social significance of the tasks the professional performs—professional activity promotes basic social values. (3) Professionals claim to be better situated/qualified than others to pronounce and act on certain matters. This claim reaches beyond the interests and affairs of clients. Experts believe that they should define various aspects of society, life, and nature and we generally agree. We defer to them (or at least our elected representatives do) in matters of public policy and national defense and, of course, expert testimony is prominent in both civil and criminal litigation. (4) On the basis of their expertise and the importance of the work that requires it, professionals claim to be and have been recognized as being governed (in their professional conduct) by role-specific norms rather than the norms that govern human conduct generally. The final element of our composite picture is (5) that most professionals work in bureaucratic institutions.

With the last point it is important to remember that institutions not only form networks but may overlap or be "nested"; that is, one institution may be housed in another (one or more) as when a hospital is part of a college in a university that is state supported. The point is important because professions themselves are institutional. Professions exist in a social context where the claims noted above are made and accepted (or not) and the results of professional activity are manifest. Professions are instituted, set up, established, and brought into use or practice. They are organized, purposeful arrangements for the channeling of human energy in the pursuit of specified ends. They standardize a set of social relations and fix social roles; they are products of the institutionalization of expertise. In a word, they are institutions.

In the sociological sense of the term, an "institution" is a more or less stable set of roles defined by complementary expectations that arise (and change) as human beings interact. The interaction is purposive; an institution has a purpose (or purposes)—realization of a value (or values) shared by the parties who interact within its relational structure. In other words, an institution answers to a perceived need. People who share values tend to behave in ways that accord with what they expect of each other and they regard this conformity as a good thing even when it seems to go against their own immediate self-interest. Thus, an institution is a particular type of normative pattern; conformity to this pattern is expected and nonconformity is generally met with moral indignation. The point can be put another way. Institutions consist of roles. A role is a position one occupies (or a capacity in which one acts) within a social relationship that is (i) neither transitory nor spontaneous and (ii) associated with a pattern of conduct—a more or less diffuse notion of appropriate conduct—recognized "in the breach as well as in the observance."[33] This is a more or less standard view. It is fine as far as it goes. But as C. Wright Mills points out, it does not go far enough: "the roles making up an institution are not usually just one big 'complementarity' of 'shared expectations.' "

For example, Mills says, an army, a factory, and a family are institutions and in each case there is an element of power—"the expectations of some [parties] seem just a little more urgent"—that the notion of complementarity conceals; "an institution is a set of roles graded in authority."[34] Institutions then, consist of roles carrying different degrees of authority. We should be cautious too not to be misled by the notion of consent implicit in talk of shared values. Consent can be managed or manipulated as well as fairly won and only the last involves the reason or conscience of the consenting party (i.e., moral cachet).[35] Moreover, acquiescence may be mistaken for consent. These last points are clearly apposite in the case of bureaucratic institutions, for, among other things, bureaucracies involve lines of authority. But they also reach to institutional arrangements that are not bureaucratic, in particular, the role relation of (an independent) professional and client—the arrangement preferred by professional ideology.

In this institutional setting, the professional has more authority than the client or patient. As individuals, both the client and the professional enter the relation with some authority—the moral authority possessed by each person that is captured in the notion of autonomy. But—the crucial point—the professional has epistemic authority as well. The client or patient recognizes this, of course. The professional is seen as a source of expert advice or help. Moreover, it often happens that the need or interest that prompts the client to seek professional help can neither be fully understood nor handled without professional assistance. Thus, the professional's expertise explains the client's entrance into the relation and the fact that the person in a professional role is in a position of authority (i.e., a position in which another defers to one's judgments as largely, if not completely, determinative of a course of action to be taken).

The authority associated with a professional role, as distinct from the individual moral authority of the person who functions as a professional, is the upshot of consent. Given the epistemic inequality of professional and client, however, it is clear that this consent may be managed or manipulated as well as fairly won. Indeed, the possibility for exploitation of the client by the professional is recognized on all sides. Thus, the points made above apply to the institutional arrangements we call professions.

According to economist Kenneth Arrow, there is a special need for the institutionalization of social responsibility in economic relations when "there is a very large difference in knowledge between the buyer and the seller."[36] Such relations often obtain in business (e.g., with automobiles, drugs, and other chemicals). Arrow argues that in such cases (i) "the simple rule of maximizing profits is socially inefficient" and (ii) the institutionalization of social responsibility can make "a great contribution to economic efficiency."[37] Although the argument itself is not directly on point for present purposes, his examples of successful institutionalization of social responsibility are on point. According to Arrow, examples of success (which he cashes out in terms of economic efficiency) in this regard are not hard to find. They are part of our everyday lives. The professions are paradigmatic cases of epistemically unequal economic relations in which social responsibility has been institutionalized.

In medicine, for example, "there is a strong presumption that the doctor is going to perform to a large extent with your welfare in mind."[38] This presumption is an upshot of an ethical code consisting of norms that "have grown up over the centuries" to limit the possibility of exploitation by a physician and assure the patient—the buyer of medical services—that she is not being exploited. Here, restraint is achieved not by appealing to individual conscience but by means of a "generally understood definition of appropriate behavior."[39] This notion of appropriate conduct is a source of benefit for both the patient and the physician; put another way, it makes the relationship "a viable one."

> The fact is that if you had sufficient distrust of a doctor's services, you wouldn't buy them. Therefore the physician wants an ethical code to act as assurance to the buyer, and he certainly wants his competitors to obey the same code, partly because any violation may put him at a disadvantage but more especially because the violation will reflect on him, since the buyer of the medical services may not be able to distinguish one doctor from another.[40]

The point respecting viability, which, Arrow says, holds for professions generally, is familiar.

As we noted earlier, professions are the products of the institutionalization of expertise. They standardize a set of social relations and fix social roles and "a role relation . . . has some notion of conduct as appropriate or inappropriate built into its description."[41] When Arrow says that a professional ethic (or a code of ethics in business) is a means of institutionalizing social responsibility, he suggests, rightly, that the moral constraints it creates attach to a position or role and thereby to an individual who occupies it rather than the other way around. The rights, duties, privileges, and immunities of a professional are institutional.

There are, of course, other means of institutionalizing social responsibility. That is to say, there are other ways of creating institutional rights, duties, privileges, and immunities. Arrow points to the law—statutes, case law, and administrative regulations; bureaucratic organization is another such means. Each of these methods for creating normative relations involves a considerable amount of formality as well as a structure of authority.[42] Yet, as with a professional ethic, the normative institutional constraints they create attach to roles.[43] Some of these roles are quite plainly professional (for example, the role of a consulting engineer, attorney, or physician); others (for example, the role of a city planner, an adviser to the president, or the director of a government agency such as the National Institutes of Health) are (arguably) not professional in the sense that they constitute a profession, though they are often occupied by professionals—engineers, scientists, lawyers, doctors. In either situation, the professional's role is governed by more than one set of institutional norms. Examples abound. Often they are the stuff of front-page news. For instance, on page one of *The New York Times* of January 3, 1993, in a story about the cancellation of an observance of World AIDS day at St. Vincent's Hospital in New York (a Catholic institution), one learns that physicians there may not advise AIDS patients respecting the use of condoms, abortion, or the cleaning of hypodermic needles used for intravenous drugs. This institutional constraint is surely not a part of their professional ethic. Indeed, according to one physician at St. Vincent's, who requested that he not be named in the story for fear of losing his job, because many H.I.V. patients continue to have an active sex life and some still use drugs, the risk of re-infection with different strains of the virus as well as the risk that others will be infected is quite real; consequently, compliance with this institutional constraint "would be tantamount to malpractice."

The case of Dr. Michel Garretta, former head of the National Blood Transfusion Center in France, illustrates the second sort of situation. In the spring of 1985 it was clear that the French supplies of a blood-clotting substance needed by hemophiliacs was contaminated with the AIDS virus. French hemophiliacs could have been protected if then-available techniques for decontaminating blood tainted with H.I.V. had been used or if the tainted supplies had been replaced. The technology was developed in the United States. So either way, the French would have been relying on American science—something that the French government was loath to do, especially given the dispute between the two countries over who first isolated an AIDS virus central to the development of commercial blood tests for AIDS—and the cost would have been substantial (one estimate put the cost at $40 million).

Although Garretta was aware of these possibilities, he ordered that the supplies be used until they were exhausted. (They were withdrawn in October 1985, after the French decontamination process became available.) As a result, some 1,500 hemophiliacs were infected; 300 have already died. In October 1992, Dr. Garretta was convicted on charges of "fraudulent description of goods" in the distribution of tainted blood and sentenced to four years in prison (the maximum sentence allowed). In Garretta's defense it was argued that his superiors were aware of the dangers and that he acted as an agent within a bureaucracy committed to safeguarding the prestige of French science. In short, he was fulfilling his role responsibilities. Though here, plainly, the responsibilities in question do not arise from the ethic of his profession and the conviction suggests that they fly in the face of the law.[44] Again, a role occupied by a professional is governed by more than one set of institutional norms.

To be sure, the claim that Garretta was fulfilling his role responsibilities may be doubted. Indeed, it might be claimed that he had no obligation to do what he did. Putting the point this way, however, discloses little; it suggests an overly simple picture of the situation and seems to say nothing else than that he acted wrongly. It also seems to ignore the fact that he did have role responsibilities; absent a reason for doing so, this is plainly ill advised. It might be reasonable to ignore the role responsibilities Garretta had as head of the National Blood Transfusion Center, if he had stood to gain financially from his action. But there is nothing in the record to suggest that he had a financial interest in the decision. Moreover, not only Garretta but others outside of the government, mostly critics of the health bureaucracy in France, have suggested that he was doing what was expected of him in his job.

The critic's point, which presupposes institutional role responsibilities, is not that Garretta himself was blameless (or less blameworthy) but that the institution itself is subject to moral criticism. This point is well taken. Especially so, since, as Dorothy Emmet observes, "to seek explanations of our misfortunes in the machinations of ill-disposed persons is the most primitive and natural way in which we all think until we have become sufficiently sophisticated to think otherwise."[45] It is welcome for another reason. The evaluation of an institution raises questions of institutional design and these, in turn, force recognition of the fact that the responsibilities of a role may be misinterpreted or mistakenly regarded as weighty enough to override others that call for a quite different decision and action.

Professional Ethics and Social Responsibility

Normative institutional constraints on professional activity arise from various sources. A professional ethic is one of these. The law, bureaucratic organization, and social morality also create such constraints. The law differs from the others in several ways, particularly with respect to the scope of its claim of authority and its coercive power. And, in any case, as far as professional responsibilities are concerned, law is properly regarded as setting out a bare minimum. Professional ethics differs from bureaucratic organization and social morality in having a narrower scope. The scope of the norms of bureaucratic organization is somewhat greater than that of a professional ethic— they govern nonprofessionals as well as professionals—and considerably less than that of social morality. Writers on professional ethics agree on this point.

However, with respect to the moral thrust of the norms in each set, they flesh it out in different ways. Apart from subtle differences, what distinguishes their accounts is their acceptance or rejection of the subsumption thesis. Subsumptionists hold that professional ethics is subsumed by social morality and that social morality, in turn, is subsumed by critical morality. Nonsubsumptionists hold that a professional ethic has a smaller domain than social morality and that its authority within this domain is a result of its moral justification as an institution. (In each case, the point holds, *mutatis mutandis*, for the norms of bureaucratic organization.) Either way, a professional ethic governs in a field that is within the jurisdiction of another (one or more) set of institutional norms that is more far-reaching. Moreover, and again on either account, a professional ethic and the institution it governs are within the scope of noninstitutional morality (i.e., critical morality or ethics plain and simple) and subject to moral evaluation in its terms. Thus, in discussions of professional ethics and social responsibility there is good reason to resist the temptation to reduce the former to the latter.

A profession is more than a collection of persons with similar expertise and jurisdiction. It is a social institution. Acting within it, a professional has special prerogatives and vital responsibilities in promoting and sustaining certain values that, rightly or wrongly, are thought to be best served by those with the expertise. Professional relations are institutional relations; these relations both stand alone—solo practice—and obtain within larger institutions. In the case of solo practice as well as practice within an institution such as a hospital, university, court, government agency, or industrial laboratory, a professional occupies an institutional role; the "license" or "privilege" and the responsibilities that attach to such roles are elements of the social charter of an institution. Yet, as Dennis Thompson remarks, "ethics, both as an academic discipline and as concrete practice, has tended to focus either on relations among individuals, or on the structures of society as a whole. It has neglected . . . institutions . . . [which] are the site of many of our most difficult moral problems, as well as the source for many of our most promising solutions." In order to address adequately the problems in this largely unexplored area, it will be necessary to "go beyond the moral principles of individual ethics, yet stop short of taking on at once the whole structure of society." In particular, Thompson continues, it will be necessary to "take the idea of roles seriously, and the relation of roles to the institutional structures in which they are situated."[46] Focusing attention on professional ethics and social responsibility, the contributors to this volume have undertaken to explore this territory.

One of the most vexing problems of professional ethics and social responsibility is the problem of dirty hands. Crudely stated, the notion of dirty hands covers cases in which an individual, usually acting in an official capacity, is obligated to do something wrong. The idea is that the agent cannot fulfill a pressing responsibility without getting her hands dirty—the act, which is necessary, has a negative moral residue. Discussing the problem of dirty hands in what many regard as its natural habitat—namely, politics—C.A.J. Coady says that the issue of dirty hands "is not special to politics, though there are some aspects of politics which perhaps raise the issue more acutely or dramatically."[47] Yet, as Kenneth Winston observes in his contribution to this volume, there is a sharp division of opinion respecting dirty hands even among political theorists. Some, whom Winston calls realists, hold that there are occasions when public officials are morally obligated to engage in acts that are morally wrong. Others, whom Winston calls idealists, deny this holding that no one is or could be morally required to act wrongly. (A similar division exists among writers on professional ethics.)

Winston suggests that, in part at least, the disagreement here is the result of confusion with respect to the claim being made. Accordingly, he undertakes to "clarify the moral geography of dirty hands." He distinguishes three quite different situations that are confounded in the debate—situations involving the necessity of (i) tragic choices, (ii) benign corruption, and (iii) moral opportunism—and argues that the issue in dirty hands cases should be framed in terms of role obligations rather than an opposition between utilitarianism and absolutism. Focusing attention on actual rather than hypothetical cases and, in particular, cases of conflicting moral demands within a single sphere of role-governed activity, Winston explains and defends the realist's position and presents some trenchant criticisms of idealists such as Alan Donagan and John Noonan.

Like Winston, Larry May addresses a perennial topic in professional ethics. And again like Winston, he challenges and presents an alternative to the traditional view in an effort to clarify "the picture of a certain part of the moral landscape we call professional life." According to the traditional view, conflicts of interest are to be avoided because they are morally problematic, and they are morally problematic because they compromise objective professional judgment. May rejects this view. Embracing the postmodern perspective of Jean-

François Lyotard, May eschews the modernist assumption that "the self can be objective and unconflicted in its judgments" and maintains that it is a mistake "to think that all, or even most, conflicts of interest should be avoided." It is a mistake, May argues, because (i) conflicts of interest are often inevitable—they are rampant in most professions—and (ii) "conflicts of interest per se are not morally problematic"; *some* conflicts of interest are morally problematic, not for the reason cited by the tradition, but because they involve deception or the infringement of client autonomy.

May's position respecting conflicts of interest runs headlong into the American ideal of professional life. This ideal is modeled on the way lawyers in our society conceive of themselves; namely, as fiduciaries who single-mindedly pursue the interests of their clients. And, as May points out, it presupposes a modernist conception of the self. Arguing that this ideal should be abandoned, May identifies several factors that make it unrealistic to think that professionals can offer "virtually total loyalty" in serving the interests of their clients. Moreover, he argues that professionals who encourage clients to believe that they can are guilty of deception—"they betray the trust they have solicited." His brief for the rejection of the modernist conception of self is prominent here, but it does not stand alone. He also points to features of professional life (e.g., that professionals provide their services for a fee, often work in large bureaucratic organizations, and are expected to serve not only the interests of their clients, but larger societal interests such as public safety or justice) that render the notion of "virtually total loyalty" quite suspicious. Having argued for the overthrow of the reigning ideal, May closes with a discussion of a new model for understanding the fiduciary duties of professionals that is in keeping with the postmodern conception of the self and the familiar idea of role morality.

John Hardwig's understanding of the professions is quite in line with the composite picture developed above. For among other things, he holds that professionals occupy social positions that involve special rights and responsibilities—prestige and above-average incomes too— because of their presumed expertise. Today, reliance on experts is ubiquitous. It could hardly be otherwise, for what is known exceeds the capacity of any individual knower and thus intellectual specialization is inevitable. Indeed, Hardwig argues that an attempt at epistemic self-reliance would be "sheer folly," even for an expert within her own field of expertise; our rationality and knowledge require reliance on experts.

Hardwig claims that there must be an ethics of expertise. In an effort to reveal its salient features, he focuses attention on the relationship between experts and those who appeal and defer to their judgment—the "expert-layperson relationship." Three points that emerge from his analysis are especially important. First, this relationship is grounded on an epistemic inequality. Power on one side is matched by vulnerability on the other. The vulnerability of the layperson is, in fact, a consequence of the epistemic superiority that justifies appeal to experts in the first place. Second, the role of a layperson is taken by experts as well as nonexperts; experts cannot avoid appealing and deferring to other experts even within their own field of expertise. Third, and most important, Hardwig shows that this relationship involves an ineluctable element of trust. Because we must trust experts as persons, there must be an ethics of expertise. In general, however, we do not know experts as persons; we know them as occupants of a social role. Moreover, experts know laypersons in the same way; though vulnerable, a layperson is also an agent. Accordingly, the ethics of expertise reaches to persons—experts and laypersons—via their roles or positions in an established form of social relationship. Some of its maxims—Hardwig discusses seventeen candidates—are addressed to experts while others are addressed to those who appeal to experts. "The ethics of expertise is not a one-way street."

As we noted at the outset, there is a distinction between the ethic of a profession and ethics plain and simple. The former has a narrow scope; it is tied to a role or occupation—it is a role morality. The latter is not similarly limited in scope; it applies to human conduct generally. There is another important difference here; namely, that the former is, while the latter is not, institutional. Unlike ethics plain and simple, a professional ethic/role morality is instituted, set up, established, by human action (which may but need not take the form of quasi-legislative action). This distinction explains a commonplace in professional ethics: a role agent may be obligated to perform an act that is wrong. It also raises the question whether the agent would/could be justified in performing the act. Or put another way, the query is whether a justification that invokes the norms of a role morality (i.e., an institutional justification) can carry the day when what it justifies is condemned by ethics plain and simple.

Daniel Wueste argues that the decision to take role moralities seriously entails an affirmative answer to this question; it involves a commitment to the proposition that role obligations may carry the day in cases where they conflict with obligations imposed by noninstitutional morality. This decision entails other commitments as well. Wueste identifies five others. They emerge in his discussion of a position that (he argues) seems to but does not take role moralities seriously. Having identified these commitments, Wueste turns to the problem of conflicting obligations. In particular, he discusses four ways of dealing with conflicts between institutional and noninstitutional obligations. He argues that two of these are ruled out by the decision to take role moralities seriously and that heuristic and idiographic considerations tip the balance in favor of the proposition that there is (or should be) a presumption in favor of institutional obligations.

The case he presents for this presumption is consistent with the commitments entailed by the decision to take role moralities seriously. Accordingly, it presupposes that the institution is morally justified. It also presupposes recognition of the fact that the stability, persistence, and vitality of an institution's justificatory capacity are human achievements rather than logical consequences. That role agents understand this and are committed to the task of maintaining the integrity of the institution is vitally important.

There is more than one source of difficulty for a professional who wonders whether a contemplated action is right. It is apparent that a professional may find that the answer varies as the matter is considered in terms of professional obligations, social responsibilities, or ordinary morality. For instance, it may happen that the ethics of a profession are silent on the matter, thereby suggesting that the action is permissible; while on the other hand, thinking in terms of social responsibility or ordinary morality, it is clear that one ought to refrain from the action. Such a case is possible but it presents little difficulty; surely the implication of silence is overridden by a clear voice on the other side. A problematic and familiar sort of case involves genuine normative discord: the ethics of a profession speak to the matter in a straightforward way permitting or requiring action (e.g., maintaining strict confidentiality) that seems to (and perhaps does) serve the interests of the profession or the client at unacceptably high cost to the interests of society.

There is another possibility; namely, that the professional is not in a position to determine whether or to what extent an action jeopardizes societal interests in, say, safety, health, or welfare. The problem here is one of competence rather than conflict; one knows what one's obligation is, or at any rate one can provide a coherent and meaningful statement of the norm that imposes it, but the difficulty remains. The question whether the action is right is unanswered. Robert Baum addresses this difficulty in his contribution to this volume. In particular, Baum argues that the paramountcy clause of engineering codes of ethics—engineers shall hold "paramount the safety, health and welfare of the public . . ."—puts an unacceptably high burden of responsibility on engineers. That there is a moral "ought-to-be" here is undeniable. Yet, this moral "ought-to-be," like the moral ought-to-be in the claim "there ought to be no undeserved suffering," seems to be unrealizable in the real world. And for much the same reason—namely, that what is sought cannot be attained by individual effort.

What is required here is collaboration among the parties whose interests are at stake. While such collaboration clearly cannot obviate the risks involved, mitigation is a real possibility. Moreover, Baum argues, such collaboration would not only make the responsibility more manageable, it would enhance the moral tenability of the engineer's position because it blunts the charge of parentalism and evinces a respect for individual rights. Like Hardwig, Baum argues that professionals and experts function in a social context where responsibility must be shared; here we are traveling on a two-way street.

At one point in his discussion of conflicts of interest, Larry May asks, rhetorically, whether if he is right that conflicts of interest are rampant in most professions, students should be advised not to become professionals. After all, we should discourage people from getting involved in activities that put their moral integrity at risk. As it happens, the question whether an individual can be both a good person and a good lawyer has been taken quite seriously. Those who suggest that the answer is negative argue that the ethical standards of the legal profession create a conception of the lawyer's role that inspires hyperzealous advocacy and gives short shrift to moral accountability. The upshot is a compartmentalization of the lawyer's life and person that makes it very difficult, if not impossible, to be both a good person and a good lawyer.

In her contribution to this volume, Serena Stier contends that this view, which she attributes to critics of role differentiation, is misguided and that the question itself is mistaken. She argues that these critics err in attaching the morality of a particular role to the personhood of the agent in the role. "Performing in a professional role is *not* a part of personhood," she writes, "it is part of the circumstances." According to Stier, this point is crucial and it holds for professions generally. Having removed this roadblock, Stier goes on to examine the question whether the ethics of the legal profession—the law of lawyering—

provides a paradigm for discussing the ethical obligations of other professionals. She believes that to a certain extent it does. She argues that two principles that apply to the law of lawyering—namely, the Boundaries Principle and the Principle of Normativity—apply to the ethics of other professions. A third principle, the Principle of Integrative Positivism, applies to legal ethics alone.

The Boundaries Principle requires professionals to respect the boundary between themselves and those they serve as independent moral beings; it affirms the moral autonomy of both the client and the professional. The Principle of Normativity says that the norms of a professional ethic have a special claim of authority on members of a profession; professionals have a *prima facie* obligation to comply with these norms. The Principle of Integrative Positivism says that the norms of legal ethics "function as positive law"; they constitute the law of lawyering. On Stier's account this principle is peculiar to legal ethics. Yet, primarily because of what she says about the Principle of Normativity, her discussion suggests that a professional ethic stands in much the same relation to morals that law does. After all, in one form or another, the notion that a citizen has merely a *prima facie* obligation to obey the law is something of a commonplace in jurisprudence.

Aggressive marketing by the pharmaceutical repackaging industry and the actions of federal officials who champion deregulation and competition have occasioned a turf battle—what Andrew Abbott calls a jurisdictional dispute—between doctors and pharmacists. The jurisdictional claims of these rivals have been heard in the legal arena—at present, physician dispensing of drugs for profit is allowed in most states, regulated in several, and forbidden in only a few—but the debate is hardly over. Indeed, there is good reason to believe that it will intensify as physician dispensing becomes more common. The issue is not merely political and economic; as David James observes, there is more at stake here than turf. In particular, as the debate so far shows, the question here—Which system of drug dispensing should we have?—has an undeniable moral dimension.

James frames the debate in terms of four "abstract principles of individualist ethics"—namely, beneficence, nonmaleficence, autonomy, and justice—and one which is central to the physician-patient relationship itself—namely, fidelity. He argues that while the first four "yield indeterminate and conflicting indications rather than a solid moral diagnosis," looking to the principle of fidelity one finds good reason to conclude that physician dispensing of drugs for profit "is ethically a poor idea." In closing, James identifies two philosophical morals that, he says, emerge from his inquiry. First, the moral principles of individualist ethics—beneficence, nonmaleficence, autonomy, and justice—are ill-suited to the task of answering systemic questions. Second, in comparison, it is easier to be clear about what a good professional (in this case, therapeutic) relationship requires. Moreover, if we look to the norms and ideals that are, as it were, built into the physician-patient relationship, it seems that the uncertainties about likely consequences and priority disputes that cause so much trouble for arguments involving the principles of individualist ethics can be safely ignored. And that is surely welcome, for, among other things, the prospect of a consensus on how to resolve priority disputes involving the principles of beneficence, nonmaleficence, autonomy, and justice, seems quite remote.

RU 486 is a chemical abortifacient commonly known as the French abortion pill. In the summer of 1992 it got national attention when a pregnant California woman, Leona Benten, challenged the federal ban on importation of RU 486. She purchased twelve pills in England and brought them to the United States for her own use under her doctor's supervision. (The ban on RU 486 is an exception to the FDA rule that allows importation under such circumstances.) The FDA, whom she had informed of her plans, confiscated the pills. Her case was heard in two federal courts and the decision of the second, favoring the FDA, stood when the Supreme Court declined to annul its holding. In October 1992, more fuel was added to the fire when it was announced that RU 486 is a highly effective "morning-after pill." While it has other uses and, according to researchers, many potential uses, the two mentioned here are the source of the controversy surrounding its development and use. There are numerous ethical issues here and many of them fall squarely in the arena of professional ethics and social responsibility. Indeed, professionals are major players in the story of RU 486; its development, use, and legal regulation, as well as the scientific investigation of its potential, involve professionals.

Kathleen Dixon approaches the moral issues involved in the use and availability RU 486 from the vantage point of professional ethics and (corporate) social responsibility. She argues that these "two pillars" support claims to enhanced clinical investigation, access, and use of RU 486. Dixon begins with a discussion of the corporate and political history of the drug and a description of its chemical function, clinical use, and effectiveness. Turning to the ethical questions, she presents three types of arguments in support of her claim that physicians and patients are entitled to access and use RU 486. The key element in the first case is the *prima facie* obligation of physicians to provide patients with the safest, most effective mode of medical treatment. In the second case the obligations of health care professionals to promote patients' responsibility for treatment decisions and health maintenance are center stage. The linchpin in the third argument is the notion of professional privilege.

Corporate social responsibility is cashed out variously in terms of (i) net social utility, (ii) obligations to produce and distribute goods and services that sustain and enhance human existence, and (iii) maximization of profit. In some cases, for example, with corporations that manufacture prescription drugs, it may be thought to include (iv) obligations to a professional constituency. Rather than championing one of these views, Dixon considers them in turn and, in each case, she argues that Roussel-Uclaf, the developer and maker of RU 486, and Hoechst AG, the German company that acquired Roussel-Uclaf in 1974, have a moral obligation to extend commercial distribution of RU 486.

Thinking in terms of applications—both medical and nonmedical—the societal impact of scientific discoveries can scarcely be doubted. So too, at the level of applications, few would deny that moral assessment is apposite. It is clear that human genetic engineering will have an impact on society through its risks and its applications. In this respect there is nothing special about discoveries in human genetic engineering; precisely the same thing is true of many other kinds of scientific discoveries. RU 486 is an excellent example. Yet, many have at least a sneaking suspicion that human genetic engineering differs from other scientific undertakings. In any case, there are many people who find it a suspicious activity.

According to Robert Wachbroit, there is something special about human genetic engineering. Something, indeed, that warrants suspicion. But that suspicion is not about the activity; its target is the traditional view respecting the responsibilities of scientists. Granting, as he must, that human genetic engineering will affect us through its risks and applications, he argues that there is a third way, independent of these two, in which its discoveries will have social significance: The scientific discoveries *themselves* will have a social significance because the knowledge that we will gain from them will alter how we see ourselves. At this juncture we confront the question of whether moral assessment is appropriate at this level as well as at the levels of risk and application. Wachbroit puts the question this way: The query

"To what extent are scientists (morally) responsible for how their discoveries are used?" is familiar and apt; but "[d]oes it makes sense to ask whether scientists have a moral responsibility concerning the discoveries themselves?" Wachbroit argues that the answer is affirmative. He discusses two kinds of cases—the detection of diseases, for which no treatment exists, in asymptomatic individuals and discoveries of new kinds of abnormalities or disabilities—to reveal the sense in which scientists' responsibility extends to their discoveries themselves. This responsibility is what he calls a "second-order responsibility"; it arises from the change scientific discoveries—new knowledge—may make in our (first-order) moral responsibilities (i.e., those respecting actions and their consequences). Such changes occur, for example, when, as in the cases Wachbroit discusses, genetic discoveries alter our understanding of normality in the biological (as opposed to its mathematical or evaluative) sense. If Wachbroit is right, there is a significant lacuna in the traditional view respecting the professional responsibilities of scientists.

According to the traditional view, science is unique among social institutions that receive public support and markedly affect society, for it possesses the means to transcend particular private interests and biases and attain universal knowledge. Thus, as William Maker observes, on the traditional view scientific autonomy is not only justified but required; society is best served when science defines and pursues its own goals. The autonomy of science is a social good. Maker argues that the traditional "image of an autonomous science, in but not of society, effectively free from all interests save an interest in universal knowledge," flies in the face of actual scientific practice. Consequently, there is reason to question science's continued claim to autonomy. According to Maker, the contemporary reality of scientific practice cannot support an unqualified justification of the freedom from external interference that science has traditionally enjoyed. The time has come to rethink the nature of the social responsibility of science.

Maker presents an "external and practical critique" of the traditional image of science. This critique is based on two sets of empirical observations. The first challenges the idea that there is a meaningful way to disentangle the pursuit of scientific knowledge from its applications. The second suggests that "for all intents and purposes [science has] become a business." The picture of science that emerges from his critique is markedly different from the traditional one. Science is under the sway of external special interests and is rarely far distanced from particular goals, even when "pure research" is undertaken. Maker argues that as science is being commodified, it comprises a rival set of values and a rival ethic. These values and this ethic conflict with rather than complement the traditional values and ethic of science. In particular, they do not comport well with two of the four institutional imperatives of the (uncodified) ethic of the scientific enterprise, namely, communalism and disinterestedness (the others are universalism and organized skepticism). Arguing that a return to the conditions that could legitimate the traditional claim to scientific autonomy is unlikely, Maker advocates the democratization of science. He closes with a discussion of the steps that can be taken to achieve this goal.

There is a tendency in discussions of professional ethics to focus on the individual practitioner. Consequently, as Joan Callahan points out, "considerations that have to do with institutional design and the moral hazards institutions create for practitioners" have often been neglected. It might be thought that the situation would be different in discussions of ethics in science. After all, it is clear that scientists work in institutions. Yet, as Callahan points out, the typical response in cases of scientific fraud is to provide a "bad apple" explanation of the culprit's conduct, though as she argues, "a hard look at the reality of scientific practice suggests that . . . the major problem might well be more with the barrels than with the apples." As in professional ethics generally, the neglect of institutional considerations is partially explained by a lack of fit between the reality of professional life and the picture promoted by professional ideology.

Like Maker, Callahan believes that the conventional picture of how science is done does not match the reality it purports to represent. She discusses the conventional ideology and several cases that belie its claim accurately to describe scientific practice. But her project is not to show that the conventional ideology misrepresents scientific practice, it is to see how the institutions that support and house contemporary science cohere with that ideology "as a set of ideals regarding standards for scientific work and standards of virtue for practitioners of science." Distinguishing several varieties of scientific malpractice and making it plain that malpractice in science may be subtle as well as dramatic, Callahan argues that these institutions create moral risks for science and its practitioners. Their standards of success and reward structures, to say nothing of the need to compete successfully for private and public funding, create enormous pressure to produce and to publish; they also largely explain the proliferation of professional journals that makes some forms of scientific fraud possible. There is more to the argument, of course. Yet, even at this juncture, since both motive and opportunity can be traced to institutional factors, there is reason to think that part of the problem is the result of institutional design.

In the final sections of her paper, Callahan discusses other professions, including her own, and suggests that some of the moral risks they are subject to are comparable to those in science. In addition, she argues that there is "an unavoidable political dimension to professional responsibility" that requires recognition of and work for changes in the "patriarchal presumptions embedded in our practices and institutions," for they only exacerbate the moral risks in professional life.

The political dimension of professional responsibility comes to the fore in the debate over the institutionalization of voluntary euthanasia. The issue here is one of social policy and, as is characteristic of things political, in deciding whether (and to whom) authority should be granted, attention is focused on social costs. Indeed, the question has been put to voters—in Washington in 1991 and California in 1992—and has been the subject of numerous polls. These polls consistently show that about 60 percent of Americans favor legalization of voluntary euthanasia. And, according to one poll, the same percentage of doctors favor it, though the same poll reveals that nearly half of these doctors would not perform it.[48]

According to the American Medical Association's "Principles of Medical Ethics and Current Opinions of the Council on Ethical and Judicial Affairs—1989," a physician is obliged to sustain life and relieve suffering. If these duties conflict, as they may, "the preferences of the patient should prevail." The code embraces the distinction between passive and active euthanasia permitting the former and forbidding the latter: "the physician should not intentionally cause death," though for "humane reasons, with informed consent, a physician may . . . cease or omit treatment to permit a terminally ill patient to die when death is imminent." In cases where death is not imminent it is permissible—"it is not unethical"—to discontinue life-prolonging medical treatment, provided that the patient is permanently unconscious and there are adequate safeguards to confirm the diagnosis.[49] At this juncture we may wonder, along with James Rachels, "what is the cessation of treatment, in these circumstances, if it is not 'the intentional termination of the life of one human being by another?' Of course," Rachels continues, "it is exactly that, and if it were not, there would be no point to it."[50]

The AMA position to the contrary notwithstanding, in itself, Rachels argues, the difference between letting die and killing does not make a difference. Or more precisely, it does not make a moral difference; legally it makes a world of difference, for active euthanasia is forbidden by law. Noting this fact, Rachels says that while doctors must be concerned about the legal consequences of their actions, they should also be "concerned with the fact that the law is forcing upon them a moral doctrine that may well be indefensible, and has a considerable effect on their practices."[51] Rachels's point here is not radical. The AMA code says much the same thing: "A physician shall respect the law and also recognize a responsibility to seek changes in those requirements which are contrary to the best interests of the patient."[52] In any case, it is clear that there is a political dimension to this issue of professional responsibility.

As Joel Feinberg points out, most of the arguments against the legalization of voluntary euthanasia are indirect. They do not deny, indeed many concede, that in many individual cases, considered on their own merits, euthanasia is morally justified. These arguments favor deliberately overlooking the merits of individual cases and cite external considerations in support of a blanket prohibition. Feinberg argues that these arguments do not justify a blanket prohibition; they do not justify overlooking the merits of individual cases. In euthanasia situations, decisions should be made on the merits. If the decision is to be made on this basis, however, we will be placing a burden on and putting trust in those professionals who, we believe, are best situated and qualified to assist the patient (or family) in the evaluation of the merits of the case, namely, physicians.

Feinberg devotes special attention to what he calls the argument from abusable discretion. This form of argument is familiar and in some applications it is persuasive. Moreover, according to Feinberg, it is the most plausible of the indirect arguments for a blanket prohibition of voluntary euthanasia. In its application to the euthanasia situation, however, Feinberg argues that it too fails. He grants that mistakes/ abuse are inevitable with a permissive rule. But the same is true with a blanket prohibition. Two types of mistakes are possible in euthanasia situations: "One creates the danger that curable patients will need-lessly be killed or killed without their real consent; the other creates the danger that incurable terminal patients will have their sufferings pointlessly prolonged." A blanket prohibition is warranted only if one can say that, isolated from other factors (i.e., in itself), the first of these two types of mistake is always more serious than the other and that, other things being equal, one of the two conflicting values (life) is always a weightier consideration than the other (surcease of suffering). But one cannot say that. Not because the second sort of mistake is always more serious or as serious (i.e., equally serious) and so on. Rather, Feinberg's point is that the comparison called for here cannot be made. "It is easy enough to speak of 'death in the abstract' or 'suffering in the abstract,' " he writes, "but real people do not live in the abstract."

In a discussion of the political dimension of professional ethics Dennis Thompson remarks that professional ethics, "as many professionals themselves insist, is too important to all of us to be left only to professionals . . . all of us must work together to formulate and interpret the ethical principles that govern how we act, individually and institutionally."[53] The papers in this volume confirm his point.

Notes

1. Paul Camenisch, "Business Ethics: On Getting to the Heart of the Matter," *Business and Professional Ethics Journal* 1 (1981): 59.

2. George Simpson, *Emile Durkheim* (New York: Thomas Y. Cromwell, 1963), 118.

3. North's conviction was overturned because he had been convicted on the basis of testimony given under a grant of immunity from self-incrimination in the course of the congressional investigation of the Iran-contra affair. "North *was* guilty. . . . [His] own testimony is that he shredded documents, aided and abetted the obstruction of Congress and took an illegal gratuity (a $13,873 security system at his home)—the things for which he was originally convicted. Yet, he now proclaims himself 'totally exonerated' because the federal courts have let him slip through the biggest loophole in the criminal law—the Fifth Amendment." Harrison Rainie, "Oliver North in America's Star Chamber, *U.S. News & World Report*, 30 September 1991, 13.

Although Rainie decries this result, particularly North's claim of exoneration, no charge of unethical conduct is leveled against North's attorneys. They were simply doing their job. See David Luban, "The Adversary System Excuse," in *The Good Lawyer*, ed. David Luban (Totowa, N.J.: Rowman and Allanheld, 1984), 85–86 (discussing the case of Richard Helms, former director of the Central Intelligence Agency, and the ingenious way in which his attorney, Edward Bennett Williams, got the government to drop an action for perjury against Helms and allow him to plead guilty to a misdemeanor. Williams's ploy has come to be called "graymailing.").

4. Simpson, *Emile Durkheim*, 118.

5. Thomas Nagel, "Ruthlessness in Public Life," in *Public and Private Morality*, ed. Stuart Hampshire (Cambridge: Cambridge University Press, 1978), 77.

6. Nagel argues that this fact cannot be explained by those who hold that public morality is derivable from private morality. The crucial point for Nagel's explanation of this fact is that although public morality is not derivable from private morality, they have a common source. From this source each derives, independently, a concern respecting the consequences of action and a concern respecting actions themselves which, *inter alia*, entails rights-based restrictions on the selection of means. For several reasons, which Nagel discusses, public morality emphasizes the former, whereas private morality emphasizes the latter. According to Nagel, the difference between the content of public and private obligations is explained by the impersonal dimension of public morality and the increased concern for results and the rigorous standard of impartiality entailed by it. See Nagel, "Ruthlessness in Public Life," 82–86, et passim; cf. Stuart Hampshire, "Public and Private Morality" in *Public and Private Morality*, ed. Stuart Hampshire (Cambridge: Cambridge University Press, 1978), 51–52 (suggesting that "the assumption of a political role, and of powers to change men's lives on a large scale, carry with them not only new responsibilities, but a new kind of responsibility, which entails, [*inter alia*, that policies] are to be justified principally by their eventual consequences [and] a withholding of some of the scruples that in private life would prohibit one from using people as a means to an end and also from using force and deceit").

7. Nagel, "Ruthlessness in Public Life," 82.

8. Ibid., 89.

9. Ibid., 79.

10. Stuart Hampshire, *Morality and Conflict* (Cambridge: Harvard University Press, 1983), 159. According to Hampshire, "there always will be, and . . . there always ought to be, conflicts between moral requirements arising from universal requirements of utility and justice, and moral requirements that are based on specific loyalties and on conventions and customs of love and friendship and family loyalty . . . moral conflicts are of their nature ineliminable and . . . there is no morally acceptable and overriding criterion, simple or double, to be appealed to, and no constant method of resolving conflicts." Ibid., 165.

11. Kenneth Kipnis, "Criminal Justice and the Negotiated Plea," in *Philosophical Issues in Law*, ed. Kenneth Kipnis (Englewood Cliffs, N.J.: Prentice Hall, 1977), 310. See Arnold Enker, "Perspective on Plea Bargaining," from *Task Force Report: The Courts*, issued by the President's Commission on Law Enforcement and Administration of Justice (Washington, D.C., 1967), ibid., especially 299–300 (identifying "several useful ends" served by plea bargaining and inviting attention to the price the system pays for these accomplishments).

12. Ibid., 90. Speaking of institutions, Stuart Hampshire makes a similar point: "An institution is a . . . formally established, and a definitely identifiable entity . . . generally governed by its own observances and rituals. The moral

claims of pure practical reason, calculating consequences, often come into conflict with the duties and obligations that arise from participation in an institution, and there sometimes is no third, independent source of moral arbitration." Stuart Hampshire, *Morality and Conflict*, 164.

13. The explanation of this fact appears to be quite simple. As Andrew Abbott points out, the "word *'profession'* in French means what 'occupation' means in English." Andrew Abbott, *The System of Professions* (Chicago: University of Chicago Press, 1988), 331.

14. Michael Bayles, "The Professions," in *Ethical Issues in Professional Life*, ed. Joan C. Callahan (New York: Oxford University Press, 1988): 27; Bernard Barber, "Some Problems in the Sociology of the Professions," in *The Professions in America*, ed. Kenneth S. Lynn and the editors of *Daedalus* (Boston: Houghton Mifflin Company, 1965): 17; Mark Abrahamson, "Introduction," in *The Professional in the Organization*, ed. Mark Abrahamson (Chicago: Rand McNally & Company, 1967): 8; Neil H. Cheek, "The Social Role of the Professional," ibid., 9. Richard Wasserstrom provides a list of six "central features of a profession." Richard Wasserstrom, "Lawyers as Professionals: Some Moral Issues," *Human Rights* 5 (1975): n. 6, 2; cf. Jack N. Behrman, *Essays on Ethics in Business and the Professions* (Englewood Cliffs, N.J.: Prentice Hall, 1988): 97–99, et passim (recognizing two groups that seem clearly to qualify as professions, namely lawyers and physicians, yet arguing that "there are no true professions today in the United States . . . [though] we still need them).

15. Andrew Abbott puts the point forcefully: "People don't want to call automobile repair a profession because they don't want to accord it that dignity. This unwillingness probably has less to do with the actual characteristics of automobile repair as an intellectual discipline—which are conceptually quite close to those of medicine—than it does with the status of the work and those who do it." Andrew Abbott, *The System of Professions* (Chicago: University of Chicago Press, 1988), 8.

16. Michael Bayles, "The Professions," 28–29. Bayles also distinguishes between consulting professions and scholarly professions. Scientists, journalists, nonconsulting engineers, teachers, and technicians, for example, are members of the scholarly professions. Such professionals usually work for a salary and either have many clients at one time (e.g., students) or no personal client, being part of a staff or a member of a department working on tasks assigned by superiors. Consulting professionals include accountants, consulting engineers, architects, dentists, psychiatrists, and psychological counselors; the consulting professions also include two paradigm cases—namely, medicine and the law. Such professionals act primarily in behalf of an individual client on a fee-for-service basis. This distinction is important because these differences between the roles of scholarly and consulting professionals "are crucial in defining the kinds of ethical problems each confronts." Ibid., 29.

17. Ibid., 29. Bayles holds that using normative features to define or

characterize professions is a mistake. In particular, he singles out claims to the effect that professionals are primarily devoted to providing a service and secondarily to making money and that a profession should be self-governing.

18. Bernard Barber, "Some Problems in the Sociology of the Professions," 17–19. Bayles would object to Barber's characterization because and insofar as it involves normative features such as community orientation and self-control. Yet, when he identifies the three salient features of the consulting professions—they (i) provide an important service (that is, serve basic values such as health, justice, wealth, comfort, safety), (ii) have a monopoly over the provision of services and (iii) are not subject to much public control but are largely self regulating "because of the intellectual training and judgement" they require—he seems to be saying essentially the same thing. Bayles, "The Professions," 29–30. (A statement of Bayles's distinction between the consulting and scholarly professions is provided in note 14 *supra*.)

19. Everett C. Hughes, "Professions," in Lynn, *The Professions in America*, 1–3.

20. Abbott, *The System of Professions*, 19.

21. Ibid., 318.

22. Ibid., 8.

23. Ibid., 102.

24. Ibid., 34.

25. Ibid., 33; see 84–86, 90–91, 111, 112. Abbott says that he is taking Hughes's logic one step further.

26. Ibid., 147, 323–24.

27. Ibid., 154, 324.

28. Ibid., 325.

29. John J. Beer and W. David Lewis, "Aspects of the Professionalization of Science," in Lynn, *The Professions in America*, 117–18; Hughes, "Professions," ibid., 10.

30. Abbott, *The System of Professions*, 61.

31. Ibid., note 11, 328.

32. Ibid., 80, 8; Hughes, "Professions," 9–12.

33. Dorothy Emmet, *Rules, Roles and Relations* (New York: St. Martin's Press, 1966; Boston: Beacon Press, 1975), 169, 14, 140, 151, 170. See Marion J. Levy, *The Structure of Society* (Princeton: Princeton University Press, 1952); Bronislaw Malinowski, *The Dynamics of Culture and Change* (New Haven: Yale University Press, 1945), 50–51; John Rawls, *A Theory of Justice* (Cambridge, Mass.: Harvard University Press, 1971), 55–56.

34. C. Wright Mills, *The Sociological Imagination* (New York: Oxford University Press, 1959), 29–30.

35. Mills, *The Sociological Imagination*, 40–41; idem, *The Power Elite* (New York: Oxford University Press, 1951), 304, 343, 360.

36. Kenneth J. Arrow, "Social Responsibility and Economic Efficiency," *Public Policy* 21 (Summer 1973), 313.

34 Introduction

37. Ibid., 309, 313.
38. Ibid., 313–14.
39. Ibid., 310.
40. Ibid., 314.
41. Emmet, *Rules, Roles and Relations*, 15.
42. In this respect, a professional ethic differs from the law and bureaucratic organization as means of creating normative institutional relations. While some of the norms of a professional ethic are the product of official action by an organized group and thus resemble norms of positive law, others develop as a consensus in interaction or discussion in various public forums such as lecture halls, professional journals, or popular media. These norms are customary or conventional; they are, nevertheless, operative elements of the professional ethos/ethic. Such norms may be recognized at law or within a bureaucracy, but prior to such authoritative recognition one would scarcely say that they were legal norms or rules of a bureaucratic organization.
43. I am ignoring several complications here, particularly with respect to the normative constraints imposed by legal norms. A discussion of the sense in which the duties, rights, privileges, and immunities created by law are institutional and attach to roles is beyond the scope of my project here. The matter receives attention in Mortimer R. Kadish and Sanford H. Kadish, *Discretion to Disobey* (Stanford: Stanford University Press, 1973): 15–18, et passim; Wellman, *A Theory of Rights*, Ch. 4; and Daniel E. Wueste, "Rights and Right Conduct, Presumptions and Validity," *The Canadian Journal of Law and Jurisprudence* 4 (January 1991), 165–85.
44. *The New York Times*, 24 October, 1992; Science & Society, *U.S. News & World Report* 18 (January 1993), 69–70.
45. Emmet, *Rules, Roles and Relations*, 203. Such explanations are common in cases of scientific misconduct. Joan Callahan calls them "bad apple" explanations and suggests that there may be a problem with the barrel. See her contribution to this volume: "Professions, Institutions, and Moral Risk."
46. Dennis Thompson, "The Nature of Practical Ethics," *Ethically Speaking* 1 (Summer 1992), 2–3. *Ethically Speaking* is published by and distributed to the members of the Association for Practical and Professional Ethics (410 North Park Avenue, Bloomington, Ind. 47405).
47. C. A. J. Coady, "Politics and the Problem of Dirty Hands," in *A Companion to Ethics*, ed. Peter Singer (Cambridge, Mass.: Basil Blackwell, 1991), 374.
48. Marcia Angell, "Euthanasia," *The New England Journal of Medicine* 319 (November 17, 1988), 1349.
49. American Medical Association, "Principles of Medical Ethics and Current Opinions of the Council on Ethical and Judicial Affairs—1989" (Opinion: "Withholding or Withdrawing Life-Prolonging Medical Treatment") in *Codes of Professional Responsibility* 2nd edition, ed. Rena A. Gorlin (Washington, D.C.: BNA Books, 1990), 191.

50. James Rachels, "Active and Passive Euthanasia," *The New England Journal of Medicine* 292 (January 1, 1975), 79–80.

51. Ibid., 80.

52. Gorlin, *Codes of Professional Responsibility*, 191 (Principle III).

53. Thompson, "The Nature of Practical Ethics," 3.

2

Necessity and Choice in Political Ethics: Varieties of Dirty Hands

Kenneth I. Winston

A sharp division of opinion exists among political theorists as to whether public officials are sometimes morally required to engage in acts that are morally wrong; that is, to have dirty hands. On one side, for example, Max Weber asserts that anyone who fails to recognize this necessity is a political infant. For the fact is "the world is governed by demons" and "he who lets himself in for politics, that is, for power and force as means, contracts with diabolical powers."[1] Other theorists, however, take the opposite as obvious—indeed, no one *could* act rightly by acting wrongly, they say—and attribute the first view to a kind of romanticism of political life. Setting aside the name calling on both sides, I think the division of opinion results in part from confusion as to the claim being made. Although in a sense it can be stated quite simply—public officials are sometimes morally required to engage in acts that are morally wrong—I believe three quite different situations are confounded in arguments about dirty hands, and though similar in important respects they are morally distinct. Therefore, any hope of resolving the theoretical controversy depends on sorting out these differences. The main purpose of this paper, accordingly, is to clarify the moral geography of dirty hands.

Overview

To introduce the general themes of the analysis that follows, I shall begin with a preliminary overview of the landscape of dirty hands. The problem of dirty hands arises for public officials only on the condition that, in Machiavelli's words, their "object is to promote the public good, and not [their] private interests."[2] The central question is

37

how ought a public official to act for the public good when circumstances are not ideal for its realization. In each of the three types of cases typically conflated in the dirty hands debate, the public official reasonably believes that an immoral act is compelled by circumstances if the public good is to be promoted. The three types are distinguished by the particular nonideal feature affecting available opportunities to act. Since Machiavelli gave more thoughtful attention than any other political philosopher to the question how public officials ought to act when circumstances are not ideal, it is natural to turn to his writings for guidance. Of the three categories of cases I shall briefly sketch, two were clearly recognized by Machiavelli and the third broadly hinted at.

First is the contingency of events. One of Machiavelli's principal themes is that what happens in politics is as much subject to chance, to fortuitous happenstance, as to human control. Even when officials manage to dominate events, what actually occurs depends on the activities of numerous parties whose intentions are not the same and may not harmonize. The result is a constant disorderliness or instability in public affairs that provides the occasion for opportunistic action. Chance offers opportunities that may not otherwise occur. The skillful official, who wishes to act effectively for the public good, will take advantage of them. Deliberation and consensus building are time consuming; opportunity is fleeting. The public official cannot always wait. And since others may not agree, indeed may not even understand what is being proposed, prudent officials find it necessary sometimes to resort to manipulation, deception, even coercion—for the public good. Thus "necessity compels them to many acts to which reason will not influence them."[3] This category of cases illustrates *the necessity of moral opportunism*.

The second circumstance identified by Machiavelli that argues for dirty hands is the fact of evil tendencies in human nature. When he speaks of human beings as "more prone to evil than to good," Machiavelli has in mind primarily the corroding influence in political life of self-interest. The wise public official knows that in a world in which others are acting badly it is not possible always to do what is right. And though it is "exceedingly rare that a good man should be found willing to employ wicked means,"[4] situations sometimes arise that require it. In the context of this last statement Machiavelli's worry is how to preserve liberty in a republic that has become corrupt. Abstracting from this context, we can observe in Machiavelli the recognition of a second kind of contingency, this one normative rather than empirical, relevant to the moral evaluation of political conduct: the contingency of obligations. To put the point simply, a public official's obligations in a given situation depend crucially on what other people in the situation are doing. If others are acting badly, the ordinary rules of morality are no longer dispositive of what the official ought to do. For one "who wishes to make a profession of goodness in everything must necessarily come to grief among so many who are not good."[5] It is here that Machiavelli utters his notorious line that public officials, since they may be required to engage in wicked acts for the sake of the public good, must "learn how not to be good," though he is careful to add that they must "use this knowledge and not use it, according to the necessity of the case."[6] This class of examples illustrates *the necessity of benign corruption*.

In the contemporary literature on dirty hands, Machiavelli's first consideration—the contingency of events—has virtually disappeared, and a third (only inchoate in Machiavelli's work) has been introduced that increasingly preoccupies political theorists: namely, that moral principles do not form a single consistent system. The point is formulated by Max Weber in what remains the profoundest essay on the problem of dirty hands, his "Politics as a Vocation," but it has been highlighted recently in the context of critiques of utilitarianism and absolutism. The central claim is that an act may be the right thing to do in utilitarian terms and yet leave a person guilty of doing wrong, because a moral rule with independent force has been violated. This happens because no single standard or measure exists that renders all moral values commensurable, or more generally because moral justification is not unitary. As a consequence, a public official may on occasion choose the morally better course of action, for the public good, and yet of necessity do something wrong. This class of examples illustrates *the necessity of tragic choices*.

These three categories of cases, although only briefly and incompletely sketched so far, reveal the basis of *realism* in politics. Dirty hands theorists are realists because at the core of their understanding of political life is a recognition of limits in human capacity—with a different limit emphasized in each of the three categories of cases. The first circumstance, supporting moral opportunism, finds a limit in the human ability to control and dominate events; the second, giving a reason for participation in corruption, locates a limit in human motivation (the influence of self-interest); and the third, leading to tragic choices, reveals a limit in human rationality. To be a realist in politics, then, is to believe that political life exceeds our capacities in certain crucial ways. (We muddle through, morally and otherwise.) By contrast, *idealism* in politics is the view that human capacities are adequate to political life. Problems can be solved; obligations can be comprehended. Of course idealists concede that human capacities are finite, that they are often only grudgingly exercised on behalf of others, that they are prone to error and confusion. But idealists estimate the effects of these limits differently. They have confidence in what human intelligence and human benevolence can do, at least if overreaching is avoided and political aspirations are brought into line with possibilities. In such a view, there is no place for dirty hands.

To formulate the difference between realists and idealists in this way appears to suggest that the fundamental cleavage between them is temperamental. I cannot entirely exclude that possibility. Yet considerable argumentation occurs before one reaches the differences that temperament might make. In what follows, I shall examine the points of argument to bring out the moral differences in the three kinds of situations I have identified. I consider the cases in reverse order, beginning with tragic choices.

Tragic Choices

In this category of cases not only is it true that something "morally disagreeable" is required but "one might say that whatever the agent did [the agent had to do something] wrong."[7] Bernard Williams refers to these as cases of tragic choice and observes that, unlike the merely morally disagreeable, these cases are exceptional in political life. That is fortunate, if true, because they are also the most puzzling of the three categories of cases I shall discuss.

A Formula and the Search for Cases

Let's begin with an abstract formula. We might say that a tragic choice arises in a situation where an agent has a duty to do *A* and has a duty to do *B*, but cannot do both. The impossibility is not generated by moral principles that are inherently inconsistent, in the sense that there is no conceivable world in which a person could act in accordance with both. Rather, the principles are incompatible in a specific situation because of contingent features of the world. The tragedy lies in one's not being able to do everything one is morally required to do because of circumstances. So runs the standard analysis.[8]

The claim that the agent "cannot do both" requires elucidation. By hypothesis, the conflict in a tragic situation is genuine, not merely apparent. It cannot be made to disappear, for example, by more careful examination of the situation or by appropriate redescription. Nor is it resolvable by a lexical ordering of principles or by other strategies of ranking. A moral requirement continues to be compelling even though there are compelling reasons to violate it. That is why it is impossible for the agent to act without doing something wrong.

Of course, not every moral conflict is a moral dilemma. In a standard class of cases, A and B cannot both be done, but A takes priority over B and the conflict is resolved. For example, protection of one person's right may outweigh a small gain in other people's utility, even though one has a duty to promote both. In a second class of cases, A is more compelling than B and so takes priority, but B is still compelling in some way, such that violating it leaves a *moral residue* and calls for reparation. For example, a medical emergency is more compelling than a promise to help a friend deal with a distressing personal crisis, but the friend is owed special consideration when the emergency has passed. In this situation, although it is literally true that the agent could not do both acts in the circumstances, the possibility of subsequent recompense leaves the moral order intact. No tragedy is involved. With a tragic choice, we are a crucial step further removed from mere conflict. In this class of cases, A is more compelling than B, but a moral residue remains for which no adequate reparation is possible. In other words, there is irreparable damage to the moral order.[9]

What would count as an example of a tragic choice in the sense indicated? Williams discusses the agony of Agamemnon at Aulis, forced to choose between his public duty as commander of the Athenian army and his private duty as father of Iphigenia. The example typifies a traditional (if not quite Hegelian) conception of tragedy as the clash of duties generated by the fragmented character of moral life. Although some minimal moral requirements have force across the entire range of human interaction, the bulk of a person's duties falls within separate spheres of activity that are autonomous in the sense that they are regulated by distinctive sets of principles. On occasion these spheres intersect, unexpectedly, and create inescapable dilemmas. Anything the agent does will rend the moral order. So Antigone is caught between her familial duty to bury her brother Polyneices and her civic duty to obey Creon's decree against burial, violation of which threatens civil unrest. So Brutus is caught between his love for Julius Caesar and his love of Rome. So Agamemnon.

The moral crises generated by the clash of autonomous spheres are of special theoretical interest because they support arguments against the idea of a comprehensive justificatory principle of morality. Thus Williams observes that Agamemnon's agony may not have resulted from his "persistent doubt that he may not have chosen the better thing [in deciding to sacrifice Iphigenia]" but from the "conviction that he has not done the better thing because there was no better thing to be done."[10] This results, presumably, because no overarching viewpoint exists from which the duties generated by the two separate spheres can be compared and weighed against one another. Yet, if there were in fact no better thing for Agamemnon to do, it would not matter, morally, what he did. Such a case would be tragic, perhaps even doubly tragic, since the necessity of doing wrong would be conjoined with the impossibility of, in Williams's words, "acting for the best." But that reading of the tale renders tragic choices even more exotic than they already are. At any rate, Williams's judgment about Agamemnon's plight is not shared by the Greek chorus. The chorus does not blame him for killing Iphigenia—thus revealing that the sacrifice is regarded as "for the best"—but they reproach him for the way he does it: He treats her as just another sacrificial animal.[11]

The alternative is to search for cases within a single sphere of activity. A good candidate in the familial sphere is Ibsen's Nora, who is forced to choose between her duties to her family and "other duties equally sacred"; namely, to herself. However, as I want to focus on political dirty hands, I need to look elsewhere. Michael Walzer concentrates on conflicts internal to political roles, but the two cases he discusses, unfortunately, do more to confuse than to clarify the issues.[12] The first is of a candidate for elected office who, to win, must make a deal with a dishonest ward boss, involving the granting of contracts for school construction. The example is not entirely inapt for illustrating conduct that is morally disagreeable, but it is not an example of a tragic choice. At best, it is a case of benign corruption, and the central question for discussion is the meaning—and force—of the claim that the act (i.e., the corrupt deal) is necessary. (The candidate has the option of not running for office without doing anything wrong.) Walzer's second case is closer to what he intends. It involves a politician, his country engaged in a prolonged colonial war, deciding whether to authorize the torture of a captured rebel leader who knows the location of bombs hidden around the colony's capital city. He does so, convinced it is the only way to save many innocent lives, even though he believes torture is always wrong, "indeed abominable," and said so many times during his campaign for office. To qualify as a case of tragic choice, the central focus must be on the juxtaposition of the claim that torture is always wrong with the decision to authorize it in the particular case. How do we make sense of that juxtaposition?

Walzer's strategy, which I shall explore in a moment, relies on the opposition of two moral theories, utilitarianism and absolutism. But his discussion of the case itself tends to put the focus either on the politician's failure to live up to his earlier campaign promises or on the inner conflict he feels as a result of acting contrary to his own initial belief. Walzer's politician thus embodies the moral sensitivity that Agamemnon appeared to lack, but neither of these foci illuminates the nature of tragic choices. A campaign promise, on any account, has little weight as against the duty to save imminently threatened innocent people. And while inner conflict of a sort plays a role in dirty hands—though not quite in the way Walzer thinks—the realization that one's former promises cannot be maintained in new circumstances does not capture the actual source of guilt.

Such rocks and shoals are warning enough of the difficulty of discovering viable examples of dirty hands. An added worry is that hypothetical or literary examples, slimmed down and tidied up for rhetorical purposes, produce rarefied and unreliable intuitions and, in any case, are weighted in favor of the theoretical arguments they are designed to support. While the selection of actual events may also, if more subtly, be theory driven, historical examples, I would argue, are more reliable because they are more firmly rooted in moral experience. To be sure, the difference between the historical and the hypothetical should not be exaggerated, since an historical example becomes hypothetical as soon as its facts are stipulated. Yet there is a crucial difference in a case that carries the potential always of overwhelming any theoretical account of it, with the discovery of new facts and new implications. What we should seek, I think, is a case that resonates with the complexity of historical reality, that elicits the desire for more facts even if they are not forthcoming, and that may also generate alternative, conflicting theories of the situation.[13]

Truman's Dilemma

Consider President Harry Truman's decision to authorize the atomic bombings of Hiroshima and Nagasaki. Is this a good candidate for the category of tragic choices?

A common strategy, as I have indicated, frames the issue in terms of the opposition of utilitarianism and absolutism. A tragic choice arises when an act is "exactly the right thing to do in utilitarian terms and yet leave[s] the [person] who does it guilty of a moral wrong" because a binding rule has been violated.[14] Thus the absolutist is correct to think the rule prohibiting the act is mandatory, but incorrect to think as a consequence that the act should not be done. The utilitarian is correct to think the act should be done, but incorrect to think the agent is justified, without remainder, in violating the rule. This happens because, although action is unitary, moral justification is not; no single standard integrates all moral principles into a comprehensive scheme. As a result, a public official may on occasion choose the morally better (i.e., the utilitarian) course of action, thereby acting for the best, yet do something wrong.

Although he objects to regarding Truman's situation as a case of dirty hands, Walzer frames his analysis just this way: "The only possible defense of the Hiroshima attack is a utilitarian calculation . . . to override the rules of war and the rights of Japanese civilians."[15] Walzer thinks the utilitarian case is too weak for the override. But the calculation is characteristically difficult to pin down. Walzer's assessment, for example, rests on the premise that Allied invasion of the Japanese mainland was not necessary for ending the war, thus undercutting Truman's principal defense that the bombings saved millions of lives. However, if one estimates differently the conditions for preventing renewed Japanese militarism, which everyone agrees was a critical goal, the force of this point becomes much weaker.[16] Walzer also balks at Truman's readiness to count American lives for more than Japanese lives. Yet such partiality is easily justified by utilitarian considerations, in the same way the preference of parents in favor of their own children over other people's children is justified. Further, Walzer says nothing about the possible long-range consequences of the bombings, such as the effects on the Soviet Union and the prospects for a lasting peace. On utilitarian grounds these may legitimately be taken into account, and may outweigh the effects on innocent victims. So if the utilitarian calculation is pursued rigorously, one may have to conclude that, while it is true (as Walzer claims) that Truman did not have dirty hands, that is because his decision was fully justified. Thus, *A* outweighed *B*, and the conflict was resolved. (The only question would be whether there was a moral residue and, if so, what form reparation might take. Since utilitarians have no difficulty recommending the cultivation of a strong psychological disposition to rule following, the recognition of moral residue on appropriate occasions has a utilitarian justification.)

Of course one might conclude instead that utilitarian calculations are always *ad hoc*, and some rather than others are employed on particular occasions because they support positions reached on different grounds. But Walzer's argument is not meant to elicit skepticism about the utilitarian enterprise, only to show that it has limits. That means, I think, that the question in Truman's case is whether one can make the limit stick *even if* a clear utilitarian case exists for the bombings. The standard analysis reaches this result by invoking certain rules—here the rules of war regarding the rights of innocent civilians—that are absolute, in the sense that they allow no exceptions and so are binding even when a utilitarian calculation seems to permit (or require) their violation. On this view, Truman again did not have dirty hands, because by intentionally killing the innocent he simply acted badly.

The absolutist claim raises its own kind of difficulties. In one version the absolutist challenge is so strenuous that it eliminates the moral possibility of politics altogether. Conceding the inevitability of dirty hands, it is said that, since one must be prepared in politics to do evil for the sake of greater good, "politics belongs . . . to the pursuits that have to be forgone."[17] Other versions of absolutism do not concede the inevitability. They focus on the moral limits of political action: What politicians do is not inherently iniquitous, but certain boundary conditions must be carefully observed. Typically, the moral error politicians commit is use of illicit means to achieve otherwise acceptable ends. Thus Elizabeth Anscombe says: "In the bombing of [Hiroshima and Nagasaki] it was certainly decided to kill the innocent as a means to an end," and that "is always murder."[18] So Truman can be condemned without condemning politics as a whole.

Why is it thought that certain rules can be discovered and articulated that state what must always be done? It would take me far afield to pursue the obstacles I see to accepting this idea. Yet there is a core of truth here that I want to hold on to. If moral experience supports the conclusion that good and sufficient reasons exist for sticking rigorously to a rule, we may say that the rule has a presumptive validity. This places a heavy burden on anyone who proposes to violate it, a burden that may never be entirely lifted even when a violation seems warranted. If the presumption is widely accepted, we may speak of the existence of a *moral convention*. In this sense, moral conventions, such as the rules of war, are collective considered judgments, the outcomes of reflection and mutual deliberation over time and across cultures. They are continuous with social customs and manners, but also distinguished from them by their overrriding importance, since they regulate the more constant and more fundamental interests of human beings. (Thus moral conventions are not to be conflated with coordination rules, such as rules of the road.) This points to what I think is true in the absolutist view: Certain moral rules—what I have called moral conventions—have a presumptive validity. Even when compelling reasons exist for violating them, the violation is likely to involve deep and unanticipated—and often indiscernible—moral costs.[19] Because such costs are involved, a moral convention retains its force even when there are compelling reasons for the violation. That is why feelings of guilt and regret are appropriate.

Where does this leave us regarding the standard analysis of tragic choices? My conclusion is that framing the problem in terms of a clash between utilitarianism and absolutism is seriously flawed. First, the frame itself has evident difficulties. The worry about the *ad hoc* character of utilitarian calculations is not easily dismissed. And even if political reasoning is predominantly utilitarian, it is not always or exclusively so. As to absolutism, while there is an important truth in this view, it needs to be restated in a way that brings out its salience. I have begun to do that by speaking of moral conventions. Second, and more importantly, the standard analysis is flawed because it suggests that tragic choices arise only for people committed to a certain theoretical schema, a moral discourse constituted by two rival theories that exhaust relevant analysis. I think a quite different frame of analysis, set in terms of role obligations, enables us to reformulate Truman's dilemma without entailing a particular theoretical construction. I shall sketch it briefly.

Truman had a duty, stemming from his role as president and commander-in-chief, to do what was needed to win the war against Japan and to do so while keeping the loss of American lives to a minimum. This duty is not to be confused with the duty to maximize overall expected benefits (or minimize costs) to Americans. The duty was interpersonal, and so in this respect similar to other role obligations. Citizens' reliance on public officials, especially in a democracy, generates a legitimate expectation that the officials will not be indifferent to their lives, even when large and important social goals are at stake. And that expectation applies with special salience when citizen-soldiers defer to the judgment of their commander. Thus the ability to use atomic weapons as soon as they were available provided Truman not merely with an opportunity but with an imperative to act, especially after the Japanese decision to continue the war despite the fire bombing of their major cities.

At the same time, based on the moral conventions of war, Truman also had a duty—equally an interpersonal duty—not to harm innocent Japanese civilians. There may of course be serious disagreement about who was innocent in the relevant sense. Combatants, those actually or potentially threatening harm, obviously were not innocent; nor were those providing the means of fighting, such as munitions workers. It is more controversial whether suppliers of food and medicine were innocent, to the extent they were sustaining soldiers in combat and not just serving basic human needs. But there is no doubt that many groups, such as children, the elderly, and the disabled, were innocent, and the fact was that atomic bombs could not be used on the two Japanese targets without killing or horribly maiming them. (Regarding the Nagasaki bomb, which fell a mile and a half off course, McGeorge Bundy observes: "Any target large enough to be thoroughly and shockingly destroyed by a single inaccurate bomb was also a target full of [innocent people]."[20]) Thus, in the circumstances, Truman could not fulfill his first duty (to American soldiers) without violating the second (to Japanese civilians)—and vice versa. To act for the best, he was forced to choose between them. That was the nature of the tragedy.

Benign Corruption

I turn now to a class of dirty hands cases in which the intractable conflict of a genuine moral dilemma is not present. In these cases it is not true that however the agent acts necessarily involves doing something wrong. Rather, the agent has the option of not doing any evil deed and thereby retaining clean hands. However, circumstances are such that an evil deed is a means to a great good, and the agent is in an especially favorable (perhaps unique) position to realize that good. Thus the situation has, we might say, a certain moral urgency. The evil deed is not unavoidable, but it is nonetheless compelling. Further, in this class of cases, it happens that the close link between the evil deed and the great good is forged (in the circumstances) by the evil deeds of other agents. Because others are acting badly, the public official who wishes to serve the public good must participate in immoral conduct. Thus, the deed is contingent on what others happen to be doing, as well as on the closeness of the relation between means and ends.

An immediate objection arises from those who dispute the claim that acting wrongly is ever required for achieving a good outcome. For example, Alan Donagan remarks that it is a presupposition of common morality that public goods have more than one way of being brought into existence; indeed they always have a way of being brought into existence that avoids wrongdoing. What is the source of this confidence? Donagan observes: "That good has come about [in the past] through crime does not show that it could only have come about through crime."[21] Which is correct. But that does not show that the good could have come about without crime, either. The peculiarity of Donagan's claim is that it attempts to counter one claim of necessity by another claim of necessity.[22] For Donagan to escape dirty hands he has to assume that morally acceptable means are always available for bringing about desired outcomes. What leads Donagan to make this assumption? At times it seems that he is worried about slippery slopes. If it is admitted that public officials must sometimes do what is wrong to achieve a public good, it follows, in his view, that "great historical crimes"—aggressive wars, religious persecutions, slavery, despotism, economic oppression (all his examples)—can be rationally justified, even retrospectively justified, if they resulted in some public good. Further, it follows, he says, that it is legitimate to include wicked actions in a political program so long as they are intended to achieve desirable outcomes. But neither of these implications holds. And, if they don't, the only ground Donagan has to stand on is the idealist assumption that history does not require choices that are morally problematic for human beings to carry out.

Lincoln's Corruption

To get to the core of this class of cases, let us discuss a specific example. The one I have selected is Abraham Lincoln's use of bribery to get the U.S. House of Representatives to pass the Thirteenth Amendment. This is an apt example because considerable disagreement exists about whether Lincoln acted properly. For example, Donagan says he did; John Noonan says he did not. This disagreement exists even though both theorists deny the necessity of dirty hands; that is, both are idealists in the sense I am using that term.

The crucial facts of the case are as follows. After issuing the Emancipation Proclamation in 1863, Lincoln committed himself to passage of a constitutional amendment that would extend liberation beyond the rebellious southern states to the entire country and would prevent any postwar effort at re-enslavement. In the spring of 1864, the Thirteenth Amendment passed the Senate with the requisite two-thirds majority, but the tally in the House was twelve votes short. Republicans constituted only slightly more than half the House membership, and a large block of Democrats and Unionists were against the measure. The election of November 1864 changed these numbers dramatically, with the Republicans winning about three-quarters of the seats, but the new Congress would not take office until March of the following year. Lincoln decided he did not want to wait and worked to get the necessary votes for the amendment during the lame-duck session. He preferred to have a bipartisan majority for the amendment, and saw passage as a gesture of wartime unity helpful, if not essential, to Union victory. So Lincoln targeted about a dozen lame-duck Democrats, inducing them either to stay away from the House chamber during the vote (which would reduce the number needed for a two-thirds majority) or to switch their vote. Although some uncertainty exists to this day as to exactly what rewards Lincoln offered to the Democrats, they appear to have included promises of government jobs for themselves or their relatives, release of rebel soldiers who were relatives, and the setting aside of pending legislation on railroad monopolies. Whatever the rewards, they were, in the words of Carl Sandburg, "gifts that would have raised a high and noisy scandal if known by the opposition."[23] The amendment passed by a margin of two votes.[24]

Donagan's favorable view of Lincoln's deals is initially quite surprising, given his assumption that it is never necessary to use evil means to achieve any end. After all, Lincoln could have waited for the new Congress to be seated, rather than engaging in secret and questionable negotiations with the lame-duck Democrats. Instead Donagan says that Lincoln was justified. "[M]ost ordinary decent men," he says, would rightly be "taken aback at the suggestion that by [engaging in these acts] Lincoln violated common morality."[25] However, John Noonan is "an ordinary decent man," and he thinks Lincoln was wrong to act as he did. So we cannot settle this case quite so quickly.

In his discussion of corruption cases, Donagan argues that it makes a difference, morally, who initiates the corruption and what is at stake. "Even in a society in which corruption is normal and lawful, it is wrong to initiate the corruption of others or to harden them in it; but it is not wrong *to defend yourself* by means of corruption against corrup-

tion already initiated by others.''[26] Although Donagan's meaning is not
perfectly clear, I think his point in this passage is that it is crucial not
only that others have initiated the corruption, but that what is at stake
is a basic civil right. Only then may one defend oneself by means of
corruption. (He offers the example of bribing a corrupt judge to keep
the judge from doing an injustice.) With qualifications, Noonan might
agree with Donagan's judgment in this case; at any rate, he offers the
story recounted by Elizabeth Anscombe of Wittgenstein's efforts to
save the lives of his two sisters. The sisters lived in Vienna. When
Germany annexed Austria in 1938, they became subject to the Nazi
laws on race. Wittgenstein went to Germany, negotiated with the Nazi
authorities, and arranged to make available a certain sum from the
family fortune in Switzerland, in exchange for leaving his two sisters
undisturbed.[27]

    Noonan formulates the general principle justifying this bribe as
follows: When one has a right to a civil good, one has a right to prevent
its unjust denial. Formulated so broadly, however, this principle covers
too wide a range of cases, including ones where corruption is not
pervasive but where an isolated individual confronts a single corrupt
official. Noonan makes it clear that he does not mean to include such
cases. He specifies that the principle applies only under conditions of
warfare, or at least conditions in which civic ties and social trust have
deteriorated to such an extent that something like a state of war exists,
at least for an oppressed group. Under such conditions, bribery is a
defensive weapon against an unjust attacker; its employment is necessary to achieve justice. But this description, he observes, does not
apply to Lincoln's case. Although Lincoln's deed occurred during
wartime, it was not directed against the enemy. And it "subverted"
the democratic process.[28]

    How could Donagan disagree? Of course, after attending to Noo-
nan's argument, Donagan could revise his judgment. If, as one learns
more of the facts, it appears correct to say that Lincoln may have been
"initiating the corruption of others" or at least "hardening them in
it," Donagan might want to admit that Lincoln was wrong and should
have waited for the seating of the new Congress. If he would be
reluctant to revise his view, it may be only because he is keen
to challenge the "Machiavellian conviction that common morality
incapacitates ordinary politicians in constitutional states."[29] Again,
common morality is assumed to be adequate to the moral work that
needs to be done. But why should we not have a different view of
common morality: Whether or not it sometimes incapacitates public

officials, it at least makes their lives more complicated, morally. The correct assessment of Lincoln's deed may be more complicated in just this way.

To preserve the judgment that Lincoln acted for the best, as I am inclined to do, and yet retain the idea that he did something wrong, we need to shift to a moral argument not available to idealists such as Donagan or Noonan. The key idea is the contingency of obligations.

Although formulated by Machiavelli, the classic statement of this idea is by Hobbes, who believed that this contingency holds for all our obligations. For Hobbes, moral duties are not unqualifiedly binding on oneself unless one can dependably rely on others to abide by them. Since merely trusting others to act morally is unreliable, at least in political society, moral duties become binding only if they are coercively enforced. In the absence of enforcement, people exist in a state of nature, where one is *not obligated to do what is morally required*. This paradoxical statement is crucial to understanding Hobbes's view. It is not that, in a state of nature, moral duties cease to be moral duties; rather, one is not obligated to act on them. More specifically, such duties are binding *in foro interno* ("to a desire they should take place") but not *in foro externo* ("to putting them in act") without enforcement or mutual guarantees.[30] Hobbes's distinction preserves the idea that the duties are binding, albeit in a qualified sense; to act contrary to them violates the natural moral order. Nonetheless, one is not required to follow them in a state of nature. Since one's own preservation is at stake, to act on them would be literally self-defeating. Hence, one cannot be blamed for failing to do what is morally required.

If we confine ourselves to the state of nature, or at least to circumstances characterized by a widespread breakdown of civic trust, Donagan and Noonan might not disagree with Hobbes's conclusion. The divergence comes with attempts to extend the analysis to "ordinary" political life. So the question we need to ask is how far the Hobbesian analysis reaches. Is political life sometimes a quasi-state of nature? One possibility is that the Hobbesian analysis applies to any social process the fulfillment of whose purpose depends on compliance by all participants.[31] In a foot race, for example, cheating by any of the runners (perhaps by use of steroids) undermines the point of determining who is capable of the best performance. Similarly, in an election, cheating by any of the candidates (perhaps by stuffing ballot boxes) undermines the point of determining who is preferred by a majority of voters. In the absence of mutual guarantees in such situations, participants are not obligated to place themselves at an unfair disadvantage.

However, it is one thing not to be obligated to place oneself at a disadvantage, another to believe that the cheating of others provides a warrant for one's own cheating—or that the corruption of others provides a warrant for one's own participation in corruption. We must be careful about the direction of the argument. For example, in Lincoln's case, some will point to the fact that corrupt practices were fairly widespead in the federal government. Technically such practices were probably in violation of law, but enforcement of the law was subject to political manipulation. Although the Democratic Party officially opposed the Thirteenth Amendment—calling it "unwise, impolitic, cruel, and unworthy of the support of civilized people"—it is fair to hypothesize that some Democrats adopted the party stand publicly only as a bargaining strategy. In actuality they were probably willing to deal, and the question for them was what could they get for their vote. So, anyone familiar with the process might well have said: "These are the rules of the game. Anyone who wishes to participate must play by the rules." This view leads naturally to the claim that, when wrong acts are sufficiently pervasive, widely expected, even sanctioned, they are not wrong after all.

But if the act were considered not wrong after all, there would be no dirty hands, and the paradox in the Hobbesian analysis would be lost. Walzer clearly holds on to the paradox. In his election case, the demand of the dishonest ward boss warrants the candidate's engaging in the corrupt deal. But Walzer indicates he should be reluctant, perhaps even extremely reluctant, to act. And if he were engaging in a widespread and long-standing practice of corruption, he would know that he should not participate at all. He should overcome his scruples only because he reasonably believes that, on this occasion, the corrupt act is necessary for success.

Now, at this point, I have to note that I am inclined to disagree with Walzer's judgment in the election example. Perhaps the situation is underdescribed; perhaps details could be added that would lead me to a different judgment. But I think one detail would continue to make a moral difference: namely, that the good to be achieved by the corrupt deal is too remote. The candidate's aim is to get elected, and since the process is corrupt it seems that the only way to succeed is also to engage in corruption. Being a good person it is expected that, once elected, he will attempt in the best way he knows how to serve the public good. Indeed, if we did not believe that, the argument would not get off the ground. But whether the candidate, once in office, will actually accomplish any good is highly uncertain. A great many factors, most of them not under any one person's control, determine whether a public official manages to serve the public good. Thus, for me, the connection between the means and the end is too distant to provide the warrant needed for the corrupt act. And meanwhile the dangers—both moral and political—of the candidate's participating in corruption are too great.

(It is worth repeating that evil acts, even when necessary, have multiple effects. They are never *simply* means to a given end. That is why the duty to avoid them is binding *in foro interno*, even when not *in foro externo*. In practical terms, I take this duty to mean that the primary obligation of an individual faced with a corrupt process is to attempt to reform it. When reform is at best a long-term goal, and meanwhile great goods are at stake, the question of dirty hands arises.)

The connection between means and end distinguishes Walzer's election case from Lincoln's case. It is not just that the good to be achieved—the prohibition of slavery by a bipartisan vote—was a great good. The connection between the means and the end was sufficiently close for a reasonable person to believe that the end could be achieved—and perhaps only achieved—with these means.[32]

In sum, I want to say that Lincoln had dirty hands for two main reasons. First, to retain the sense of wrongdoing. The situation—and Lincoln's deed within it—was morally undesirable. It would have been better had the corrupt act not had to be performed. Even if we stipulate that the members of Congress were already corrupt, we cannot get around the point that Lincoln "hardened them in it." Second, I want to stress the psychological point that corrupt acts, even when done for the best, undermine stable moral character if they are repeated. People who engage in such acts and fail to feel guilt or regret do not have the moral character that enables them to recognize—and refrain from— acts that are purely corrupt.[33]

Moral Opportunism

I turn finally to a class of dirty hands cases involving opportunistic conduct. This is the most controversial, and hence in some respects the most interesting, category of cases, because it involves people taking advantage of others without their knowledge or consent. Whereas with benign corruption everyone acts, as it were, with eyes open, here the agent with dirty hands engages in deceit, operates in secret, or manipulates others against their wishes—in order to serve the public good.

The Ideal of Public Deliberation

To set the frame for the particular case I have selected, I shall begin by describing briefly a background ideal of decision making from which the case represents a falling away. The ideal may be called *public deliberation*. I shall emphasize two related components of this ideal.

One component is democratic participation. The idea is this: Decisions by public officials that affect the interests or responsibilities of other parties, including other public officials, require their participation and consent. The concerns, the points of view, the "local knowledge" of affected parties are all legitimate ingredients of collective democratic decision making.

The demand for democratic participation has a special saliency in administrative decision making, because the authority of administrators is weak and divided. It is weak because administrators are not directly accountable to the electorate. What formal authority they have is derivative, being based on delegation by one or more elected officials. (I am not saying that administrators never attain great power; weak authority is compatible with great power when other parties acquiesce in it.) And administrative authority is divided because, in the typical case, administrators are appointed by an executive branch officer but operate under a statutory mandate granted by the legislative branch. Often enough the two branches have divergent, if not actually conflicting, agendas. In such circumstances, consultation with affected parties becomes, I think, a special obligation of administrators, the absence of which decreases the legitimacy of any decision taken. Or, to put the point in a way relevant to the case that follows, to the extent a decision is derived from a personal agenda, with indifference to the administrator's sources of authority, it violates the ethical conditions of the office.

The second component of public deliberation is the idea of epistemic responsibility, which is something in the nature of a constraint on the kind of deliberation that occurs among the diverse parties. Democratic decision making should be based on open consideration of the merits of alternative proposals. Such deliberation requires reasoned argument—publicly conducted—and assessment of the best available information. This, in turn, presupposes honesty and good faith by all participants. It is undermined if agents engage in strategic acts.

Now, the ideal of deliberation may be criticized on at least two grounds. One is that it makes administrative decision making look too much like a philosophy seminar on ethics, which seems to some observers to be just so much jaw-jaw.[34] The other criticism, which I take more seriously, argues that advocacy—putting a favorable face on an issue—is a legitimate role adopted by public officials, including administrators. Advocacy allows partial, even misleading accounts of the truth, leaving it to other parties (who are also advocates) to detect and rectify any distortions or misrepresentations. It thus appears to rest on an implicit assumption about the self-correcting nature of a system of decision making in which the single-mindedness, not to say excesses, of some participants is countered or balanced by the single-mindedness of others. Whatever one makes of the assumption, the advocacy conception of public decision making is a major step away from the ideal of deliberation.

The realist takes yet another step in that direction. The realist sees the necessity of moral opportunism, including deception and manipulation of the decision-making process. Here the theory of adversariness, in a sense, is still at work, but not a benign conception of it. It is no longer assumed necessarily to be self-corrective.

There are at least two types of cases in which the step to opportunistic dirty hands may be warranted. In the first, deliberation might be desirable but events require that action be taken immediately, before deliberation can occur; or in secret, where deliberation would risk public exposure of plans and thereby preclude effective action. In the second type, attempts at deliberation are undesirable because it is reasonably anticipated that they will fail. Failure may be due to entrenched interests, unshakable ideological commitments, or simply limited rationality. Let me suggest a candidate for this second type.[35]

Hermann's Case

It is the case of "Robert Hermann" (a pseudonym), who became acting administrator of the State Department's Bureau of Security and Consular Affairs (SCA). The SCA had been created in 1952 by the McCarran-Walter Act to monitor requests by foreigners to visit the United States and by U.S. citizens to travel abroad, with an eye to national security concerns. Hermann succeeded to the position of acting administrator in March 1966, after a stormy three-and-a-half year period in which his predecessor, Abba Schwartz, was finally forced out of office by conservatives at the State Department and in Congress who found his efforts to liberalize passport and visa policy insufficiently sensitive to the threat of Communist subversion. Hermann shared Schwartz's goal of promoting an "open society" by expanding freedom of travel; he also had a strong desire to develop a personal reputation for managerial competence. So, despite Schwartz's difficulties, and despite the absence of a public mandate for change, he set as one of his policy objectives a liberalization of the terms on which visas for entering the United States would be issued to foreign citizens. (Compared to its major allies and trading partners, existing U.S. visa policy was quite restrictive.)

Hermann succeeded brilliantly, and the story of his success is employed as a model for students of public management of how to devise strategies, build coalitions, and generally act effectively in an administrative setting.[36] Part of the story, however, is Hermann's skill at exploiting opportunities and manipulating deliberative (or nominally deliberative) encounters with key players whose interests or responsibilities would be affected by the change in visa policy—or, when he reasonably anticipated the failure of such encounters, short-circuiting the deliberative process altogether.

Central to the story is the way Hermann managed the relationship with his boss, Secretary of State Dean Rusk. As administrator of SCA, Hermann had the legal authority, delegated to him by the secretary of state as authorized by the McCarran-Walter Act, to prescribe rules governing the issuance of visas. However, legal authority defines the powers of an office, not its obligations. Hermann knew that Rusk was accountable for any SCA policy change; he therefore owed it to Rusk to discuss his proposed initiatives on liberalization. The two officials had not established a working relationship, however, and Hermann had reason to believe that Rusk actually distrusted him because he was Abba Schwartz's chosen successor. More importantly, perhaps, Hermann knew that Rusk gave SCA business very low priority on his own full agenda. This inattention could be interpreted as a kind of window of opportunity: So long as Hermann pursued his initiatives without making trouble for the secretary, Rusk would probably acquiesce in his accomplishments. When, in the event, Hermann succeeded in establishing the coalition he needed to put the new visa policy in place, he finally turned to the question of Rusk's approval. He had two options. One was to send Rusk an "action memorandum," which would require Rusk's signature; the other was an "information memorandum,'' which simply informed Rusk about the policy change. Hermann sent an information memorandum and said that the change would be announced to the press in three days. When no response was forthcoming, he called a press conference.

Such was Hermann's relation to his boss. A comparable story could be told about Hermann's strategic behavior in relation to his subordinate, Ted Zelenka, director of the Visa Office. However, in the space I have, I shall focus instead on certain deliberative encounters (or nonencounters, as the case may be) that resemble situations belonging to the previous category of dirty hands cases. In these encounters, the other parties have already departed from the governing ideal of public deliberation and so may be regarded as warranting Hermann's departures. The contrast between these encounters and the Rusk story will help illuminate this third category of cases.

Thus, Hermann had to decide how to deal with J. Edgar Hoover, director of the FBI. There was no question that the change in visa policy would affect the bureau's responsibilities. But Hoover was a central and highly influential member of the security-conscious conservative faction, and Hermann reasonably believed that Hoover would not be moved by—indeed would not listen to—the arguments for liberalization. So he decided to bypass the FBI by going to Hoover's boss, Attorney General Nicholas Katzenbach, with whom he had already developed a personal relationship. Katzenbach gave his support to the visa plan without consulting Hoover. Also, Hermann had to deal with Representative Haynes Gaighan of Ohio, head of the House Subcommittee on Immigration, who had been instrumental in Abba Schwartz's ouster. It was reasonable to assume that Gaighan also would be against the policy change, especially if he thought the FBI opposed it. Hermann overcame Gaighan's resistance by concocting the story that the president supported liberalization of visa policy in order to increase foreign tourism, as a way of helping to resolve the ''balance of payments'' deficit—thus, using one ''phony issue (balance of payments) to combat another phony issue (national security).''[37] Hermann also gave Gaighan a false impression of the degree of support in the executive branch for his plan.

Hermann's excuse for these machinations might be that the other parties, Hoover and Gaighan, had disqualified themselves from good-faith treatment, as it were, by adopting immovable ideological positions. If Hermann had acted in accordance with the ideal, the process of deliberation would have been dominated by people obsessed by a nonexistent threat of subversion and not open to arguments on the merits. Now, it might be objected that I make the mistake (on Hermann's behalf) of thinking that the ideological commitments are all on one side. Hermann also had such commitments, it could be said, and therefore no more validity should be granted his assessment of the public interest than Hoover's and Gaighan's. But, even if this point is conceded, it is not clear what follows. How should officials act if all sides are committed to immovable ideological positions? Does it mean that everyone is permitted to act strategically? In any case, the objection misconstrues my point. My emphasis is not on "ideological" but on "immovable." I take it as a corollary of the ideal of deliberation that public officials have a duty of openness. The question here is how one should construe one's obligations when other parties do not acknowledge this duty.

I think no one would dispute, at any rate, that Hermann's conduct was manipulative. By regarding it as a case of dirty hands, I mean to add that he should have felt guilty for having done something wrong, even though he acted for the best. Guilt was warranted because, by acting strategically, Hermann failed to honor fundamental obligations of his role, specifically the honesty and good faith required by the ideal of deliberation.

At this point one might object, I suppose, that this conclusion gives too much moral weight to the claims of the deliberative process. The duty to engage in open decision making, it may be said, is a *prima facie* duty and must be weighed against the duty to achieve good outcomes. One is obligated to meet the demands of both process and substance, if possible, but when they conflict the right thing will be sometimes to give more weight to process and sometimes to give more weight to substance. Hermann was simply giving appropriate weight to substance.

The difficulty I have with this objection is that, in the absence of a process of collective deliberation, judgments about the good to be achieved by adopting one policy or another are made by isolated individuals. Individuals are not privileged sources of knowledge about the public good, and in a democratic society one person's idea of the public good has no more standing than anyone else's. Exploiting an official position to realize a particular idea of the good is indistinguishable from promoting a personal agenda. Like matters of personal conscience, personal agendas are inappropriate in public decision making, except as a possible starting point for garnering collective support.[38] Indeed, one may go further and say that the only relevant judgments about the public good are just those judgments that emerge from deliberative processes. Hence, process in a way has priority over substance. It is true that a commitment to deliberation, by limiting managerial discretion, limits an official's potential effectiveness. When consultation is required, success is more problematic. But the commitment to process is in the service of fundamental values. By constraining the pursuit of personal policy agendas, deliberation diffuses power, generates conflict, and requires accommodation. But it does this because liberty and democratic decision making are at stake. I do not mean to suggest, of course, that these values cannot be overridden in some cases—my point is just the opposite—but one needs to keep in mind the seriousness of any such violation.

Another objection to my conclusion is based on the idea that the justification of political action is retrospective. If Hermann's policy initiative is accepted and survives, then he was justified in what he did. If it is repudiated, then he was not justified and must be prepared to accept blame. This is a variation on the "verdict of history" argument, according to which realization of the expected public good relieves the agent of the guilt that would otherwise accrue for the deeds involved in achieving success—with this twist: that the criterion of realizing the public good is acceptance of the policy. In this view, the dirty hands official is a moral risk taker, an entrepreneur for the public interest. As with business entrepreneurs, public acceptance of the product means success (justification) and public repudiation means ruin (blame).

I accept the view that Robert Hermann was a moral entrepreneur, but there are a number of problems with the idea of retrospective justification, as others have pointed out.[39] First, since actual outcomes have multiple causes, the combination of which may be fortuitous, this view gives moral credit to individuals on the basis of luck. Second, the idea that justification is retrospective appears to be incoherent. Any deed that can be justified by its outcome can be so justified before the deed occurs. If it cannot be justified before, it cannot be justified afterwards. Finally, the agent would not be justified if indeed the act was wrong. The agent may have acted for the best—but have dirty hands. I think that was true in Hermann's case.

Nonetheless, this last objection gets indirectly at an important point. The question left open by my analysis of Hermann's conduct is the question of accountability. As I have described the values at stake in the ideal of deliberation, Hermann's act has to count as an affront to democratic government. Even if he acted for the best, there is a need for a public reaffirmation of the validity of the morality that has been violated. For that to happen, the act cannot remain secret. Which means that, at some point after the deed is done and the circumstances have passed, the public must be given the opportunity to approve or repudiate—or, rather, to approve *and* repudiate—the dirty hands opportunist. When that happens, the opportunist should graciously accept the public's (dis)favor.

Questions

This brief exploration of the landscape of dirty hands raises many difficult questions. In this concluding section, I shall discuss only two, and even those incompletely: What does it mean to act "for the best" when faced with a dirty hands situation? And who exactly makes that judgment? These questions are not easily answered, and I shall do no more than indicate the current direction of my thinking.

Consider tragic choices. Since the situations I have in mind often involve third parties whose evil deeds force the agent into the tragic choice, it seems fair to describe many of them as a choice of the lesser evil. In such situations, therefore, to act for the best is to choose the lesser evil. In the typical case, it is not simply that the agent must do one of two acts both of which are wrong; the agent must do something wrong, or else another person will do something even worse. However, this description does not fit all cases of tragic choice. It does not apply, for example, to Truman's case, since the alternative to use of the atomic bombs was continued incendiary bombing of Japanese cities and invasion of the mainland by the United States. More importantly, when the lesser-evil description is apt, it entails a clear priority between *A* and *B*; one should of course do the lesser rather than the greater evil, if those are the only alternatives. Thus it appears to settle in advance several moral questions that should remain open. It suggests, for example, that the two evils are commensurable, and that we have a single measure to determine which is the greater and which the lesser. It thereby predisposes us to a utilitarian account of resolution. While in most of our examples the utilitarian act may turn out to be for the best, this result should not be presupposed. The most I want to say now is that, when a moral dilemma occurs, two conflicting acts are found compelling; typically one is more compelling than the other, but the other does not cease to be compelling. That holds for the other categories of dirty hands as well.

Regarding the second question—Who exactly makes the judgment about what is for the best?—I think there are three alternative formulations worth exploring. For example, the conflict may be thought to occur, as it were, within the agent. It is the agent who believes the wrong act is wrong, and yet must be done in order to achieve what the agent believes is for the best. Thus the conflict is internal. To do the wrong act would violate the agent's own principles and would result in a feeling of guilt. As Walzer says: "[H]e will believe himself to be guilty. That is what it means to have dirty hands."[40] The difficulty with this formulation is that the presence or absence of the feeling of guilt may be unwarranted. Perhaps the agent should feel guilty but doesn't. Those who believe Truman had dirty hands are alarmed that he considered as "perfectly justified" his decision to drop the bombs on Japanese civilians. (There is considerable evidence that Truman in fact deluded himself about the nature of his decision, because he described the targets as "purely military."[41]) Or perhaps the agent feels guilty but shouldn't. The guilt may be neurotic, or simply the result of confusion about the situation. In both cases, the agent's point of view needs to be supplemented, if not replaced, by the view of an outside observer.

A different formulation sees the conflict as occurring between the agent and the public on whose behalf the agent is acting. We might call this an example of political conflict, and it can happen in a number of ways. One scenario is that the agent and the public have different moral standards; perhaps the public is utilitarian, for example, but the agent is absolutist, insisting on adhering to certain rules no matter what the consequences. In Walzer's example of the candidate who must make a corrupt deal in order to get elected, he observes that the candidate has scruples. "But we [the public] view the campaign in a certain light, estimate its importance in a certain way, and hope that he will overcome his scruples and make the deal."[42] If we leave the case there, we have a moral standoff, and everyone has clean hands. Another scenario is that the public is making contradictory demands: It wants the agent to act for the best but doesn't want the agent to do the evil deed necessary to bring that about. Donagan seems to think of dirty hands cases this way, and he complains of the hypocrisy involved in the public's punishing officials who were acting according to their wishes.

If this description were accurate, the point would be well taken, but the public's making contradictory demands is not the kind of moral conflict we are interested in. In yet another scenario, both the agent and the public grasp the conflict. It is not just that the public wants the politician to make the dishonest deal; the public realizes that the act is wrong—but wants it done nonetheless, because it is necessary for achieving the public good (e.g., electing a "good person" who will work to eliminate corruption). In this scenario, the conflict is internal to the mind of the public. But this understanding of the conflict leaves the same problem left by the first formulation: the possibility that the public is simply mistaken or confused in its judgment. So we still need another point of view.

The final formulation sees the conflict as internal to an ideal deliberator. It is the ideal deliberator who believes the wrong act is wrong, and yet must be done in order to achieve what the ideal deliberator thinks is for the best. By an ideal deliberator I mean simply a person deliberating under conditions favorable to moral judgment. The ideal deliberator provides an external standard by which the motives and reflections of actual persons may be assessed—placing a check on mistakes, neurotic guilt, and the like—but without dissolving the moral conflict. And that is because the conflict is a conflict in morality itself. After ideal deliberation, the agent acts for the best but experiences guilt (the moral residue) for having done damage to the moral order. That happens because morality is not a single consistent system. Or so the ideal deliberator must conclude. (Thus the limits of human rationality, though most acute in tragic choices, infect all dirty hands cases.)

At this point the idealist impulse emerges in many theorists, leading them to devise intellectual strategies to deny the claim of a limit to human rationality. The thrust of idealist criticism is captured by Donagan when he attacks those "moralists [who] have always been tempted to find fault with the contingencies of the world rather than with their moral thinking."[43] Certainly the variety of idealist strategies for turning apparent dilemmas into resolvable conflicts is impressive. One strategy is appeal to the rules governing ordinary use of such concepts as *ought* and *obligation*, which (it is said) prevent claims from remaining compelling if they are not otherwise permissible (i.e., if they conflict with stronger claims). Another strategy, often connected to the first, converts the conflicting moral claims into *prima facie oughts*, with the conflict resolved at a "higher" level of analysis, for example by application of the principle of utility. A third strategy simply puts all moral principles in order. Every principle is ranked, so that when apparent conflicts occur one needs only to discover the correct arrangement of principles. In other words, morality forms—or, rather, is fashioned by a theorist into—a single consistent system; all very tidy. A fourth strategy, which Donagan uses effectively, reflects the casuistical resources of reason. He proceeds case by case and demonstrates each time what the resolution of the conflict is. As a result, dirty hands cases dissolve: Either the act in question turns out on examination to be wrong and so should not be done (e.g., torturing the rebel leader in the case Walzer describes), or it is perfectly justified and legitimately overrides the conflicting act (e.g., Lincoln's bribery of members of Congress). However, I have just completed the kind of casuistical examination Donagan recommends and have generated very different results.

In the end, what strikes me about all of these idealist strategies is that they are simply dogmatic assertions of the power of rationality. The experience of intractable moral conflict, I think, remains unaffected. To be sure, it won't do simply to appeal to "the fact" of intractable conflict, when the correct description of the fact is in dispute. We need an explanation of the phenomenon. But that is different from explaining it away.

Notes

This paper gestated during the five years that I taught mid-career students at the Kennedy School of Government, from 1986 to 1991. Their fascination, not to say preoccupation, with the problem of dirty hands led me to devote greater attention to it with each succeeding year. The paper was finally prepared for the Conference on Professional Ethics and Social Responsibility at Clemson University, November 21–23, 1991. I am grateful to the organizer of the conference, Daniel Wueste, for his invitation and to the participants for their helpful comments. I am especially indebted to Philip Selznick and Kenneth P. Winkler for a careful reading.

1. Max Weber, "Politics as a Vocation," *From Max Weber*, edited by H. H. Gerth and C. Wright Mills (New York: Oxford University Press, 1958), p. 123.

2. Niccolo Machiavelli, *The Prince and The Discourses* (New York: Random House, 1950), p. 138.

3. Machiavelli, p. 129.

4. Machiavelli, p. 171.

5. Machiavelli, p. 56.

6. Machiavelli, p. 56.

7. Bernard Williams, "Politics and Moral Character" in *Moral Luck* (Cambridge: Cambridge University Press, 1981), p. 60.

8. See Christopher Gowans (ed.), *Moral Dilemmas* (New York: Oxford University Press, 1987).

9. An alternative use of "tragic choice" confines it to situations where no

one does anything wrong but great misfortune results. For example, a fire-fighter able to save only so many people in a burning building has to choose which ones. Guido Calabresi and Philip Bobbitt discuss cases of this type in *Tragic Choices* (New York: Norton, 1978).

10. Williams, "Ethical Consistency," in *Problems of the Self* (Cambridge: Cambridge University Press, 1973), p. 173.

11. Here I am following Martha Nussbaum's account in *The Fragility of Goodness* (Cambridge: Cambridge University Press, 1986), pp. 32–41. The agent's moral sensitivity is often placed at the center of discussion in dirty hands cases; I shall explain below why I think that view is misleading.

12. Michael Walzer, "Political Action: The Problem of Dirty Hands," reprinted in *War and Moral Responsibility*, edited by Marshall Cohen et al. (Princeton: Princeton University Press, 1974), pp. 67–68.

13. For an opposing view, see Frances M. Kamm, "Ethics, Applied Ethics, and Applying Applied Ethics," in *Applied Ethics and Ethical Theory*, eds. David M. Rosenthal and Fadlou Shehadi (Salt Lake City: University of Utah Press, 1988), p. 164. Kamm prefers "unrealistic hypotheticals" because "real-life cases" tend to involve "details inessential to a theoretical point."

14. Walzer, "Political Action," p. 63.

15. Walzer, *Just and Unjust Wars* (New York: Basic Books, 1977), p. 266.

16. McGeorge Bundy, *Danger and Survival: Choices About the Bomb in the First Fifty Years* (New York: Random House, 1988), p. 652.

17. R. F. Holland, *Against Empiricism* (Oxford: Basil Blackwell, 1980), p. 137. Socrates expresses the same view in the *Apology*.

18. Elizabeth Anscombe, "Mr. Truman's Degree" in *Ethics, Religion, and Politics* (Minneapolis: University of Minnesota Press, 1981), p. 64.

19. Philippa Foot makes this point when she observes: "[T]he breaking of promises, even when necessary, usually has bad effects." See "Moral Realism and Moral Dilemma" in *Moral Dilemmas*, p. 258.

20. *Danger and Survival*, p. 80.

21. Alan Donagan, *The Theory of Morality* (Chicago: The University of Chicago Press, 1977), p. 185.

22. This point is made by Dennis Thompson, "Democratic Dirty Hands," in *Political Ethics and Public Office* (Cambridge: Harvard University Press, 1987), p. 14.

23. Quoted by Donagan, *The Theory of Morality*, p. 187.

24. See the brief account by James McPherson, *Battle Cry of Freedom* (New York: Ballantine, 1988), pp. 838f. It is worth stressing that the argument for a military *benefit* to be gained by passage of the Thirteenth Amendment is morally distinct from the argument of military *necessity* that Lincoln employed to justify the Emancipation Proclamation. On the latter argument, see Garry Wills, *Lincoln at Gettysburg* (New York: Simon and Schuster, 1992), pp. 137–47.

25. *The Theory of Morality*, p. 187.

26. *The Theory of Morality*, p. 186.
27. John T. Noonan, Jr., *Bribes* (Berkeley: University of California Press, 1984), pp. 685f.
28. *Bribes*, pp. 694–95.
29. *The Theory of Morality*, p. 186.
30. Thomas Hobbes, *Leviathan*, ed. C. B. Macpherson (London: Penguin, 1968), p. 215.
31. This possiblity is suggested by Norman Gillespie, "The Business of Ethics," *University of Michigan Business Review* 26:6 (November 1975), p. 3. See also Amy Gutmann and Dennis Thompson, "The Theory of Legislative Ethics," in *Representation and Responsibility*, edited by B. Jennings and D. Callahan (New York: Plenum Press, 1985), p. 182.
32. Some historians have recognized that Lincoln possessed sufficient subtlety of mind to appreciate the complexity of dirty hands situations, but because of their own confusion about the moral issues, they end up unwittingly presenting a portrait of Lincoln as an unprincipled opportunist. Such a portrait is offered by David Donald in "Abraham Lincoln and the American Pragmatic Tradition," *Lincoln Reconsidered*, 2nd ed. (New York: Vintage Books, 1961), pp. 128–43.
33. It is important to distinguish the type of case discussed in the text from circumstances in which a public official is aware of but fails to do anything about the corrupt acts of others, because exposing the corruption would likely imperil the official's honest efforts to do his or her job. In this situation, the honest official may feel corrupt simply for acquiescing in others' corruption. Sometimes one does indeed have an obligation to expose the evil deeds of others, but in political life there is also what I would call *an economy of responsibility*, captured in the political maxim that one can't fight every battle.
34. So Martin Shapiro remarks in *Who Guards the Guardians?* (Athens: University of Georgia Press, 1988), p. 149.
35. In the analysis that follows, I am especially indebted to a teaching note on the case written by Mark Moore and incorporated into his casebook on leadership. However, Moore frames his analysis in terms of the opposition between consequentialist and deontological theories; as above, I eschew that frame. Also, Moore does not reflect on the case in the context of dirty hands. See Mark Moore and Malcolm Sparrow, *Ethics in Government* (Englewood Cliffs, N.J.: Prentice-Hall, 1990), pp. 89–95.
36. "Bureau of Security and Consular Affairs" (1975) is available from the Case Program of the Kennedy School of Government (Harvard University). It was prepared by Jeanne Johns, under the supervision of Philip B. Heymann and Stephen B. Hitchner. For Philip Heymann's own account, see *The Politics of Public Management* (New Haven: Yale University Press, 1987), pp. ix-xiii.
37. *Ethics in Government*, p. 92.
38. See my discussion of the status of public officials' personal convictions in "The Religious Convictions of Public Officials," *Canadian Journal of Law and Jurisprudence* 3:1 (1990), pp. 129–43.

39. See, for example, Thomas Nagel, "Moral Luck," *Mortal Questions* (Cambridge: Cambridge University Press, 1979), especially p. 28n.

40. "Political Action," p. 68.

41. See, for example, *Danger and Survival*, p. 79.

42. "Political Action," p. 68.

43. Donagan, "Consistency in Rationalist Moral Systems," in *Moral Dilemmas*, p. 281.

3

Conflict of Interest

Larry May

The splitting of the self would, at least, have the finality of
destroying its presumptuousness.
—Jean-François Lyotard, *The Differend*

Conflicts of interest are to be avoided, so the prevailing wisdom has it,
because the professional's objective judgment is compromised. When
a professional has a conflict of interest, the professional's self is
divided, with one part of the self pulled toward serving the interests of
one's client, and the other part of the self pulled toward personal gain
(or some other interest) at the expense of serving the client's interests.
Black's Law Dictionary defines such conflicts in terms of "a clash
between public interest and the private pecuniary interest of the
individual concerned."[1] Most codes of professional conduct urge
people to avoid conflicts of interest in order to be more integrated
professionals, and to be more likely to avoid the violation of their
professional duties. Generally, the conflict of interest literature is in
agreement with the codes. For example, in their monograph, *Conflicts
of Interest in Engineering*, Wells, Jones, and Davis write that "[m]ost
conflicts of interest can be avoided. We can take care not to put
ourselves in a position where contrary influences or divided interests
might undermine our ability to do what we are supposed to do."[2]
 In this paper I will draw on some very recent work in postmodern
social theory[3] that challenges the view that conflicts within the self are
to be avoided or minimized. The postmodern approach to the world is
generally to celebrate conflicts, to think of them as part of what
constitutes the self. The self is just the diversity of conflicting interests
that are constantly operating over the course of a life, if indeed there
is such a thing as a stable and coherent concept of a single self at all.
While some postmodernists think of the self as an incoherent notion, a

view that I do not endorse, postmodernism has important insights nonetheless, which moral philosophers would do well to take seriously. Postmodernism contains at least two divergent strains. Some postmodernists think of the self as a fiction, or even as an incoherent notion. Jacques Derrida is the best-known defender of such a view. Derrida and his followers have largely eschewed talk of morality and politics, opting instead for a version of nihilism. But there is another postmodern strain that is highly critical of the modernist conception of the self, but which still thinks that there is enough coherence to the self to provide a basis for moral and political obligation. Jean-François Lyotard is the best example of a postmodernist of this sort. In what follows I will follow the latter rather than the former strain in postmodern social theory.

Most modernist discussions of conflicts of interest merely assume that they are bad things to be avoided, especially when they adversely affect the independent judgment of the professional. But there are some exceptions. Charles Wolfram, for instance, begins his hornbook, *Modern Legal Ethics*, by noting that

> conflicts of interest are part of the world around us, always have been and inevitably must be. . . . In a sense, every representation begins with a lawyer-client conflict. If the representation is for a fee, the lawyer's economic interest will be to maximize the amount of the fee and the client's will be to minimize it.[4]

I wish to argue that we will seriously misunderstand the moral difficulties of conflicts of interest if we do not realize the extent to which some conflicts of interest are "inevitable" or at least not necessarily problematic in professional settings.

The inevitability of some conflicts of interest in professional settings should not lead us to think that all conflicts are morally permissible. And, indeed, I will attempt to explain which conflicts can and should be avoided. But the thesis of this essay is that conflicts of interest per se are not morally problematic. What makes some conflicts of interest morally problematic is that they involve deception or they infringe client autonomy, but not all conflicts of interest are of this sort and hence not all conflicts are morally problematic. In presenting this thesis I will consider and reject the standard accounts of what is wrong with conflicts of interest. Let us first turn to some cases that will begin to illustrate why the extreme view, namely, that all conflicts of interest are morally problematic and should be rejected.

Real Estate Brokers—Constant Conflicts?

Quite recently my wife and I had the unhappy task of selling one house and buying another. I was struck by the fact that the real estate brokers with whom we worked in buying our St. Louis home were involved in what would standardly be called a conflict of interest. Most of such a broker's work involves showing houses to prospective buyers and advising the buyer whether to place a bid on a certain piece of property and at what price. Some real estate brokers who claim to work for the buyer will actually be paid by the seller. Assuming a zero-sum game, every decrease in price offered by the buyer clashes with the pecuniary interests of the buyer's broker, since the broker's commission is determined as a percentage of the selling price. There is indeed a conflict of interests here since there will surely be situations where it is in the buyer's best interest to offer a lower price or back out of a sale, whereas it is clearly in the personal interest of the buyer's broker to advise the buyer to accept a higher-price counter-offer and go through with the sale. Yet, these brokers see nothing wrong in these situations. My view is that their claims should not be lightly dismissed.

The identity of a real estate broker is conflicted. On the one hand, due to the sheer time they spend with buyers, guiding them through house after house, they clearly work for, or at least with, the buyers. But on the other hand, it is quite clear that their business and personal interests coincide with the seller's interests. As long as real estate brokers are paid by the seller, it is in a sense inevitable that there will be a conflict of interest between the broker's personal interests and the interests of their buyer-clients. The brokers I met, however, continued to talk as if they worked for the buyers. Nevertheless, it was clear that they did not take an adversarial role toward the seller, nor did they have any desire to do so. It was as if they assumed that everyone knew, or at least should have known, that the brokers had personal interests in being paid as high a commission as possible, and that this common knowledge meant that it was not problematic to maintain nonadversarial relations with both parties. Such an arrangement places brokers into a different category than some other professionals.

Real estate brokers who work with buyers could reasonably claim that their main professional duty is to facilitate housing market transactions, rather than to serve in an adversarial process in which they "represent" one person's interests against another person's interests. If facilitation and cooperation are indeed the goals they seek to serve, and if it is assumed that both buyer and seller have an interest in houses being sold rather than not, then the broker's interest in his or her own greater monetary gain is not necessarily, even though it is traditionally thought to be, in conflict with their buyer client's interests. In a sense, real estate brokers can take a communitarian rather than contractarian view of the world, and this may at least partially explain why they are less troubled by their potential or actual conflicts of interest. The problem is that many real estate brokers continue to talk as if, and often claim explicitly that, they do "represent" the interests of the buyer. Because of this fact, these professionals remain entangled in very problematic conflicts of interest.

There is a sense in which many other professionals are caught in conflicts of interest from the beginning of their relationships with their clients. Lawyers, doctors, engineers, accountants, etc., generally do not work for free and are, therefore, as Charles Wolfram points out, already in a conflict of interest the minute they begin work for a client, since their interest in making a larger income clashes with the client's interest in paying as little as possible to solve their legal, medical, safety or financial problems. More important though, many professional lawyers, doctors, engineers, accountants, etc., work for large organizations and corporations. Their salaries are not paid directly by a client, and so their relationship to their clients is often one that involves a conflict of interest since the interest in serving the organization or corporation, which pays the professional, is often at odds with serving the interests of the client. This is evident, for instance, where doctors work for health maintenance organizations that put pressure on them to minimize expensive diagnostic testing, even though such testing may be in the interests of their patients.

In addition, engineers, for instance, are not only supposed to serve their clients' interests but also the larger societal interest in public safety. This latter interest often comes into conflict with the former interest, when, for example, an engineer is urged by her company to use the least costly, and weaker, material in a product even though public safety would dictate a stronger and more costly material. Similarly, lawyers like to forget that they are supposed to be serving the interest of justice, a paramount societal interest, while also serving their client's interests. Yet, they are paid by those whose interests are often at odds with the societal interests these professionals are supposed to be serving, as is true when criminal lawyers are told by their clients of the location of missing bodies, for instance. If I am right about there being rampant conflicts of interest in most professions, should we advise our students not to become professionals at all, so as not to risk entering into morally problematic behavior?

There are several strategies that could be employed to avoid these difficulties. The American Bar Association's code of professional responsibility stipulates that lawyers only need to concern themselves with conflicts that have a "reasonable probability" of interfering "with a lawyer's professional judgment"[5] by compromising the lawyer's chief professional duties of loyalty and confidentiality. Michael Davis sees the ABA standard as a way to capture what it is about some conflicts of interest that is morally problematic.[6] We could formulate a general rule; namely, that professionals should only be concerned with those conflicts of interest that are likely to have a material effect on their professional judgments. But even if the inherent ambiguity of the word "material" is overlooked, would such a strategy substantially limit the cases of conflict of interest that professionals should worry about?

Such a strategy runs into the following difficulty: one's professional judgment can be materially affected by almost any personal monetary incentive. If real estate brokers working for buyers are being paid by the sellers, then their professional judgment is always at risk of being clouded and they are always in such a compromised position that, from the perspective of the way that conflicts have been viewed, they should not continue in their profession. And yet, it is worth considering whether or not there is any insight to be gained from the moral intuitions of these brokers, which clearly tells them that they are not being morally compromised.

Lawyers have long recognized that not all conflicts of interest are morally problematic. Not only has their code distinguished between conflicts that are likely to affect professional judgment and conflicts that are not, but the judges who interpret the lawyers' obligations have recognized that in many cases the informed consent of the client to a conflict relieves the conflict of interest of its morally problematic character.[7] In the following sections, we will build on this insight in conjunction with some insights gained from the standpoint of postmodernism.

Postmodernism and the Interests of the Self

My view is that what makes conflicts morally problematic is not merely that judgments are compromised, but in addition, that the professionals continue to assert that they are able to serve the interests of their clients unambiguously, even though they know, or should know, that their judgments are likely to be clouded. As I will argue, it is the deceptiveness or the infringement of client autonomy that is morally problematic, not merely the compromised judgment. The alternative I advocate, informed by the postmodern perspective, is to accept rather than decry such potential conflicts, worrying only about the possible deceptions or infringements of client autonomy that might result. Instead of engaging in the often futile attempt to eliminate conflicts, I follow Lyotard who calls for a "metalepsis," a change in the "level of one's take." From my own perspective, the change in the way we respond to conflicts should allow clients to become fully informed about them through a full and open disclosure of the conflict of interest.

Professionals should only feel the need to avoid a conflict of interest if those who have been made aware of these conflicts, and who are likely to be adversely affected by the judgments rendered in such conflict situations, are not willing to accept or for some other reason cannot consent to the situation. In such cases, the professional should either remove the cause of the conflict or terminate his or her relationship with the person whose interests the professional is supposed to serve. Otherwise, the chief professional duty will be that of full and open disclosure of potential and actual conflicts (along with a correspondingly diminished fiduciary duty—to be explained later), rather than the more strenuous and sometimes impossible task of eliminating or evading all possible or actual conflicts.

From a postmodern perspective, selves are always multiply interested and they are also often involved in conflicts concerning those multiple interests. Lawyers, for example, are so often involved in various conflicts of interest that they should discontinue the practice of advertising themselves as persons who act only in the interest of a client. And the American ideal of professional life, which is modeled on the way the lawyers in our society have conceived of themselves, should no longer glorify the single-minded pursuer of a client or patient's interest. Rather, there should be a great deal more honesty in the way that professionals present themselves to their clients and patients.

Lyotard and other postmodern theorists argue that modernists make the mistake of assuming that the self can be objective and unconflicted in its judgments, and that the self can blind itself to, or remove, all of its egoistic motivations.[8] For Lyotard and other postmodernists, the self is always seen as "in progress,"[9] pulled toward several different poles at once. It is never fixed or settled, and if one were to take away all of the various poles, or interests, to which it is attracted or repelled the self would be lost altogether. Similarly, if one were to try to make of the self something that is not drawn in several directions at once, the lack of tension would often destroy the self.[10] It is characteristic of the modern point of view, which Lyotard wholeheartedly rejects, to think that the self or mind can attain an objective, universal, and hence unconflicted standpoint.

The postmodernist's target is well presented by Wells, Jones, and Davis when they write:

A conflict of interest is like dirt in a sensitive gauge. For the same reason rational persons want reliable gauges, they want those upon whose judgment they rely to avoid conflict of interest (insofar as practical) . . . though conflicts of interest cannot always be avoided, they can always be escaped. We can end the association, divest ourselves of the interest, or otherwise get beyond the influence that might otherwise compromise our judgment.[11]

The postmodernist would deny that the self is indeed like "a sensitive gauge," which, with the proper care, can be kept clean insofar as it is unconflicted.

Lyotard uses the term "differend" to refer to an impasse or unresolveable conflict that often characterizes social interactions.[12] Occasionally, a self is able to communicate with another self in such a way that conflicts are resolved. But in most cases, it is "not possible to evade the differend by anticipating it."[13] While Lyotard's analysis of differends is meant to concern all forms of conflict that would involve some sort of stated claim by two parties, I find it especially useful in understanding why conflicts of interest are often inevitable and, contrary to prevailing sentiment, why they are not things which professionals can or should always avoid.

Lyotard, as is characterisitic of postmodern thinkers, seriously considers the proposal that since we have such intractable problems with conflicts of interest, we should dispense with the idea of professional obligations and duties altogether in such cases. He writes:

Instead, obligation should be described as a scandal for the one who is obligated: deprived of the "free" use of oneself, abandoned by one's narcissistic image, opposed in this, inhibited in that, worried over not being able to be oneself without further ado. But these are phenomenological or psychoanalytic descriptions of a dispossessed or cloven consciousness. . . . They maintain the self even in the very acknowledgement of its dispersion.[14]

Lyotard does not follow the nihilistic postmodernists. While he does propose that we give up our "nostalgia for the self"—that is, our nostalgia for an unconflicted self that knows its obligations absolutely—he nonetheless urges that we retain the notion of obligation, although it is a more time-bound notion of obligation.

Lyotard argues that we should reject modernist conceptions of universal moral obligation.[15] But he also contends that obligations are like the rules of a language game, binding on those who choose to play the game. This fits nicely with the notion of professional duties sometimes envisioned in codes of professional conduct.[16] Professionals take on special duties by agreeing to project themselves into the world as having unique expertise.[17] But there is no reason to think that these duties should involve unrealistic self-sacrifice on the professional's part. In keeping with Lyotard's brand of postmodernism, I will argue for a revised understanding of the fiduciary relationship between professional and client. First, let me say a bit more about the core problem in conflict-of-interest cases, deceptiveness, and the infringement of client autonomy.

Deception and Client Autonomy

Michael Davis correctly states the major moral difficulty with conflicts of interest when he writes:

> if a lawyer does not at least warn his client of the conflict, he does more than weaken a guarantee worth preserving. He presents himself as having a judgment more reliable than in fact it is. He invites a trust the invitation itself betrays.[18]

As I shall argue in this section, Davis is largely correct, but for the wrong reasons. Davis goes wrong, as do most modern theorists, in believing that there is a type of professional judgment that is trustworthy and reliable in that it is uninfluenced by the material considerations of one's other interests.

Lawyers have perpetuated the view that professionals can and should be expected to serve absolutely the interests of their clients. Wolfram states the point well when he says:

Whatever may be the models that obtain in other legal cultures, the client-lawyer relationship in the United States is founded on the lawyer's *virtually total* loyalty to the client and the client's interests. . . . The entrenched lawyerly conception is that the client-lawyer relationship is the embodiment of centuries of established and stable tradition.[19]

Other professionals have come to model themselves on the Anglo-American law profession.

The idea that professionals should serve "virtually total[ly]" the interests of their clients is at best unrealistic and at worst deceptive. It is unrealistic, as we will see, because it asks lawyers to blind themselves to their own interests in ways that are nearly impossible to meet, and because it ignores the fact that there is often no objectively right way to conceive of someone's interests. It is deceptive because it creates false expectations on the part of the clients, expectations of loyalty that, when thwarted, lead clients to a position where they lose control over their cases. The clients unknowingly render themselves vulnerable to possible abuses of trust that they would otherwise remain vigilantly on guard against. Lawyers betray the trust they have solicited when they act as if they are capable of rendering judgments in behalf of their clients' interests that are unaffected by their other interests.

There are many factors that intrude upon a professional's judgment, rendering the notion of a "virtually total loyalty" in serving the client's interest itself quite suspicious. Consider again the case of lawyers. Lawyers who are in private practice must be constantly concerned about paying the rent—indeed many lawyers find themselves spending so much time getting, keeping, and billing clients that they come to regard the practice of law as a type of business. Yet rarely is this the picture of lawyers that lawyers themselves present to the public. In addition, the lawyers I have known are also highly ambitious individuals who often see the pursuit of a particular client's case as a means of furthering their own careers. Furthermore, lawyers also have political agendas. As Wolfram and others have pointed out "even in pro bono representations, the ideological or altruistic motives that induce a lawyer to offer legal services" can often obscure the pursuit of the client's interests.[20] All of these factors make it unrealistic to think that lawyers can offer "virtually total loyalty" to their client's interests, a loyalty lawyers nonetheless continue to claim to be the hallmark of their profession.

It is an infringement of client autonomy for professionals to deny

clients the knowledge they need to decide whether to entrust themselves to a particular professional. It is deceptive of professionals to
present themselves as capable of rendering objective judgments when
they are aware of conflicts that will make it even more likely than
normal that their "objective" judgments are compromised. This is why
some conflicts of interest are morally problematic. But if a professional
is quite open about the interests that he or she has, or is likely to have,
that are at odds with the client's interest, and secures from the client
an understanding and consent to the lawyer's continued service under
these circumstances, conflicts of interest are no more troubling, from
the moral point of view, than other cases of consensual client services.

It may be objected that in order for possible conflicts to be disclosed
my proposal calls for professionals to be able to identify what all
of their interests are, a feat sometimes not feasible. On my view,
professionals need to be, or to become, self-reflective concerning their
interests. But this is no more troublesome for my view than it is for
any other view of conflicts of interest. The traditional view, for
instance, which calls for professionals to *avoid* all conflicts of interest
surely must also call for professionals to be, or to become, aware of
what their interests are that may conflict with the client's interests. My
view is no worse off than the traditional view.

It may be further objected that I have misidentified the morally
suspicious feature of conflicts of interest. Some might claim that the
difficulty with all conflicts of interest is that they create temptation for
wrongdoing. There are two things to be said about such a view. First,
my postmodern orientation leads me to think that at least some
conflicts of interest are not occasions for wrongdoing at all, but
manifestations of the perfectly legitimate situation where one has
multiple and conflicting motivations. Second, wrongdoing occurs,
when it does, because of a presumed promise that all the professional's
other interests have been subordinated to the client's interests. But
when professionals stop claiming that they can subordinate all of their
other interests, the basis of the wrongdoing also begins to disappear.
Disclosed conflicts that are consented to are not temptations for
wrongdoing because the client has waived the right that would otherwise be the basis of a claim of wrongdoing based on the conflict
of interest.

From the standpoint of deceptiveness and client autonomy, real
estate brokers are better off than lawyers. Real estate brokers make it
quite well known that they are working toward the consummation of
real estate sales and that their income depends on securing higher

rather than lower prices for these pieces of real estate. While they sometimes claim to represent the interests of the buyer, and in this sense perpetuate a deception, they do not claim to serve these interests absolutely. Those who are in the market for real estate are made much more aware of the conflicted nature of the brokers that they encounter than is true of those who find themselves in need of legal counsel. In contrast to the case of real estate brokers, lawyers make it very difficult for clients to see the possible ways in which the client's interests will not necessarily be served. In this way, lawyers infringe client autonomy especially when they continue to assert so strongly that they are uniquely situated to devote themselves to the client's interests.

Next consider a different kind of case taken from engineering. A mechanical engineer is asked to give an informal opinion about a matter that the company he works for is planning to bring before the product standards committee of his profession at large. This engineer helps his work associates draft a letter of inquiry, which is then submitted to his profession's product standards committee for review. As it turns out, this very engineer serves on the relevant product standards committee and is assigned the task of responding to the inquiry (which he had helped draft) in behalf of the professional committee. The engineer gives a ruling that is favorable to the drafters of the inquiry, who also happen to be his associates at the company for which he works. A competing company is placed in a disadvantageous position as a result of the ruling and eventually goes into bankruptcy. Needless to say, the ruling also works to the advantage of the engineer's own company. In 1982, the U.S. Supreme Court reviewed a similar case, and held that the professional association had acted wrongly in allowing the engineer to review an inquiry that he himself had helped to draft.[21]

Since it is true that professional engineers must staff such committees as the professional product standards committee discussed above, and since most engineers are employed by private organizations that will need to get rulings from such committees, it will inevitably happen that conflicts of interest manifest themselves in such contexts. It is my view that there is nothing initially wrong with the engineer in question consulting with his work associates and also drafting a response to the inquiry made by his work associates. Surely it is a mistake to think that professionals must never assume roles that will possibly conflict with other roles they *may* play. In the case at issue, the engineer needed to inform the professional organization as well as the parties who would possibly be affected by the professional organization's ruling.

The postmodern perspective I am advocating in this paper finds it odd indeed to think that all, or even most, conflicts of interest should be avoided. If, for instance, engineers avoided such conflicts as those described above, their professional lives and the world in which they live would become tremendously impoverished. Engineers could only serve on those professional standards committees that would never hear cases brought by the companies these engineers work for. Or, perhaps, such committees could not be staffed at all by engineers working in the private sector, even though it is just these engineers who are most likely to retain a day-to-day understanding of the likely problems of the products in question. In other professions, perhaps including real estate brokerage, avoiding conflicts of interest might mean that the very profession itself would disappear.

Deception and infringement of client autonomy are the key moral problems when personal interest conflicts with client interest. If the engineer in the case discussed above had informed all relevant parties that he had a special, work-related interest in the outcome of the product standard review he was preparing, and if these people had consented to let him continue to serve them, and to notify others who might come to rely on the report, then the writing of this report would have posed no special moral problems. As it was, though, the people who relied on the report did not have sufficient knowledge of the writer's interests to be able to assess it properly; their autonomy was infringed through the lack of such disclosure. They were put into a vulnerable position that they would otherwise have wanted to guard against. In what follows, I attempt to set out a new model for understanding the fiduciary duties that have traditionally been seen as the basis for requiring professionals to avoid potential and actual conflicts of interest.

Fiduciary Duties and Professional Responsibility

In law and other professional contexts, there is thought to be a fiduciary relationship between professional and client. *Black's Law Dictionary* defines "fiduciary" as follows:

> The term is derived from the Roman law, and means (as a noun) a person holding the character of a trustee, or a character analogous to that of a

trustee, in respect to the trust and confidence involved in it and the scrupulous good faith and candor which it requires.[22]

A "fiduciary relation" establishes a situation where various professionals "in equity and good conscience" are "bound to act in good faith and with due regard to interests of one reposing the confidence."[23] When professionals are viewed as fiduciaries, they are thought to be bound to act as if their interests were those of their clients and hence to sacrifice their own interests for the sake of their client's interests.

It is instructive to contrast this situation with that of the standard way that two parties are viewed if they are not in a fiduciary relationship. In his book, *The Critical Legal Studies Movement*, Roberto Unger rightly points out that in law, nonfiduciary relations are ones in which neither party is thought to owe anything to the other: "the other party's interests can be treated as of no account as long as the rightholder remains within his zone of discretionary action."[24] The contrast between normal commercial relations and fiduciary relations is quite striking—surely there is a middle position that would more appropriately apply to conflict-of-interest cases. Like Unger, in this section I will strive for a view of fiduciary relations that takes account of the reality of professional life.

Unger proposes a fiduciary standard that "requires each party to give some force to the other party's interests, though less than to his own."[25] This proposal is a compromise between the overly minimalistic notion of simple contractual obligation that some might apply to professional-client relationships, and the unrealistic selflessness of the legal model of fiduciary duty. Unger goes too far here. Surely, it is not too much to require professionals to place the interests of their clients at least on a par with their most strongly held personal interests. The special status afforded professionals calls for some serious attempt to serve the client's interest. In order to give proper care to the client, the client's interest must be given serious weight, and this means that it should be at least *equal to* the professional's most strongly held personal interests.

Those who have voluntarily placed themselves into positions of trust concerning the interests of others must give careful consideration to those interests. But it is simply a mistake to demand selfless service to the client's interest. Since "virtually total loyalty" is not a realistic possibility in professional life, the chief duty of professionals cannot be absolute service to their client's interests. Hence, the chief professional duty concerning conflicts of interest should be merely the duty of full disclosure, along with the duty to withdraw from serving the client if the client finds the disclosed conflict objectionable. It is too much to expect professionals to have a duty to be totally loyal or to place the interests of their clients significantly above their own interests. As I have indicated, the perpetuation of the myth that professionals have these more strenuous duties is both unrealistic and deceptive.

It is important to note that many of the most serious harms that occur in conflict-of-interest cases result because one party becomes less vigilant on the assumption that another party is serving absolutely the first party's interests. When the professional raises expectations of total loyalty and trustworthiness, then it would indeed implicate the professional in whatever harms result from the diminished vigilance of the client. This is also true of those expectations raised by the profession of which a given professional is a member. But as with other collective responsibilities, an individual can diminish or extinguish his or her personal responsibility by taking steps to overcome the expectations raised by the profession at large. By explicitly stating the interests the professional has that are likely to conflict with the interests of the client, the professional at least partially distances himself or herself from the expectations of objectivity that the rest of the profession may raise. This heightens the vigilance of the client and makes it less likely that the client will be harmed.

Professional responsibility is not merely a matter of conforming to the fiduciary duties one has, even if we understand these duties in the way in which I have suggested. Rather, it is important that elements of shame exist alongside of the guilt that is associated with the direct violation of a professional duty. Even when a professional has done all he or she can do to avoid harm to a client, professionals should deeply regret whatever harms nonetheless occur, and when those harms result from actions taken by the profession as a whole, shame is often not at all misplaced.[26] But the appropriateness of such shame should not lead us to think that professionals have a *duty* to serve absolutely the interests of their clients, such that they should feel guilt whenever they let personal interest interfere with the pursuit of the client's interest. As I have argued, such guilt is appropriate only in certain cases involving deception or infringement of client autonomy.

I have tried to provide a new basis for understanding what is morally problematic about some conflicts of interest in professional life. In arguing that the deceptiveness and infringement of client autonomy of certain conflicts of interest is their undoing, I have indicated a straightforward strategy for rendering many conflicts of interest morally unproblematic; namely, full and open disclosure of potential conflicts by the professional. In general, professionals have for too long mistakenly thought that they can and should avoid all conflicts of interest, as if it were possible for the professional thereby to provide objective judgments and absolutely loyal service for the client. I have provided a challenge to this assumption that has drawn heavily on a postmodern perspective of social and personal conflicts. But, at least in this case, reliance on some postmodern ideas has not thrown us into a moral abyss,[27] but has rather clarified the picture of a certain part of the moral landscape we call professional life.[28]

Notes

1. *Black's Law Dictionary*, fifth edition (St. Paul, Minn.: West Publishing Co., 1979): 271.

2. Paula Wells, Hardy Jones, and Michael Davis, *Conflicts of Interest in Engineering* (Dubuque, Iowa: Kendall/Hunt Publishing Co., 1986): 21.

3. By "postmodern social theory" I mean roughly what Lyotard means by "the postmodern perspective" on social bonds. Among other things, Lyotard says that there are irreconcilable voices in society, but that "the self does not amount to much" in trying to resolve these conflicts. He writes: "Consensus is an outmoded and suspect value. But justice as a value is neither outmoded nor suspect. We must thus arrive at an idea and practice of justice that is not linked to that of consensus." Lyotard, *The Postmodern Condition*, trans. Geoff Bennington and Brian Massumi (Minneapolis: University of Minnesota Press, 1984): 15, 66.

4. Charles Wolfram, *Modern Legal Ethics* (St. Paul, Minn.: West Publishing Co., 1986): 312–13.

5. See Canon 5 of the American Bar Association's *Code of Professional Responsibility and Code of Judicial Conduct*, 1976; and see Wolfram, *Modern Legal Ethics*, 316, 324.

6. Michael Davis, "Conflict of Interest," *Business and Professional Ethics Journal*, vol. 1, no. 4, (Summer 1982): 17–27.

7. Wolfram, *Modern Legal Ethics*, 337–49.

8. See Iris Young's excellent book, *Justice and the Politics of Difference* (Princeton: Princeton University Press, 1990).

9. Jean-François Lyotard, *Peregrinations: Law, Form, Event* (New York: Columbia University Press, 1988): 6.

10. Lyotard, *Peregrinations*, 5.

11. Wells, Jones, and Davis, *Conflicts of Interest*, 20–21.

12. Lyotard, *The Differend*, trans. George Van Den Abbeele (Minneapolis: University of Minnesota Press, 1989): 9, 13.

13. Ibid., 19.

14. Ibid., 109–10.

15. Ibid., 127.

16. Dorothy Emmet ably argues for the conclusion that professional codes are matters of role morality and not universal morality. See her book, *Rules, Roles and Relations* (Boston: Beacon Press, 1966): 158–63.

17. For a more detailed analysis of the moral basis of a professional's duties, especially concerning negligence, see Chapter 5 of my book, *Sharing Responsibility* (Chicago: University of Chicago Press, 1992).

18. Davis, "Conflict of Interest," 21.

19. Wolfram, *Modern Legal Ethics*, 146. Emphasis added.

20. Ibid., 313.

21. See *American Society of Mechanical Engineers v. Hydrolevel Corporation* (72 L Ed 2d 330) 1982. For an extended discussion of this case see my essay "Professional Action and the Liabilities of Professional Associations: ASME v. Hydrolevel Corp.," *Business and Professional Ethics Journal*, vol. 2, no. 1 (Fall 1982): 1–14. Also see Wells, Jones, and Davis, *Conflicts of Interest*, 1–24.

22. *Black's Law Dictionary*, 563.

23. *Black's Law Dictionary*, 564.

24. Roberto Mangabeira Unger, *The Critical Legal Studies Movement* (Cambridge, Mass.: Harvard University Press, 1983): 83.

25. Unger, *Critical Legal Studies*, 83.

26. See my paper "Metaphysical Guilt and Moral Taint" in *Collective Responsibility*, ed. Stacey Hoffman and Larry May (Savage, Md.: Rowman and Littlefield Publishers, 1991).

27. See Edith Wyschogrod's *Saints and Postmodernism* (Chicago: University of Chicago Press, 1990), for another attempt at arguing that postmodernism can be conceived as a nonrelativistic standpoint. Also see my review of Wyschogrod's book in *Ethics*, July 1992.

28. I am grateful to Roger Gibson, Paul Gomberg, Dan Wueste, Bill McBride, Marilyn Friedman, and Bruce Russell for helpful comments on earlier versions of this paper.

4

Toward an Ethics of Expertise

John Hardwig

Most professions rest on the expertise of their members. Professionals are professionals primarily because they know more than most of us about something of importance to our society or to many members of it. Professionals are given power, respect, prestige, and above-average incomes. If professionals are worthy of this status, it is largely because of their special knowledge and the way they use it. And if professionals have special rights and responsibilities, it is also primarily because of the social positions they occupy due to their presumed expertise.

I hope the broad claim that most professions rest on expertise is plausible. For I plan to embark on an exploration of the ethics of expertise under the assumption that the ethics of expertise will throw at least some light on professional ethics. But I cannot justify this basic assumption here, nor can I enter into a discussion of whether various professions really do have the knowledge on which to base their claims. Instead, I must simply state that I believe that understanding the expert-layperson relationship will provide an important part of the explanation of why we need to consider professional ethics at all. An ethics of expertise should also provide common denominators for the ethics of many different professions. Perhaps the differences among the ethics of different professions can also be traced in part to differences in various forms of expertise.

As my title indicates, I do not have a fully developed ethics of expertise. I will, however, offer some reflections on the form of an ethics of expertise and then propose maxims for inclusion in such an ethics. But before I can do either, I must explain what I take the expert-layperson relationship to be, since the features of an ethics of expertise will flow out of the nature of that relationship. So, bear with me while I discuss the epistemology of expertise. There will be an ethical payoff for these labors. Or that is my hope, at any rate.

I.

I find myself believing all sorts of things for which I do not possess evidence: that acid rain and global warming are things to worry about; that my house will not be safe unless it is rewired; that we have no sure way to dispose of high-level nuclear waste; that my irregular heartbeat is premature ventricular contraction and hence nothing to worry about; that my son's failure to do well in school is a sign of insecurity and hence *is* something to worry about; that mass media and increasing mastery of the techniques of persuasion threaten democracy; that money in my retirement account is safely invested so that it will be there when I retire.

The list of things I believe without having the evidence for them could be extended indefinitely. And I am finite. I *might* be able to gather the evidence necessary to support one of these beliefs. But I could not gather the evidence that supports all of them. Too much is known; the evidence is too extensive; much of it is available only to those with special aptitudes and skills honed over years of study and practice. And I lack the competence, the skills, the sheer intellectual capacity, as well as the time. Usually, I lack the ability to evaluate critically the merits of evidence presented to me. Often I cannot even understand it. Thus, if any of the beliefs I have just mentioned is a rational belief, it is not because *I* possess the evidence to justify it. It is because I believe, with good reason, that *others* possess the necessary evidence.

I am not alone in this. More is known than anyone can know by herself, and this forces intellectual specialization: those who invest the necessary time, energy, and focused attention in a particular area come to have better opinions than those who have not similarly invested themselves in that area. I do not see how we can deny the epistemic superiority of expert opinion without denying the efficacy of inquiry with respect to the relevant subject matter. If inquiry is efficacious, more inquiry is likely to lead to a more reliable opinion. And we generally do acknowledge our need for more reliable opinions than our own: this acknowledgment is the force that creates social support for all kinds of "knowledge industries"—including this book.

As I understand it, then, the idea of expertise is based on an epistemological inequality between two opinions—an expert opinion and a nonexpert or lay opinion. (I will use "nonexpert" and "layperson" interchangeably.) Within her area of expertise, an expert's opinion is better than a nonexpert's opinion. By "better," I mean more reliable, but not necessarily correct. Even though it is not necessarily correct, an expert opinion is still better than a lay opinion because it is less likely to be mistaken and likely to be less mistaken. Areas in which expert opinion exists and is available are areas in which one ought not to make up one's own mind—without first becoming an expert.[1] For to insist on relying on the evidence that one can gather or even assess for oneself would be to hold relatively crude, unchecked, unreliable, and therefore *irrational* beliefs.

Although it matters greatly *to me* that many of my beliefs rest on trust in others, *my* beliefs about most matters are of no great import . . . except to me. But our leaders, our government officials, our public and corporate policymakers are in a similar epistemic position. They, too, must rely on expert opinion. They, too, are often not able to assess the merits of the arguments given them by experts. And that is a matter of much greater import. Trust in experts goes on—and must go on—even at the highest levels.

So far, I have been talking as if nonexperts were the only ones who must trust the experts within a given field. But this is not the case. Expertise rests on specialization, so an expert about one thing will be a layperson about another. Even more important: experts become experts and remain current *in their own fields* primarily by assuming the role of laypersons and accepting the testimony of other experts, standardly in the form of books and journal articles. No one could be competent in, say, physics or automobile repair, medicine or psychology, if she insisted on accepting only propositions that she had verified for herself.

An attempt at epistemic self-reliance—even by the experts *within their own fields* of expertise—would be sheer folly. Experts, too, must rely on others to possess the evidence for their beliefs within their disciplines or even their subspecialties. In a culture as complex as ours, even *knowledge* is often unavoidably based at least partly on trust in the testimony of other experts.[2]

I hasten to add that this does not mean that scientists and scholars have only a poor, second-best substitute for direct first-person evidence. It means that "hearsay evidence" is often the best evidence *anyone* could have. For example, an attempt to measure the lifespan of charm particles takes about 300 person/years and is such a complicated process that no one university has physicists with all the competences necessary to run the experiment.[3] Any individual physicist attempting to measure the lifespan of charm particles without relying essentially on the testimony of others could produce only a hopelessly inept and crude measurement, no matter how brilliant and industrious she might be.

Even experts must, then, rely on what they are told by other experts, even within their own disciplines. This leaves us with a terminological difficulty: it seems perversely wrongheaded to call a full professor of chemistry at Harvard a layperson in chemistry. But all chemists can be competent only by accepting the opinions of other chemists and by deferring to their judgment—i.e., by taking the role of laypersons. Even a top-flight chemist cannot validate for herself all of the opinions she accepts in chemistry, for reasons not only of time, but also of competence.[4] Indeed, she standardly will not be able to validate for herself even the premises on which her own research rests. In the following, I will continue to talk in terms of "the expert-layperson relationship." But we will need to remind ourselves that the role of a layperson is not limited to those outside a field of expertise.

II.

The relationship between expert and layperson is grounded on an epistemic inequality. The expert knows more than the layperson about matters within the scope of her expertise. And if the layperson appeals to the judgment of the expert, he usually does so because he acknowledges the superiority of the expert's judgment to his own. Thus, the epistemology of the expert-layperson relationship can be focused on the concept of rational deference to epistemic authority. This rational deference lies at the heart of the particular form of power that an expert has and is also the center of the particular form of vulnerability that each of us, as a layperson, is in.

The concept of rational deference presupposes that the layperson appeals to the expert and acknowledges the rational authority of the expert. Obviously, someone must appeal to the expert; some layperson must acknowledge the authority of the expert, or the expert's knowledge will be socially irrelevant and useless. So, the ideas of appealing to epistemic authority and rational deference may suffice for the epistemology of expertise. But when we turn to the ethics of expertise, we must not forget that often an expert's expertise is applied to those who have not appealed to the expert. They may well not even agree that this opinion represents a form of expertise. Indeed, expert opinion alters many people's lives without their knowledge, much less their consent.

If we limit ourselves to considering beliefs in propositions for which reasons can be given, the essential structure of rational appeals to the authority of experts is this:

If A has good reasons to believe that B has good reasons to believe p, then A has good reasons to believe p.

Let's look more closely at this structure of rational deference. A has good reasons to believe that B has good reasons to believe p. It is B's good reasons that make B an expert and distinguish her authority— epistemic authority—from other forms of authority and other grounds for deference. And A defers to B because he believes that she has good reasons; it is these good reasons that make her opinion count in his eyes. In fact, A defers to B because he believes that she has *better* reasons than he has—or even could have—by himself. Clearly, the whole point of appealing to the testimony of others is that they know things we don't. If this were not the case, basing belief on the testimony of others would be pointless at best, hence nonrational or irrational. The appeal to B must be able to *strengthen* A's reasons for believing p.

Nor is this conclusion based entirely on the limited competence of A about p. As we have seen, even the most knowledgeable people in many specialties must base their claims to expertise and their own work primarily on appeals to the knowledge of *others* in their field.[5] If the best reasons for believing p are sometimes primarily testimonial reasons, if knowing requires having the best reasons for believing, and if p can be known, then *knowledge* will also sometimes rest on testimony.

Basing belief on expert testimony has potential problems as well as strengths, however, and they arise from the same feature of testimony: in order for testimony to be useful, A *cannot* already have B's reasons. So, if A accepts p on B's say-so, those reasons (B's reasons) that are necessary to justify p and A's belief that p are reasons that A does not have. Sometimes it is feasible for B to share with A all the evidence necessary to justify the claim that p. But usually not. Indeed, if A and B come from different disciplines or even different specialties within the same discipline, A often will not know what B's reasons are, much less why they are good reasons for believing p.

Thus, there is a certain blindness in A's belief that p, since he lacks much or all of the evidence that justifies the claim that p. The vulnerability of laypersons who rely on experts thus grows out of the same features that justify appeals to experts in the first place: A doesn't know what B knows. And since he doesn't, his ability to check up on what she says, to criticize her opinions rationally, or even to answer back effectively is really quite limited. I may suspect that my cardiologist is incompetent, that she is not being honest with me, or that she is ordering unnecessary tests. But one must know much of what cardiologists know in order to rationally confirm or dispel my suspicion.

Given all this, what can we say about layperson A as he appeals to expert B? A's position is really this:

1. A knows that B *says* p.
2. A has good reasons to believe that B (unlike A) is in a position to know what would be good reasons to believe p and to have the needed reasons.
3. A believes (and has good reasons to believe?[6]) that B is speaking truthfully, that B is saying what she believes.
4. A believes (and has good reasons to believe?) that B actually has good reasons for believing p when she thinks she does.

At this point, it is obvious, though important, to note two things about B and her contribution to A's good reasons. 1. Unless B is likely to believe what she is saying, her knowledgeability about p will not give A good reasons to believe p. Thus A's reasons must include the (implicit) belief that B is truthful or at least being honest in this situation. This truthfulness is no simple or single thing to assess; it can involve a good deal of B's character. This becomes clear if we consider various reasons that an expert might not be honest. In certain situations, B cannot be relied upon to be honest if she is greedy, or cowardly, or too concerned about her status and reputation, or lazy, or too friendly with some who have important interests at stake in her testimony, etc.[7]

2. Even B's truthfulness will not give A good reasons to believe p if B believes she has good reasons when she does not. Experts are generally most knowledgeable about what constitutes good reasons in the domain of their expertise. So that's not the main issue. B must, of course, be competent, keep herself up-to-date, and she must have done her own work carefully and conscientiously. But the point I wish to emphasize is this: A's reasons must also include the (implicit) belief that B is not subject to epistemic vices—the tendency to deceive

herself about the extent of her knowledge, for example, its reliability, or its applicability to whether p.

If questions about B, about her truthfulness, her competence, or her appreciation of the limits of her knowledge, arise in A's mind, he can, to an extent, check up on B. He can, for example, find out about B's reputation in her field. But generally one must know what someone in B's field knows in order to know whether B is competent and whether her reasons are, in fact, good reasons to believe p. A, as a nonexpert, cannot know this, without first becoming an expert himself. Thus, although B's claims are subject to cross-checking, that cross-checking must generally occur *within* the community of experts. Therefore, A's attempt to check up on B cannot avoid reliance upon experts. It only refines and extends it. The way in which a layperson can check up on an expert can be expressed as follows: A has good reasons to believe that C has good reasons to believe that B has good reasons to believe p.

A's good reasons must include beliefs that B is of a certain character. A judgment about B's character, both ethical and epistemic, must be part of A's good reasons for believing p. (Or, if A appeals to C to check on B's personal reliability or professional competence, then A's good reasons must include a similar assessment of C's character. This becomes plain if we think about the phenomenon of physicians covering for incompetent or unethical physicians.)

Thus, even our attempts to be rational rest on an ineluctable element of *trust*. Trust in persons and the trustworthiness of those persons is epistemically basic and inescapable. Because more is known than anyone can know by himself, we must trust experts. And we must trust them *as persons*, not just rely on their knowledge, since their honesty and their lack of self-deception about the limits of their knowledge are always at issue. Those who do not trust cannot be fully rational—they often cannot have the best evidence for their beliefs. Those who do not trust often cannot know. Those who do not trust usually cannot be experts; they cannot be competent members of most professions.

And yet, this trust in experts is, like any trust, subject to abuse. There are untrustworthy experts and also many who fraudulently or mistakenly claim more expertise than they possess. There are many cases where experts have proven to be inaccurate, biased, of limited vision, and even dishonest. And sometimes we are, in fact, so vulnerable that we can't even tell whether the experts are serving us well or merely enriching themselves, whether they are helping us or leading us down a path to very serious problems later on.

III.

Because trust in persons is epistemically basic and yet can be abused, there must be an ethics of expertise. There must be principles or maxims for the expert to follow—so as not to abuse the power inherent in expertise or to undermine the attempts of laypersons to be rational. Following the principles or maxims of this ethics would be part of what makes an expert trustworthy and her testimony reliable.

But the layperson is an agent, too, his vulnerability notwithstanding. So there is also an ethics of appealing to experts—principles or maxims defining what constitutes an ethical appeal to experts. A complete "ethics of expertise" would, then, be composed of two branches— maxims for experts and maxims for those appealing to experts. This ethics of expertise would have epistemological, as well as ethical import: in cases where our rationality rests on trust, the epistemological is not separable from the ethical. For these maxims would be maxims for arriving at rational belief in cases in which expert opinion exists.

There is obviously going to be some play in the connection between the ethics of expertise and the rationality of trusting experts. Occasional lapses from the practice of the ethics of expertise would not ordinarily make an expert's testimony completely untrustworthy. Similarly, a few untrustworthy experts would not undermine the rationality of appeals to the authority of that kind of expert, not even if the layperson cannot tell which experts are untrustworthy.

Nonetheless, we must recognize that the temptations to render untrustworthy testimony will often be greatest when the experts' testimony counts for most. Moreover, the result of widespread failure to practice the ethics of expertise would be a culture that would not be able to utilize its own knowledge, due to pervasive distrust of its knowers. If its knowers are indeed often untrustworthy, it might well be rational for a culture to refuse to rely on them. But that distrust would bar the culture from arriving at maximally rational beliefs and decisions.

What would an ethics of expertise look like? An ethics for experts must be an ethics that acknowledges that where there is expertise, knowledge is not in fact open and accessible to all; an ethics that recognizes that the expert's reasons cannot be checked by the layperson and often will not even be intelligible to him. It must be an ethics sensitive to a kind of power in knowing, a power unlike that of any of our epistemic peers, whose opinions we can usually test for ourselves. It must also, then, be an ethics sensitive to the very basic vulnerability that comes with deciding to let others make up our minds, for that kind of reliance on others undermines even the internal independence necessary to decide not to accept what the other says.

The ethics of expertise will not, then, rest on a metaethics applicable to relationships among equals. For example, a contract theory that presupposes that each party will look after her own interests will not be adequate to expert-layperson relationships. Since the layperson has surrendered a portion of his autonomy in deferring to the expert, the ethics of expertise cannot be just an ethics of voluntary agreements, not even when expert and layperson begin their relationship with a voluntary agreement. The ethics of expertise must also acknowledge that laypersons often have no real choice but to rely on an expert—for example, when someone needs open-heart surgery or when his car has broken down far from home. There must be an element of benevolence in the ethics of expertise. It must be an ethic of fidelity to laypersons' interests, of service to nonexperts. At the very least, it must be an ethics of fairness to the often unprotected interests of laypersons.

Despite this need for loyalty to the interests of laypersons, an ethics of fiduciary relationships is not adequate for the ethics of expertise. Medical ethics and legal ethics have usually been constructed on the basis of the claim that in exchange for a client's trust, a physician or lawyer is to pursue the best interests of that client and no one else. However, a strict fiduciary ethic requires that we be able to identify a single client to whom the expert owes fidelity and that this client's interests not conflict with others to whom the expert also owes moral consideration *qua* expert. Given the conflicting interests of various stakeholders, there is, for most experts, no single answer to the question, *To whom* is fidelity owed? Despite its widespread acceptance within medical ethics, a strict fiduciary model is not adequate even in medicine.[8]

Finally, the ethics of expertise must resist a certain individualistic cast present in much popular American thought about ethics: an ethics for experts cannot be limited to concern for one's own conduct. Instead, experts must also be concerned about the conduct of *other* experts in their fields; they have a professional responsibility to "blow the whistle" on incompetent or unethical experts. This responsibility arises from the fact that often only another expert in the same discipline can really judge the trustworthiness of expert testimony.

The form of an ethics of expertise is still unclear. So, instead of pursuing these reflections on the form of this ethics, I will proceed to a list—admittedly an unsystematic list— of maxims for experts and for those who appeal to the authority of experts. The maxims may well be more important than the metaethical form, anyway. And the process of examining and refining a proposed set of maxims may also help to clarify the form required by an ethics of expertise.

IV.

Before moving to specific maxims, I must make two general points about maxims for an ethics of expertise. First, I do not intend a legalistic ethics; I think of the maxims as guidelines for responsible professional behavior, not as hard and fast principles specifying moral obligations. Second, I do not take these maxims to be new discoveries on my part. Rather, I am attempting to formulate some of the principles that already guide the conduct of responsible experts. Reflective experts may well find little new here.

Maxims for the Expert:
    1. Admit when you don't know, when you're guessing, and when your opinion is only a reasonable estimate. Don't overestimate the scope or certainty of your knowledge, or the inferences that can be validly drawn from it. Refuse to give opinions when you are being asked for opinions that are beyond the range of your expertise. Distinguish cases where no one knows from those where you don't know and make proper referrals in the latter cases.
    This may be a difficult maxim for experts to obey, since their sense of their professional worth and also their social status depend on knowing more than others do. Also, loyalty to the community of experts is often combined with a sense that you are letting the community down if you admit the limits of the community's knowledge. But it is an ethical vice to pretend to know more than you do; it is an epistemic vice to believe that you know more than you do.
    2. Tell the truth as you see it in your professional judgment, but don't give the impression that you speak for the community of experts when you do not. When the community of expert opinion is divided, there is an obligation to say that it is. When your opinion is a minority view within the community of experts, you should make that clear.
    3. Tell the truth as you see it in your professional judgment, even if you have to tell your employers, clients, or those in power things they don't want to hear. The money you are paid must not be taken by

either you or your employer to mean that you will tell her what she wants to hear. Nor that you will publicly support positions or propositions that you do not believe the evidence supports.

Truthfulness is important in any relationship. But truthfulness may be even more important for experts than it is among those who are epistemic peers. The arguments of those who are in positions of relatively equal expertise can more readily be tested and evaluated. Hence, it doesn't matter as much if they are lying, inquiring in bad faith, or misrepresenting what they know. We can usually check up on what they say and so trust in their reports is less necessary. But if your lawyer says you should plea bargain or a group of engineers says that a reactor has adequate safety devices, it is much more difficult to find out (soon enough) whether they are being truthful.

4. Recognize the human propensity to rationalize: you will be tempted to *believe* what your employers or those in power want to hear you say. Where possible, make allowances for this tendency by checking your opinion against that of other members of the community of experts who operate under fewer or different incentives, or against other communities of experts.

5. Consider the effects of your statements on those who are not your employers or clients. Especially if they are likely to be put at risk by the application of your knowledge and most especially if they are likely to be put at risk without their knowledge or consent. Obligations to employers or clients do not outweigh more basic considerations of justice. You must not use your knowledge to treat others unfairly or to arm your employers to do so. Remember that only organized interests can afford your services and that the least advantaged and also unorganized interests tend not to be able to make themselves either heard or considered.

Although failure to obey this maxim would not destroy the trust necessary for the expert-employer relationship, the belief that experts serve only the interests of their employers would undermine the trust of everyone else in the testimony of experts. We would all then have good reason to be suspicious of expert testimony about issues in which more than one party has an interest. If, for example, the researchers Dow-Corning hires to investigate the safety of silicon breast implants see themselves as responsible only to the interests of Dow-Corning, the rest of us will have reason to suspect a whitewash.

Nor will an ethics of advocacy silence these concerns. An expert cannot simply say, "I'll represent my clients' interests, let those with opposing interests hire their own experts," because that would leave the interests of the poor and disorganized defenseless. Business ethics recognizes that you never owe absolute fidelity to the desires or interests of those who employ you (or accord status to you, etc.). But we have given less thought to what a responsible chemist, psychologist, or political scientist may and may not do. Perhaps we've thought less about this because we tend to think of the pursuit of knowledge as a purely theoretical quest for truth, thus often ignoring the uses to which it is put. But, as a friend of mine puts it, "when a layperson wants to know whether or not p, there's almost always a reason why he wants to know."

6. Know your own ethical limits. Try to avoid positions where you might not be able to obey the above principles because you are susceptible to the temptations of the position or too afraid of the possible costs of following them. Recognize that the use of experts is dependent on a climate of trust. Don't pollute the atmosphere of social trust by abusing it for personal gain, increased respect, or support for your discipline.

If an expert suspects that she will be giving biased answers, she should not be working on that set of questions. Biased research has come back to haunt Dow-Corning and the Department of Energy. And each new case of untrustworthy research that comes to light fuels public suspicion that scientists and other experts are distorting their messages to serve their own interests or those of special interest groups.

Failure to practice the preceding maxims would have the long-term effect of undermining the social trust needed to sustain the epistemic authority of experts. However, we must also acknowledge that these will often be very difficult maxims to obey. Moreover, one of the prices we pay for blindness to the ethics of expertise is that we have not selected graduate students and colleagues for their character, their ethical commitment, or their ability to withstand the temptations of their positions. Nor have we made any serious attempt to give them the ethical training they might need.

Maxims for Those Appealing to Experts:

The ethics of expertise is not a one-way street. A layperson is usually not simply a passive recipient of expert activity. Even if he cannot very well evaluate the testimony of an expert, a layperson remains an agent, and an important part of the ethics of expertise is the ethics of one who appeals to experts. Indeed, there are ways in which laypersons can make it more likely that experts will offer trustworthy testimony.

I would argue, then, that we need to think much more about the ethics of the *recipient* of all kinds of professional services—about the ethics of the patient, the person retaining a lawyer, the analysand; about the ethics of the company or government agency hiring an engineer or chemist, a firm to do an accounting audit or environmental impact statement. The ethics of the recipient of expert opinion is also an important part of a complete professional ethics.

1. Try to find the best-qualified expert and recognize that agreement with your values, desires, policies, plans, or hunches is not a qualification for an expert. Selecting an expert whom you think will likely support your position is an epistemic vice, a form of rationalization. Selecting an expert because you know she will support your position is a form of deliberate deception (or of self-deception) and hence an ethical vice.

Appealing to experts who will support the views we already hold is a common failing, but it defeats the rational purpose of appealing to experts. If A selects an expert because he knows she will support his original views, he presupposes that he already knows enough to be able to tell whether p is true. Thus, an environmentalist should seek out the best experts on the effects of Dioxin, even if they maintain it is less dangerous than it was previously thought to be.

Of course, if A will be the only one affected by decisions based on the expert's opinion, selection of an expert who agrees with his basic beliefs and values may be acceptable. But even in this special case, it is often a form of rationalization. A common example is "doctor shopping" for a physician who will not object to one's smoking or unhealthy eating habits.

Where others will be affected, if experts are hand picked for their support of antecedently held positions, cynicism about the whole process of appealing to experts is promoted. Suppose our interests conflict or we disagree about what should be done. Then, if you are not persuaded to my position on the basis of what I've said, why should you be persuaded by an expert I have selected if she has been selected because she will support my position? The tendency will be for you to select "your" expert who you know will support your position. You, then, refuse to accept anything my expert says, and I refuse to accept anything your expert says. We're then back to our original position of disagreement, except that we have undermined the credibility of those who might have been able to throw genuine light on the issues we confront. Unfortunately, the use of expert witnesses in legal cases provides many clear examples of this phenomenon.

We must distinguish, then, two very different appeals to the authority of experts: (i) appeals to experts in a context of genuine inquiry, where the layperson is trying to find out whether or not p, and (ii) appeals to experts to promote acceptance by others—or even by the layperson himself—of a position he already holds. The first is rational, an essential ingredient in achieving rational belief. The second is rationalizing, a form of deception or self-deception. As clear as the distinction between these two may be in theory, in practice these two different appeals to experts probably represent opposite poles of a continuum. And important as the distinction is to the ethics of expertise, it is seldom a simple matter to know where either you yourself or others are on this continuum. For the experts who agree with my position will always seem to me to have the best arguments.

2. Although you appeal to experts to reduce your uncertainty and to enable you to act with greater assurance, recognize that what you would like to know simply may not be known. Recognize, too, that even the best experts may be divided. Do not generate pressure on experts to pretend to know more than they do, to overestimate the relevance of what they know, or to feign consensus within the community of experts where there is none.

We usually appeal to experts in the context of decisions and decision makers have practical and often urgent needs for conclusions. Facing the need to decide about issues involving complex and technical matters and recognizing the insufficiency of our own knowledge, we find it very difficult to refrain from trying to get more information or certainty from experts than they have to offer.

3. An expert's educated guess may or may not be a sufficient basis for action. Try to distinguish these two types of situations. When a decision must be made, the educated guess of the experts will be the best basis for a decision—an educated guess is better than an uneducated guess. Also recognize, however, that even the best, most-informed judgment can be mistaken. Where relevant expert opinion exists, it is the best opinion you have. But it is not infallible. Don't expect more than you can get from an expert or try to hold an expert accountable for more than you can reasonably expect.

Experts will have better reasons than laypersons (within their domains of expertise). But better reasons are not always sufficient reasons to act—for example, when no action is an option or the decision can be postponed; when other, less uncertain alternatives exist; when the risks or costs of their having guessed wrong are great. It seems that we must act on the problem of the depletion of the ozone layer because the risks are so high. However, we could decide to do further research before permanently disposing of high-level radioactive waste. Sweden, for example, has decided that we do not now know enough to design long-term storage facilities for high-level radioactive waste and will store its waste above ground while trying to develop more certain science and technology.

4. Recognize that experts either directly or indirectly in your employ will be tempted to tell you what you want to hear and that those trained to be experts have not been selected for their courage or their ability to withstand the heat of nonacademic battle. Make allowances for that. Try to make experts understand that you want their candid assessments, not support for your position.

I think we have tried to substitute good money for good character in the experts we appeal to. If the expert is well paid by us, she will have no reason to lie to us, and hence we don't need to worry about whether she might distort her testimony if she had reason to. But the ability of good pay to substitute for good character is limited. And it brings into play new incentives for the expert. Laypersons thus need to ask what a given expert has to gain by being believed.

Maxims for the Community of Experts:

First, a word about the phrase "community of experts." The "community," as I understand this term, is defined by field or subject matter. It is based on disciplined attention, sustained inquiry, and consequently, better knowledge of the relevant subject. The community of experts does not, then, rest upon or require agreement. However, contemporary philosophers of science in the Kuhnian tradition have made us sensitive to the degree of conformity in both procedure and belief that communities of experts often in fact require of their members.

1. Never use rewards and punishments to stifle dissent within the community of experts.

Rewarding mere conformity or punishing disagreement would seriously compromise the community's quest for truth and hence its claim to be a community of *experts*. It should be equally obvious, however, that there will be a temptation to encourage conformity, both because professional consensus presents a better face to the public and also because of our natural tendency to see those who agree with us as more competent and more ethical than those who disagree with us.

2. Beware the gap between social expectations of your community and what your members can in fact do. Combat unrealistic social expectations. Do not attempt to generate social support for your work by overestimating what is known, what is likely to become known, or the relevance and applicability of either to practical problems.

Social acceptance of the knowledge possessed by a community of experts depends on a climate of trust in that community. Trust that has been lost or destroyed is extremely difficult to reestablish. However, the short-term interests of the community (and its members) may be enhanced by unrealistic social expectations, by the appearance of consensus, or by the appearance of trustworthiness. But at the cost of the long-term interests of the community that suffer when those unrealistic expectations cannot be met, disagreements surface, or shoddy conduct comes to light.

3. Take steps to ensure that your members are worthy of the social trust placed in them. Take your responsibility for certifying experts seriously. Ensure that your members remain competent and current, discipline those who misuse their positions as experts, decertify those who are no longer fit to be included in your community. Certification, disciplining, and decertification all involve an ethical component. Those who abuse the power inherent in their specialized knowledge must be censured, penalized, and ultimately excluded from the community of experts.

Granted, however, the lines between mistakes and culpable mistakes, between mistakes and incompetence, between incompetence and disagreement, and between disagreement and improper behavior will not often be easy to draw.

4. Recognize the obligation to be a ''whistleblower'' and the sacrifices that often must be made by whistleblowers. Resist the temptation to ''circle the wagons'' and defend the reputation of the community by withholding information about the misconduct of members of your community. Work for institutions and social settings that minimize temptations to abuse the power of expertise and that protect those who blow the whistle on untrustworthy members of the community.

This responsibility follows from the fact that one must usually know what an expert knows in order to be able to tell whether the expert is competent and working carefully and conscientiously. The idea that experts are responsible for the competence and conduct of *other* experts is foreign to our individualistic orientation—''mind your own business," "don't rat on your buddies." The idea that peer review necessarily involves ethical review is especially troubling to many who believe that ethics is all subjective. Moreover, the work of monitoring one's peers seems irrelevant to the real task of the expert—to advance or apply knowledge in her field. But these attitudes fail to take seriously the element of trust in appeals to experts and the dependency of the community of experts on that climate of trust. They also ignore the dependency of one expert on the integrity of others in her field.

In the "Baltimore case" involving the fraudulent medical research of Thereza Imanishi-Kari, many members of the scientific community rallied prematurely to the defense of one of their esteemed colleagues, charging a "witch hunt." By contrast, Margot O'Toole—who blew the whistle and whose charges were eventually substantially upheld—was very nearly driven out of the scientific community. She was fired, she was unable to find another research job, she lost her house, and for a time, she was reduced to answering the telephone for her brother's moving company. Arguably, she was more severely punished than the fraudulent researcher whose misconduct she reported.

Maxims for a Society or Group that Relies on Experts:

1. Create settings for experts that protect experts who take responsible but unpopular positions, and that minimize the temptations to abuse the power of expertise. Support those experts who are conscientiously engaged in peer review.

An example of an unpopular but responsible position is that of Jerry Szymanski, a geologist, who questioned the suitability of the Yucca Mountain site for a high-level radioactive waste repository. His report has gradually been given a full hearing, despite its controversial nature.

2. Do not permit expertise to be monopolized by the wealthy or powerful or to be used as a tool of oppression or exploitation.

The danger is that money and power will command expertise and thus an appearance of rationality so skillfully woven as to be virtually undetectable. Access to the information provided by experts can itself be a tool of injustice. Therefore, although this will be especially difficult:

3. There is a responsibility to finance the education and information (through experts) of opposing and potentially opposing groups.

Unless money and power are to resolve the discussion of questions of truth, the knowledge-buying power of different groups must not be grossly unequal. To avoid that danger and to quiet suspicions about possible bias, a Martinsville, Illinois, group that opposes selection of a low-level radioactive waste disposal site in its vicinity has been given $500,000 to finance the development of its own expert knowledge. (However, the site's proponents have had many millions to finance *their* experts.)

Obviously, the last two maxims apply both to different groups within a country and to different countries within the international community.

These, then, are the maxims that I would propose as elements in the ethics/epistemology of expertise. I am confident that the present list represents a beginning, at best. Major corrections and additions will undoubtedly be necessary. Moreover, I have said nothing about how laypersons should proceed in conditions where experts are not trusted and very little about how a layperson is to determine *whom* to trust in a specific instance.

In closing, let us briefly recall the purpose of trying to construct such a list of maxims: in the long run, trust in experts will be well placed and rational to the extent that these maxims are generally followed, and misplaced, often irrational to the extent that they are not followed. Thus, if something like this set of maxims were found to be acceptable for an ethics of expertise, we would face a very important question of fact: to what extent do people in our society follow this ethics of expertise? I can't answer this question. But it is worth noting that one could read this paper as providing a strong argument for *not* trusting the members of our professions, on the grounds that those in professions in the United States do not even come close to following this ethics.

However that may be, if the main argument of this paper is acceptable—if, that is, deference to the authoritative opinions of experts is essential to our rationality and knowledge, and if that deference unavoidably rests on trust, not only in the competence, but also in the epistemic and ethical characters of our experts—then it is high time that we get to work on the ethics of expertise. Indeed, it is past time.

Notes

I wish to thank Joan Callahan, E. Roger Jones, John Nolt, Dan Wueste, the members of the philosophy department at East Tennessee State University, and especially Mary R. English for helpful discussion of many of the points in this paper. Research for this paper has been supported by the National

Endowment for the Humanities through a Fellowship for College Teachers and Independent Scholars and by East Tennessee State University through a Tennessee Board of Regents grant-in-aid.

1. I develop this point in "Epistemic Dependence," *Journal of Philosophy* 82 (July 1985): 335–49.

2. See John Hardwig, "The Role of Trust in Knowledge," *Journal of Philosophy* 88 (December 1991): 693–708.

3. For a discussion of this example, see my paper, "Epistemic Dependence," referred to above.

4. For example, Rustum Roy, head of a chemistry laboratory at Pennsylvania State University, said, in response to the suggestion that research directors should be responsible for the quality of work coming out of their own labs: "Fifteen years ago I would look at all the raw data myself. Now I'm not close enough. I wouldn't catch it if someone were deliberately trying to falsify results. Every head of a large lab is in the same position. I can't even run half of my machines." (P. S. Zurer, "Misconduct in Research; It May Be More Widespread Than Most Chemists Like to Think," *Chemical & Engineering News* 1987 [April 13]: 15.)

5. In cases where B's expertise rests on what she has learned from others (e.g., in the literature), rather than on evidence she herself has gathered, the structure of an appeal to her authority is this: A has good reasons to believe that B has good reasons to believe that C (and D and E) have good reasons to believe p. This may seem baroque to the point of silliness. But it is not. The chain of authority implicit in most appeals to experts is even more complex and remote than this. Our rationality rests on trust in many (the Cs, Ds, and Es) whom we have never met.

6. The reason for the parenthetical question in this statement and the next is that I am unsure about what to say about implicit trust. If A trusts B implicitly, he will often not have or even feel the need to have good reasons to believe in B's honesty. Obviously, that can be dangerous. But I think communities in which a climate of implicit trust prevails also have some real advantages over those in which good reasons for believing in the truthfulness of its experts are felt to be needed and are then supplied.

7. Often we try to substitute judgments about B's situation for judgments about her character—"B would have no reason to lie in this situation." But as we shall see, this substitution cannot be completely adequate. There are almost always reasons for the expert to exaggerate, if not to lie.

8. John Hardwig, "What About the Family?" *Hastings Center Report* 1990 (March/April): 5–10.

5

Role Moralities and the Problem of Conflicting Obligations

Daniel E. Wueste

Introduction

A role morality is an institutional morality. Accordingly, the justificatory capacity[1] of a role morality is also institutional. To say this is to recognize and insist upon a distinction between a justification that invokes the norms of an institutional morality and a justification made out in terms of critical (i.e., noninstitutional) morality. That distinction explains a commonplace in professional ethics; namely, that a role agent may be obligated to perform an act that is wrong. The act is mandated by the norms of an institutional (role) morality and condemned by the norms of the morality that applies to human conduct generally (i.e., critical morality). The distinction also invites the query whether such an action is justified; put more precisely, the question here is whether an institutional justification can carry the day when what it justifies is condemned by "ethics plain and simple."[2]

There is more than one answer to this question. Obviously, whether the answer is affirmative or negative matters for role agents whose conduct is governed by conflicting norms. It also matters for students and teachers of professional ethics: if the answer is negative, the legitimacy of their project is dubious (what should be studied and taught is ethics *simpliciter*[3]); if the answer is affirmative, there is a considerable amount of theoretical work to be done respecting the scope of the justificatory capacity of role moralities. After all, like the claim that there is no limit to the justificatory capacity of positive law, the claim that there is no limit to the justificatory capacity of institutional morality is clearly untenable. Indeed, that there are limits here is granted on all sides. In this connection, what distinguishes those who answer our question negatively from those who answer it affirmatively is that the former, but not the latter, take it that, *ipso facto*, what the limits are is a moot issue. Another way of marking this distinction is to say that those who answer the question affirmatively take role moralities seriously, while those who answer it negatively do not.

The decision to take role moralities seriously entails certain commitments. In what follows, I identify six of these commitments. I do this by examining a position that seems to, but does not, take them seriously. Then, turning to the problem of conflicting obligations, I show that two of the four ways of dealing with this problem are ruled out by the decision to take role moralities seriously and argue that heuristic and idiographic considerations tip the balance in favor of one of the two live options.

A Contrast Respecting Scope

A role morality is an institutional morality. It is, for example, the morality of a profession; speaking in general terms, it is the morality of an enterprise or undertaking. Its norms are either (i) "created, applied and enforced by some organization," or (ii) "generally accepted, followed and sanctioned informally within some community."[4] They are applicable to the conduct of those who are engaged in the enterprise (agents who occupy specific roles).[5]

Noninstitutional or critical morality is not similarly limited in scope. Its standards are addressed to human conduct, full stop. Thinking in its terms, whether an action is right or wrong does not turn on the role one occupies. It will be granted, of course, that one has certain obligations in virtue of one's role. A father, for example, has certain obligations in virtue of his role that a male who is not a father does not have. However, such obligations, if genuine, do not require action that would not be right in any case.[6] If an action is wrong by the standards of noninstitutional morality, there can be no bona fide obligation to perform it; the fact that one occupies a specific role within an institution is morally jejune. That is to say, the fact that one occupies a certain role is not, indeed it cannot be, morally decisive for the question whether an action is right or wrong.

Role Differentiation Without Ethical Differentiation

It is an ancient notion that persons within society occupy social roles or stations that are distinguished from one another by their functions and, as a result of this functional differentiation, further distinguished by the duties or role obligations they impose. The notion of a role *morality*, on the other hand, like the notion of professional ethics, is recent. Indeed, the notion of role differentiation is found in Plato, whereas the notion of a role morality or an ethic of an occupation or profession arises from the work of late nineteenth- and early twentieth-century sociologists—in particular, Durkheim and Mead.[7]

For Plato, role differentiation does not entail ethical differentiation in the sense suggested by talk of business ethics, or legal (i.e., lawyer's) ethics. In Plato's thought the criteria of right action do not vary with one's role or occupation; there is one notion of justice that is instantiated in different activities—in the role of the physician and the role of the lawyer, for example. Consequently, following Plato, one will reject the claim that a lawyer is justified in maintaining client confidentiality even if doing so will result in substantial harm to innocent third parties or allow his client to retain ill-gotten gains. Why? Because in both cases the result of the lawyer's action is unjust. His role as a lawyer makes no moral difference.

Continuing along these lines, one might bring the point home with a stark example: A loan shark's collection agent occupies a role. He has certain duties or role obligations. Yet surely it cannot be said that he acts rightly when, fulfilling a role obligation, he breaks the legs of a delinquent debtor. While a role determines what an individual *qua* role agent ought to do, the "ought" here is nonmoral. Of course, a "role-generated-ought" may have a moral thrust—it may flag an obligation or *duty*, for example—but such moral force is explained by the sanction of critical morality; it cannot be explained by pointing to the bare fact that the conduct in question is required of a role agent. It seems that, thinking in terms of critical morality, role moralities are not taken seriously,[8] for so far as the imposition of obligations is concerned, they are unnecessary, the work of obligation is done by the sanction of critical morality.[9] Moreover, when the norms of a role morality come into conflict with the norms of critical morality they always lose. In short, as moralities, role moralities appear to be otiose—they are normatively impotent.

Justified Institutions, Transitivity, and Role Moralities

One way of responding to the point of the example just considered is to say that, of course, the loan shark's collection agent does not act rightly when, fulfilling a role obligation, he breaks the legs of a delinquent debtor; as in the case of a "concentration camp commandant" or "professional strikebreaker" the immorality of the job is so substantial, indeed, patent, that the role and its "morality" generate an accusation rather than an excuse. But not all roles are like this. For example, as David Luban observes, "we do not call it murder when a soldier kills a sleeping enemy, although it is surely immoral for you or me to do it."[10] Similarly, while I would be guilty of a moral offense were I to kill someone by means of a lethal injection, when an executioner in Texas administers a lethal injection he is not culpable. It is his job. The suggestion here is plain enough: an institutional role morality cannot do the job of justification unless the institution is justified. Surely, this suggestion is well taken. Yet, according to Luban, this is how the story *begins*; it cannot end here. That the institution is justified is not enough. If it were, granting that justification is transitive, instantiations of the "transitivity argument" that "will not do," such as the one below, would go through.

> It is true that I am wronging you. But that is required by my role-obligations, which are essential to my institutional task, which is necessary to the structure of the institution, which is justified
> because it is there.
> because it's the way we do things around here.
> because it's not worth the trouble to replace it.[11]

The problem here is that this sort of justification—Luban calls it pragmatic justification—is not strong enough. It does not provide the *sine qua non* of what he calls institutional excuses (i.e., "moral cachet").[12] According to Luban, to get what is needed, "an institution must be justified in a much stronger way, by showing that it is a positive moral good."[13] Thus, to put Luban's point another way, the argument above will not do because, though the mechanism of transmission—the transitivity argument—is sound, the signal being transmitted is altogether too weak.

Is Luban taking role moralities seriously? Is the difference between his position and Plato's a difference that makes a difference? I think not. For in both cases, the justificatory work—the work of obligation—is done by the sanction of critical morality. The difference between the positions is that for Plato the sanction of critical morality does this job immediately, whereas for Luban it does the job mediately—the institution is mediatized. But Luban's mediatization of the institution is such that an institutional role morality itself is either justificatorily impotent, being nothing more than a conduit for the transmission of the sanction of critical morality, or eliminable. In either case, it is scarcely appropriate to say that role moralities are being taken seriously.

There are two closely related problems here: (i) the eliminability problem: whenever it appears that role moralities are doing the work of justification, it is nothing more than appearance—critical morality is doing the job; (ii) the function-identity problem: as institutional *moralities*, role moralities are generators of justification rather than mere conduits for the transmission of justification; a Lubanian role morality does not function as a morality.

The eliminability problem emerges when, having argued that the adversary system is only pragmatically justified and hence incapable of generating institutional excuses, Luban says that

> [i]f a lawyer is permitted to puff, bluff, or threaten on certain occasions, this is not because of the adversary system, . . . but because *in such circumstances, anyone would be permitted to do these things*. . . . [Moreover,] when professional and moral obligation conflict, moral obligation takes precedence. When they don't conflict, professional obligations rule the day.[14]

If Luban is right, such permission is not role-specific. But if the permission is not role-specific, then so far as the real business of justification is concerned, the lawyer's role morality is eliminable. Moreover, one wonders why professional obligations deserve the attention of ethicists. Why not focus on bona fide moral obligations? After all, on this view, professional obligations carry the day when and only when they do not conflict with morality. Perhaps it will be said that if one focuses exclusively on moral obligations something important will be missed, namely the *professional* obligations. But here the critic is likely to say that this is not a problem, for these obligations fall outside the province of ethics. They are no more than the "obligations" of a craft, for they are imposed by strategic principles (i.e., principles that mark the most efficient means for the accomplishment of a particular task). Indeed, strictly speaking, the system of professional obligations is not a role *morality*.[15] So, again, thinking in terms of *moral* justification, the lawyer's role morality is eliminable.

The other problem with Luban's mediatization of institutional role moralities emerges from his example of a bona fide institutional excuse. Here too, the critic denies that the system of professional obligations constitutes a morality. However, in this case, the denial is based on an observation respecting the function of the institution *qua* normative system[16] rather than the strategic character of the obligation imposing principles.

In Luban's example, the institution is a "charitable organization whose sole function is to distribute food to famine-stricken people in impoverished areas of the world." The division of labor within the institution creates different institutional tasks; these, in turn, specify "duties or *role-obligations*," which a role agent fulfills by performing "*role-acts*." Luban asks us to consider the case of the organization's logistics officer. It is his role obligation to procure means of transporting food. In order to get food to a remote village he has to obtain several trucks from a local gangster. The logistics officer overhears the gangster dispatching an assassin to murder the husband of a woman he lusts after. (This is just one of "a number of unsavory activities" the gangster is involved in.) Having discovered that the logistics officer has overheard him, the gangster tells him, in no uncertain terms, that the trucks will not be provided if the man whose death he has ordered escapes because the logistics officer has warned him. It is reasonable to assert that the logistics officer has a moral obligation to warn the man. Yet here, "if anywhere," Luban writes, "we may wish to permit an institutional excuse." In other words, here, if anywhere, an action that would otherwise be wrong, namely, complying with the gangster's demand, can be justified by reference to an institutional role morality.

The justification in this case is spelled out as follows: the logistics officer "points out that the role-act of complying with [the gangster's demand] is required by his role obligation, which in turn is necessary to perform the institutional task, which (finally) is justified by the positive moral good of the institution—the saving of many individual lives."[17] The trouble here is that not only moral philosophers, particularly utilitarians, but nearly anyone who considers the case is likely to ask, "Why not cut to the chase?" Compliance with the gangster's demand is justified, if it is, because the act itself produces (or is likely to produce) a positive moral good. If the logistics officer is justified in complying with the gangster's demand, this is not because of the institution and the role obligations it imposes, but because, in such circumstances and thinking exclusively in terms of merit,[18] anyone would be justified in acting this way. But then, Luban's claim to the contrary notwithstanding, the institution is not doing the job of justification; it is not a generator of justification but—at best—a conduit for the merit-based sanction of critical morality. Thus, the institutional morality here is a morality in name only; more precisely, the term "institutional morality" is a misnomer. The point is familiar. It was made earlier in the discussion of the eliminability problem, though as was noted above, in that instance it was based on the strategic character of the obligation imposing principles rather than, as here, the function of the institution as a normative system.

Taking Role Moralities Seriously

Luban is right about this: While the story *begins*, it does not end, with the observation that an institutional role morality cannot do the job of justification unless the institution is justified. The type of justification makes a difference, in particular, as Luban argues, a pragmatic justification is not strong enough. Now, if I am right, one who has decided to take role moralities seriously cannot overlook the eliminability problem and the function-identity problem. The connection between this point respecting strength—which is well taken—and the two problems is, then, a matter of concern. But this concern is easily defused, for one thing that emerges from our discussion of the problems is that they are the upshot of Luban's commitment to the viability of the transitivity argument rather than the point identified above. Thus, it seems that one who has decided to take role moralities seriously is free to embrace the point. One question remains, however. The question is this: Luban claims that a pragmatic justification is not strong enough, in particular, not strong enough to justify the role acts of an institutional functionary. But that claim presupposes transitivity, which is now being jettisoned. How is it that, absent transitivity, this condition respecting strength is still apposite?

The answer, I believe, is as follows. The satisfaction of this condition respecting strength, like the fertilization of an egg, is necessary and sufficient for "conception" only; it provides the wherewithal to mark a basic distinction between roles that possess justificatory capacity and roles, such as that of concentration camp commandant, that do not. In this case, as in the case of punishment as an institutional practice, there are two justificatory tasks: (i) the justification of the practice/institution and (ii) the justification of instances of the practice.[19] The latter depends on the former. But the justifications generated by the practice/institution are made out in terms of the norms of the practice; they are *institutional justifications*. The justification of the institution, on the other hand, is noninstitutional. We should insist upon satisfaction of the Lubanian strength condition because the justification of the practice makes institutional justification possible. There is, however, something else that we must insist upon, lest we fail to take role moralities seriously, namely, that institutional justifications are not noninstitutional justifications transmitted by institutional means. Happily, these points are compatible. They are compatible because justifying a practice and justifying an instance of a practice are distinct tasks with different conditions. The normative homeostasis of an institution and the persistence and robustness of the justificatory capacity that arise from and are sustained by it are not logical entailments; they are human achievements. Neither is self-sustaining. The justificatory capacity of institutional role *moralities* is not established once and for all by a showing that the institution is (or produces) a positive moral good; it is something that, once established, must be maintained by human effort.

The decision to take role moralities seriously entails certain commitments. Some of these commitments have emerged in the discussion: (i) acceptance of the Lubanian strength condition, (ii) rejection of the transitivity argument,[20] (iii) insistence upon the distinction between justifying a practice and justifying an instance of a practice, and (iv) a view of the justificatory capacity of institutional moralities that emphasizes the connection between the persistence and robustness of the capacity and conscious efforts to maintain the integrity of the institution. Moreover, and of immediate practical import, if we take role moralities seriously we are committed to this pair of propositions: (v) role moralities impose genuine moral obligations and (vi) in a case of conflict between the obligations one has in virtue of an institutional morality and those one has in virtue of noninstitutional morality, the role obligations may carry the day. That is to say, we cannot know *a priori* how such a conflict will be resolved.

This pair of propositions raises the question how cases of conflict should be viewed and handled. That is a large question, for, among other things, conflicts may arise between distinct role moralities or within a single role morality, as well as between a role (institutional) morality and critical (noninstitutional) morality. Answering this large question—actually a collection of questions—constitutes a major part of the theoretical work that confronts us if we decide to take role moralities seriously. Here I can do little more than suggest an answer that is both consistent with the commitments identified above and seems to have promise.

The Problem of Conflicting Obligations

As far as I can tell, there are four ways of dealing with conflicts between institutional and noninstitutional morality. Two of these are ruled out by the decision to take role moralities seriously. Put forward as claims, the four options are as follows.

A. There is (or should be) a presumption in favor of institutional obligations.
B. There is (or should be) a presumption in favor of noninstitutional obligations.
C. Institutional obligations never carry the day when they are in conflict with noninstitutional obligations.
D. Only one of the two allegedly conflicting obligations is a genuine obligation (i.e., one is an obligation in name only).

Because it denies the reality of conflict, option D also denies the status of morality to a role morality. After all, it can scarcely be supposed that the single morality presupposed in this option is an institutional morality. With option C the possibility of conflict is recognized. However, this recognition does not come to much; in this case, noninstitutional morality subsumes institutional morality, thereby denying its raison d'être and rendering it superfluous, if not spurious. Thus, as I said, two options are ruled out by a decision to take role moralities seriously. Consequently, the live options are A and B. Deciding between these options is a matter of deciding whether to ask for reasons that would overcome (rebut) the presumption in favor of an obligation of noninstitutional morality—option B—or reasons that overcome (rebut) the presumption in favor of an obligation of institutional morality—option A.

Option B is not ruled out by the decision to take role moralities seriously, because, in a particular case of conflict, the presumption might be rebutted and role morality might carry the day. Beyond this, however, little more can be said on its behalf. It is otherwise with option A. As we shall see, in addition to being consistent with the commitments identified above, this option is recommended by heuristic and idiographic considerations.

Consider again the commonplace in professional ethics discussed briefly at the outset; namely, that a role agent may be obligated to perform an action that is wrong. The distinction between institutional and noninstitutional morality both explains this commonplace and invites the query whether an institutional justification of such an action can carry the day when the action is condemned by the norms of noninstitutional morality. As we have seen, the decision to take role moralities seriously entails an affirmative answer to this question. It also raises a question about the scope of the justificatory capacity of role moralities. For here, as with positive law, the claim that there is no limit to this capacity is clearly untenable. In short, the crux of the matter is the question of limits. Indeed, that is the reason for speaking in terms of a presumption. It is also a reason for thinking that option A holds more promise than option B.

That noninstitutional morality imposes limits on institutional morality is a claim few would question. The converse of that claim, on the other hand, is quite mysterious. Moreover, in addition to being easy to understand and accept, the former claim comports well with option A. The crucial idea here is that a source of empowerment is also a source of constraint. The Constitution of the United States, for example, empowers and constrains the executive, legislative, and judicial branches of the federal government. So too, when commitment to a purpose or cause empowers persons, in the sense of providing legitimation for action, the empowerment is limited. The purpose itself establishes some boundaries: a connection between the act as means and the purpose as end is a necessary condition of legitimation. More important, nonfanatical commitment to a purpose involves accepting criteria of appropriateness in the selection of means (e.g., criteria of efficiency) and, particularly when pursuit of the purpose is an ongoing affair, the criteria of appropriateness will raise the question whether that pursuit will be jeopardized by the selection of a means. Expertise is also a source of empowerment; indeed, we speak of experts as authorities with respect to their area of expertise. But here, again, the source of empowerment is also a source of constraint: experts do not speak with authority outside their area of expertise.

The decision to take role moralities seriously entails acceptance of the Lubanian strength condition. It also entails rejection of the transitivity argument and a commitment to the distinction between justifying a practice and justifying an instance of a practice. Thus, if we take role moralities seriously, whether this condition is satisfied is a question respecting the justification—normative capacitation—of an institution. As we noted earlier, this condition provides the wherewithal to distinguish roles that possess justificatory capacity from roles, such as that of concentration camp commandant, that do not. It serves this purpose because satisfaction of this condition is both necessary and sufficient for possession of this capacity. An institution is justificatorily capacitated if but only if it is morally justified. Satisfaction of the Lubanian strength condition is, then, a matter of empowerment. But a source of empowerment is also a source of constraint. Thus, in a particular case of conflict, it is appropriate to regard noninstitutional morality as a source of constraint on institutional morality.[21] It is a source of constraint in the sense that a potentially decisive rebuttal of the presumption in favor of an institutional obligation can be made out in its terms—much as the Constitution provides the stuff of a potentially decisive rebuttal of the presumption of constitutionality respecting contested legislation in modern constitutional law.[22] In any case, with respect to the question of limits this presumption—option A—has some heuristic value; the same cannot be said for the alternative presumption—option B.

A second (related) reason for thinking that option A is a better choice than option B is that it aptly frames the central issue in actual cases of conflict between the obligations of a role and those imposed by noninstitutional morality. Such conflict is, of course, concrete rather than abstract; it arises in a case—a fact situation—and an essential element of the case is that the agent experiencing the conflict is functioning in a role. The role agent is bound by the norms of a role morality. But, as Dorothy Emmet rightly points out, the institutional commitment that explains this fact is not total, it does not entail an abrogation of judgment and conscience. If it did, it would be morally indefensible.[23] Moreover, if the commitment were total, it is difficult to see how a conflict would arise. To be sure, there would be a moral question of some moment here. But that question would be about the commitment—whether, morally, it ought to have been made—rather than what ought to be done. The latter question would be decisively answered by the institutional role morality to which the role agent is totally committed. There would be no problem of conflicting obligations; at any rate, the role agent would not recognize it.

In the class of cases under consideration here, where there is a problem of conflicting obligations, the conflict arises when a role agent bound by the norms of a role morality recognizes (on her own or at the prodding of another) that judged by criteria of noninstitutional morality the performance of the role act (doing what is expected of the role agent in the circumstances) would be wrong. For example, an attorney is "duty bound to exert his best efforts in aid of his client."[24] Thus, in a criminal case, he ought to submit proposed instructions to the judge if, under the applicable law, his client could be convicted of a lesser offense (e.g., involuntary manslaughter) and thereby receive a lighter sentence. Further, even though the attorney knows that a statement made by his client is false (because his client told him so), if that statement is adduced as evidence by the prosecution he is obligated to argue it, along with the other evidence, to the jury. The rub comes when, believing that his client is guilty as charged and applying criteria of critical morality, the attorney concludes that it would be wrong to facilitate the imposition of undeserved (because insufficiently harsh) punishment and wrong "to get up before a jury and try to argue that the statement [adduced as evidence by the prosecution] was true when [my client] had told me that it wasn't."[25]

There is a problem of conflicting obligations here. The attorney knows what his role obligation is. In past cases he has and in future cases he will fulfill it. As he has in the past, in the future he will endeavor to effectively represent his client "according to the customary standards prescribed by attorneys and the courts."[26] That is how it should be. Indeed, because of his institutional commitment, for him that it should be so is a given; in his ethical decision making this and other role obligations are taken for granted. Yet, because his institutional commitment does not entail an abrogation of judgment and conscience, taking them for granted does not amount to regarding them as absolute. There is a presumption in favor of his role obligations; this presumption is strong, but rebuttable.

This case of conflict between the obligations of a role and the obligations imposed by noninstitutional morality is typical. Role agents, particularly professionals, take their role obligations for granted in the sense indicated. Moreover, clients and patients believe that professionals take their role obligations seriously—they act in reliance on the bindingness of role obligations. Professionals know that. Indeed, recognizing that a stable framework of interaction is a foundation for confidence, reliance, and trust, they have done much to encourage this belief. The crucial point is that for clients and patients too, role obligations are primary.

Patients and clients disclose deeply personal and sensitive information, information that is often quite valuable (e.g., business plans for expansion or product development) and such as to be potentially harmful to the patient's or client's interests if revealed to others. Of course, this is done with an eye to accomplishing something, something that they believe, rightly or wrongly, cannot be accomplished without professional assistance. Yet it is equally clear that patients and clients would not disclose such information if there were no check on the personal—including moral—idiosyncracies of the professional. When such information is shared with a spouse or close friend, one knows (or believes that one knows) the person well, well enough to be comfortable in disclosing the information, well enough that a pledge of silence is unnecessary; indeed, in such a situation one need not even say, "this is just between the two of us." But the relationship here is personal. The relationship between a professional and her client or patient, on the other hand, is impersonal. In both cases, however, so far as disclosure of sensitive information is concerned, what one knows about the other is key: this knowledge is the fount of one's interactional expectations. In a personal relationship one knows the other person more or less intimately, including quirks and so on, and acts accordingly. In a professional relationship, because it is impersonal, what one knows is that the other occupies a role and thus has certain role obligations; one knows the persona rather than the person, and acts accordingly.[27]

For the client or patient as well as the professional, then, role obligations are basic. They are, as it were, presupposed on both sides of the relationship. Moreover, we have seen that in cases of conflict between the obligations of a role and the obligations imposed by noninstitutional morality the question is not whether a noninstitutional obligation stands in the face of a contrary institutional obligation; rather, the question is whether one's institutional obligation stands in the face of a contrary noninstitutional obligation. Thus, in addition to the point respecting heuristic value that emerged in the discussion of noninstitutional morality as a source of empowerment and constraint, there are good idiographic reasons to think that option A—where there is a presumption in favor institutional obligations—is a better choice than option B—where there is a presumption in favor of noninstitutional obligations. Taken together, these considerations tip the balance in its favor.

Conclusion

The case I have presented for a presumption in favor of institutional obligations is consistent with the commitments entailed by the decision to take role moralities seriously. Thus, it presupposes the satisfaction of the Lubanian strength condition (i.e., that the institution is morally justified). An institution is normatively capacitated if and only if this condition obtains. The stability, persistence, and vitality of an institution's justificatory capacity are another matter. They are human achievements rather than logical consequences. Thus, the argument also presupposes that role agents understand this and are committed to the task of maintaining the integrity of the institution. That commitment—the fourth of the six identified above—is important for another reason: At the level of practice, it is both evidence that a role morality is being taken seriously and a reason for thinking that this is appropriate. Indeed, at the level of practice it is much the most important thing for the question whether a role morality should be taken seriously.

Notes

This paper is a slightly revised and expanded version of "Taking Role Moralities Seriously," *The Southern Journal of Philosophy* 29 (1991): 407–17. Reprinted with the kind permission of the editor.

1. Here I mean to include the capacity to "generate" normative relations—for example (i) right-duty, (ii) immunity-disability, (iii) power-liability, and (iv) liberty-no-claim, familiar to students of Hohfeld's conceptual scheme—as well as the capacity to excuse. See Wesley Newcomb Hohfeld, *Fundamental Legal Conceptions* (New Haven: Yale University Press, 1919). For an analysis and reinterpretation of Hohfeld's conceptual scheme see Carl Wellman, *A Theory of Rights* (Totowa, N.J.: Rowman and Allanheld, 1985): 7–15; 17–60.

2. This is the designation Paul Camenisch employs for normative constraints arising "from what it means to be a decent human being." Paul Camenisch, "Business Ethics: On Getting to the Heart of the Matter," *Business and Professional Ethics Journal* 1 (1981): 59. Constraints arising from an enterprise or undertaking in which one is engaged (i.e., one's role) constitute a different sort of ethic; accordingly, we speak of —— ethics, or the ethics of ——, the —— being filled in with an adjective or a noun that more or less definitely marks the difference by, for example, specifying the enterprise or undertaking (e.g., "professional," "medical," "business," "medicine," "advocacy").

3. See, for example, Richard Wasserstrom, "Lawyers as Professionals: Some Moral Issues," *Human Rights* 5 (1975): 12; Richard Wasserstrom, "Roles and Morality," in *The Good Lawyer*, ed. David Luban (Totowa, N.J.: Rowman and Allanheld, 1984); cf. Gerald Postema, "Moral Responsibility in Professional Ethics," *New York University Law Review* 55 (1980): 71–73 (criticizing the approach that recommends the "deprofessionalization" of professional roles on the basis of an argument to the effect that "the duties and responsibilities of a professional are [or should be] no different from those of any lay person facing a similar moral problem").

4. Wellman, *A Theory of Rights*, 118.

5. The norms of a role morality are "dual aspect norms." That is to say, they are standards for action and for reaction: they apply to a role agent who, in his/her capacity as a role agent, is deciding what to do; they also apply to the reaction of others who observe or become aware of deviation from or conformity to them by role agents. Thus, the notion of applicability here embraces the directive and the evaluative functions of norms. See Wellman, *A Theory of Rights*, 113.

6. Here one may be reminded of the jurisprudential thesis of the natural lawyer: an unjust law is no law at all, hence incapable of imposing an obligation. Natural law thinkers, of course, say essentially the same thing about the norms of what John Austin called positive morality. Since role moralities are institutional moralities, they fall under Austin's rubric and are within the scope of the natural lawyer's claim. Thus, to be reminded of this thesis at this juncture is entirely appropriate. So, too, looking to jurisprudence for assistance in answering the question about the scope of the justificatory capacity of role moralities is entirely appropriate. After all, essentially the same question respecting the justificatory capacity of positive law is and has been at center stage in the competition between the rival jurisprudential theories of natural law and legal positivism.

7. See Emile Durkheim, "Some Notes on Occupational Groups," preface to the second edition of *The Division of Labor in Society*, trans. G. Simpson (New York: The Free Press, 1933) (the first edition was published in 1893, the second in 1902) and George Herbert Mead, *Mind, Self and Society From the Standpoint of a Social Behaviorist*, ed. Charles W. Morris (Chicago: University of Chicago Press, 1934). Also see Steven Lukes, *Emile Durkheim*, (New York: Harper and Row, 1972): 265–68 (discussing Durkheim's views on domestic and occupational ethics); 296–302 (discussing the less than warm reception of Durkheim's ideas by the Sorbonne moral philosophers); and George Simpson, *Emile Durkheim* (New York: Thomas Y. Cromwell, 1963): 117–18 ("Moral Facts and Professional Ethics"); 126–27 ("Economic Anomy and Modern Society"); 128–29 ("The Contemporary Moral Dilemma").

8. One might go further, claiming, for instance, that role moralities should not be taken seriously. An examination of recent history reveals that, for the devotee, professional ethics is nothing but a means to escape from moral responsibility; the elements of a professional ethic serve the single purpose of exculpation. That is to say, the obligations of one's profession come into play only if one is challenged to justify one's action in the face of a moral indictment. Here one would be making a moral argument for abandoning the notion of a role morality.

9. There are two ways in which this work may be done: immediately or mediately. The sanction of critical morality generates obligation immediately when a critical moral norm enjoins action; mediately when action is enjoined by a norm of an institution sanctioned by critical morality. Both means are

considered *infra*; the former in the discussion of Plato's understanding of role differentiation, the latter in the discussion of the transitivity argument.

10. David Luban, "The Adversary System Excuse," in Luban, *The Good Lawyer*, 87. The examples of the commandant and the strikebreaker are Luban's.

11. Ibid., 115. What Luban calls the transitivity argument goes as follows: "1. The institution is justified. 2. The institution requires its functionary to do A. 3. Therefore, the functionary is justified in doing A." Ibid., 114. See note 12 *infra*, for an example of how the argument is put to work; cf. the text at note 17.

12. Ibid., 116. Fully spelled out, an institutional excuse takes this form: "the agent justifies the role-act by showing it is required by the role obligation, justifies the obligation by showing it derives from an institutional task, justifies the institutional task by appealing to the structure of the institution, and justifies the institution by demonstrating its moral goodness." Ibid., 114. In such a case, the sanction of critical morality is generating obligation mediately rather than immediately—the action is enjoined by a norm of an institution sanctioned by critical morality. See note 9, *supra*.

13. Ibid., 113.

14. Ibid., 118. Emphasis added.

15. The critic's objection here is quite like H.L.A. Hart's objection to Lon Fuller's claim that the principles internal to the lawmaking enterprise constitute a *morality*. According to Hart, Fuller's morality designation rests on and is likely to perpetuate a "confusion of principles guiding any form of purposive activity with morality." H.L.A. Hart, review of *The Morality of Law*, by Lon L. Fuller, *Harvard Law Review* 78 (1965): 1285–87. Cf. Daniel E. Wueste, "Fuller's Processual Philosophy of Law," review of *Lon L. Fuller*, by Robert S. Summers, *Cornell Law Review* 71 (1986): 1214–17; Robert S. Summers, "Summers's Primer on Fuller's Jurisprudence—A Wholly Disinterested Assessment of the Reviews by Professors Wueste and Lebel," ibid., 1235–38; Wueste, "Morality and the Legal Enterprise—A Reply to Professor Summers," ibid., 1252–63 (discussing, *inter alia*, Hart's criticism, Summers's interpretation of Fuller's claim, and the question whether—as I argue, contra Hart and Summers—the principles Fuller identified as the internal morality of law constitute a role morality).

16. I follow Philip Selznick in using the term "normative system" to refer to "groups, institutions, and activities. . . . [that,] as vehicles for the realization of human values . . . embody ideals varyingly fulfilled." In this sense, a normative system is not simply a set of related norms. For instance, as Selznick points out, "science as a distinctive enterprise has this character, invoking ideals of logical order, verifiability, and accuracy. Constitutional democracy and university education are also normative systems in this sense." Philip Selznick, review of *The Morality of Law*, by Lon L. Fuller, *American Sociological Review* 30 (1965): 947. Cf. Philip Selznick, "Sociology and Natural Law," *Natural Law Forum* 6 (1961): 84.

17. Luban, "The Adversary System Excuse," 113–14.

18. It seems that where merit alone is decisive, the fact that an agent occupies a specific role will be morally otiose—the institutional rules thought to impose moral role obligations (or authorize certain conduct) would in fact do no such thing. Indeed, if merit alone is morally decisive, it is hard to see how talk of roles and the obligations they impose has any moral significance. Thus, granting the moral significance of roles and the obligations they impose, it follows that where they matter, merit alone is not decisive. In such contexts, justification requires something more than that the action is meritorious; in particular, a showing that within the institutional context of the role it is appropriate for the role agent to undertake the action. For a discussion of this last point see Mortimer R. Kadish and Sanford H. Kadish, *Discretion to Disobey* (Stanford: Stanford University Press, 1973): 5–36.

19. John Rawls is credited with having introduced this distinction in his famous article, "Two Concepts of Rules," *The Philosophical Review* 64 (1955). According to Dorothy Emmet, Rawls's distinction is well taken, because "some things can only be done through established institutions operated by rules so that one has to work within the pattern they prescribe." She goes on to suggest that this is "the main point of [Rawls's] distinction when applied to social morality." Dorothy Emmet, *Rules, Roles and Relations* (New York: St. Martin's Press, 1966; Boston: Beacon Press, 1975), 58–59. Emmet also points out, rightly, that while it might be thought that "no breaking of a rule of an institutional practice could be justified, or even possible, unless we abolish the institution altogether," Rawls's distinction does not entail such a conclusion. Ibid. If it did, it would be difficult indeed to embrace it. For, among other things, this conclusion flies in the face of the fact that legal systems have endured in the face of civil disobedience, in particular, civil disobedience that brings about moral reform of the positive law.

20. The rejection in question is wholesale. That is, taking role moralities seriously we will reject this *form* of argument altogether rather than particular instances of it. Luban does the latter.

21. See Emmet, *Rules, Roles and Relations*, 200–201 (suggesting that a view of abstract principles of critical morality as constraints on moral judgment "best fits the complexities of moral situations in institutional and organizational life").

22. See 16 C.J.S. Constitutional Law Sec. 97 ("it is the generally accepted rule that every statute or regularly enacted legislative act, is, or will be, or should be presumed to be valid and constitutional") and 16 C.J.S. Constitutional Law Sec. 98 ("The presumption of constitutionality of statutes is strong, but rebuttable. . . . [it] may be rebutted by evidence showing the actual existence of a state of facts or circumstances under which the statute, as a matter of law, is unconstitutional").

23. Emmet, *Rules, Roles and Relations*, 204. Emmet argues that if a *total* commitment to an institution or organization entails the "abrogation of

judgment and conscience in putting the demands of the organization before all other considerations in all contexts," it should neither be exacted nor given. At "the end of that road," she writes, "can stand Eichmann, who went to his death protesting that he was being punished for obedience, and that obedience is praised as a virtue." Yet, something more than what "can be stated in a bare contract" is required if an institution or organization is to function. Accordingly, Emmet speaks of "loyalty and deep involvement" in the purposes of the institution or organization. Ibid. This sort of commitment does not entail an abrogation of judgment and conscience; it is something more than what can be stated in a bare contract but less than a total commitment.

24. *Johns* v. *Smyth* 176 F. Sup. 949 (E.D. Va. 1959), 953. The example in the text is based on this case. In 1942, Johns was convicted of murdering a fellow inmate in the Virginia State Penitentiary. He was sentenced to life imprisonment. His attorney was court appointed. In this case, Johns sought a writ of habeas corpus claiming, among other things, that the actions of his attorney were such that he had not received a fair trial. Johns prevailed. The U.S. District Court decision was based on the testimony it heard from Johns's court-appointed counsel. (I have included a portion of this testimony in the text.)

The case is excerpted in *Ethics and the Practice of Law*, ed. David E. Schrader (Englewood Cliffs, N.J.: Prentice Hall, 1988), 116–20. All subsequent citations to this case are to this source. For a discussion of the case and the issues raised by it see John T. Noonan, Jr., "The Purposes of Advocacy and the Limits of Confidentiality," and Monroe Freedman, "Perjury: The Criminal Defense Lawyer's Trilemma," in Schrader, *Ethics and the Practice of Law*, 301–7, 308–20, respectively.

25. Schrader, *Ethics and the Practice of Law*, 118.

26. Ibid., 120. Apropos of the points made in the text: at the time of Johns's trial in 1942, the court-appointed attorney had been practicing for approximately fifteen years. When *Johns* v. *Smyth* was heard in U.S. District Court in 1959, this attorney had been practicing law for roughly thirty-two years.

27. For a discussion of the development of the notion of persona, its place in discussions of role morality, and the problems respecting the person in the persona, see Emmet, *Rules, Roles and Relations*, Chapter 8.

6

Engineers and the Public: Sharing Responsibilities

Robert J. Baum

The focus of this paper is the profession of engineering, and particularly one aspect of most of the major engineering codes of ethics. However, the central point of the paper is one that can and should be generalized to most (and possibly all) other professions; namely that the *primary* responsibility of the profession is that of assisting efforts of the general public—individually and collectively—to obtain information about risks associated with specific technological artifacts and systems that may be relevant to the public's health and welfare. The secondary thesis of this paper is that individuals, singly as well as collectively, bear the primary responsibility for protecting their own interests, that they ought not take the role of dependent children and assign a parental role to engineers and other professionals.

Physicians and lawyers are generally more visible than engineers—in everyday life as well as in movies and on TV—and when people think of problems in professional ethics, they think of medicine and law. However, the public is reminded of the significance of ethical practice in engineering when the lead news stories are about dramatic life-taking disasters such as the Ford Pinto fuel tank, the DC-10, 3-Mile Island, the Hyatt-Regency in Kansas City, Chernobyl, and the Challenger Space Shuttle. Engineering is concerned with the design, construction, and maintenance of artifacts and systems that are usually intended to improve the overall quality of life, but that not infrequently involve risks to human life (as well as property). Engineers are necessarily involved—as much as and sometimes even more than physicians—in the process of making decisions that can result in or prevent deaths and serious injuries. Even such common activities as the construction of bridges and high-rise buildings routinely involve the loss of lives (for example, as many lives were lost in the construction

121

of the Sears Building in Chicago as in the Challenger explosion[1]).
Although deaths and injuries related to construction and manufacturing
are usually classified as "accidents" and do not receive the same press
coverage as "disasters," many workers and their relatives are quite
aware of the dangers associated with working on projects designed and
supervised by engineers even if they are not fully aware of the role(s)
of the engineers. And although consumers are increasingly conscious
of a broad range of threats to their health and safety related to various
technologies, they are more likely to assign responsibility for these
threats to the corporations and managers rather than the engineers
involved.

Some Conceptual and Terminological Clarifications

Before we examine the ethical aspects of the work of engineers, it will
be useful to clarify several terms and concepts. One terminological
point is that cases such as those mentioned above are often referred to
as involving "moral decisions" or "ethical decisions" (for the purposes of this paper, the terms "ethical" and "moral" can be assumed
to be interchangeable). While these may be quite common colloquial
expressions, they can also be confusing. Strictly speaking, *every*
decision is grounded on a variety of judgments, as indicated in Figure
1. (This schematization is grossly oversimplified—for example, each
of the areas listed can be broken down into subareas and a number of
areas might be added that are not included in Figure 1.)
    Each of these kinds of judgment can be made about *every* decision.
For any particular decision, *some* ethical/moral judgments can be
made about it, but every other kind of judgment can be made about
the decision as well. There are no decisions about which *only* ethical
judgments can be made,[2] and ethical judgments can be made about
every decision; thus, it is misleading to describe any decision as
"ethical" (or "moral") if this is intended to distinguish it from decisions that are (mistakenly) considered to be *purely engineering*—legal,
economic, or scientific. In most contexts, the assertion that a decision
is an ethical one means that its ethical dimensions/aspects are the most
significant or problematic elements. Sometimes we (correctly) speak
of an "ethical decision" when this is intended to indicate that the
ethical judgments on which the decision is based are reasonable or
sound—that is, to distinguish such a decision from one that is *un*-
ethical.

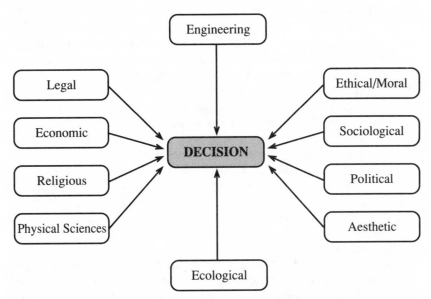

Figure 1   Partial Listing of Kinds of Judgments That Enter Into All Decisions.

Another point that needs clarification is that while decision making clearly involves responsibilities on the part of the decision makers, it also—and more importantly for the purposes of this paper—involves *rights*. Making decisions necessarily involves the exercise of power and control on the part of the decision makers and the possible infringement of the rights of other individuals. In most societies in which engineers (and other professionals) play significant roles, it is recognized that each individual has the basic right to make (or to participate to an appropriate degree in the making of) decisions that have effects on her/his welfare. The burden of proof is on agents who wish to preempt or override other persons' powers or rights to make decisions affecting their own lives—to intrude upon their sphere of autonomy.

A third point that needs to be clarified is that in an *ideal* universe a morally sound decision-making process should always produce morally good results. But in the *real* world of finite individuals making decisions based on limited information, a morally sound process will sometimes produce undesirable results. Thus, the observation of a negative consequence of a particular decision cannot be taken as conclusive grounds for the rejection of the process leading to that decision.

The Inevitability of Risk

Returning to the front-page disaster cases, we should note that engineers (individually and collectively) often feel a degree of responsibility that is probably comparable to that felt by physicians at the death of a patient or by a lawyer upon losing a capital case. However, it must be recognized that the concern with responsibility for harm caused by technological artifacts and systems (space shuttles, nuclear power plants, highways, breast implants, or whatever) is not merely a matter of name calling or guilty consciences. In addition to harm to the direct victims of the technological failures, lawsuits directed at obtaining just compensation for these victims or their survivors can result in significant, and sometimes disastrous, penalties for parties judged to be guilty of causing the disasters. Individual engineers can be sued, fired, and/or have their licenses revoked; the companies they work for can be forced out of business.

Engineers involved in such cases often feel as though they are totally alone and being judged—negatively—by the rest of society. For example, Roger Boisjoly, one of the engineers at Morton Thiokol, suffered a serious emotional collapse after the Challenger disaster, even though by all accounts he had done more than any other individual to try to prevent the failure of the O-rings, which led to the loss of the seven astronauts' lives.[3]

The stress experienced by engineers due to the possible harm that their work can cause has been well expressed by Henry Petroski in his book *To Engineer is Human.*

> When I was a student of engineering I came to fear the responsibility that I imagined might befall me after graduation. How, I wondered, could I ever be perfectly sure that something I might design would not break or collapse and kill a number of people? I knew my understanding of my textbooks was less than total, my homework was seldom without some sort of error, and my grades were not straight As. . . . I avoided confronting the issue by going to graduate school instead of taking an engineering job right away.[4]

Something deeper than concern with public image—and even more powerful than the threat of legal liability—is operative here; namely, a moral sensitivity on the part of the individuals who self-select into the profession of engineering.

Engineers derive great satisfaction from being able to see that their efforts have *produced* something—but even more, they derive satisfaction from seeing that what they have made is *good*. The world is full of pitfalls and (as Petroski realized while still a student) human beings inevitably make mistakes. Engineering—like every other profession—involves risk. It is nonsense to ask what can be done to eliminate risk. The most meaningful question that can be asked concerning engineering ethics is "What can reasonably be done to minimize the risks associated with the work of engineers?" It is important to notice that this question does not include the qualification "by engineers"; the question being asked is what can reasonably be done *by any and all interested parties* to minimize the risks associated with the work of engineers?

Let me begin to answer this question by looking briefly at the answers that engineers themselves have given.

The Evolution of Engineering Codes of Ethics

As a formally organized profession, engineering is only about one hundred years old, although of course many highly skilled and creative individuals—including Archimedes, Roger Bacon, and Leonardo da Vinci—had done very impressive engineering work long before the establishment of professional schools of engineering and engineering professional societies. The members of the first engineering societies in the United States began to clarify and delineate the scope of the responsibilities of professional engineers in formal codes of ethics a mere eighty years ago. As in most other aspects of their efforts to establish engineering as a legitimate profession, they used the medical profession as their model. The code of ethics of the AMA at the turn of the century was still firmly grounded in the tradition of the ancient Hippocratic Oath, the essence of which was an overriding parentalistic responsibility for the welfare of each individual patient.

> I will follow that method of treatment which, according to my ability and judgment, I consider for the benefit of my patients, and abstain from whatever is deleterious and mischievous. I will give no deadly medicine to anyone if asked. . . . [5]

Notice that it takes only a few word changes—essentially replacing "patient" with "client or employer"—to transform this statement into one that expresses the same meaning as those contained in the 1912 code of the American Institute of Electrical Engineers and the 1914 code of the American Society of Mechanical Engineers, namely that

The engineer should consider the protection of a client's or employer's interests his first obligation, and therefore should avoid every act contrary to this duty.

This wording puts a significant burden of responsibility on the engineer to make a judgment as to what is in fact in the best interest of the client and then to act on this judgment. The code is as highly parentalistic as the medical code in that it makes no acknowledgment of the rights of the clients and employers to decide for themselves what is in their own best interest. It is also important to note in this context that the early engineering codes pay little attention to the general public, and what little they do say about the public has to do primarily with public relations and promoting a favorable public image of the profession.[6]

As the various engineering societies matured, they continued to discuss and critique their codes. By 1947, the major engineering societies—with the exception of IEEE—agreed upon a new code, worked out by the Engineers Council for Professional Development, which explicitly recognizes the complex realities of the practicing engineer.

As the keystone of professional conduct is integrity, the engineer will discharge his duties with fidelity to the public, his employers, and clients, and with fairness and impartiality to all. It is his duty to interest himself in public welfare, and to be ready to apply his special knowledge for the benefit of mankind.[7]

(It is interesting to note that the American Medical Association did not make similar modifications in its code until 1980, at which time its code was completely reformulated so that it now begins with a preamble that states

The medical profession has long subscribed to a body of ethical statements developed primarily for the benefit of the patient. As a member of this profession, a physician must recognize responsibility not only to patients, but also to society, to other health professionals and to self.[8]

Although the 1947 engineering code more accurately reflects the complexities of the real world of professional practice, it puts an even more substantial burden on the individual engineer, who is no longer required or even permitted to simply do whatever she/he judges to be in the best interests of her or his clients/employers. The new burden is that engineers are required to make a judgment as to when the interests of the public should be given priority over the interests of the clients/ employers and when the clients'/employers' interests should have priority. Because this code offers no further guidelines as to how to "fairly and impartially" fulfill the engineer's duties to the public and to her/his employer/client, the full responsibility is placed on the individual engineer to determine exactly how to do this in individual cases. There is neither consideration nor acknowledgment in this code of any rights of members of the general public to make their own decisions based on their own judgments of what is in their best interest; once again the engineers' taking on of excessive responsibilities is simultaneously a preemption of the rights of others.

The ECPD code (and those of the various other societies that had adopted it) was substantially revised again in 1974. This version (ECPD has subsequently been renamed the Accreditation Board for Engineering and Technology—ABET), which is still the model for most of the major engineering societies (again with the IEEE being the main exception), now explicitly states that "Engineers shall hold paramount the safety, health and welfare of the public in the performance of their professional duties."[9]

Interpreting the Paramountcy Clause

While this new formulation may seem at first glance to simplify the situation for individual engineers by eliminating any questions about the relative priority of responsibilities to the public over responsibilities to the employers/clients, a moment's consideration reveals that it does not really make it easier for engineers to apply the code to specific cases. In addition, this modification makes the code less plausible, insofar as it is not very difficult to think of cases in the real world in which the engineer's responsiblities to an employer may outweigh the importance of the safety, health, and welfare of the public. For example, consider the case of an engineer who has invented a technique that decreases her employer's production costs for a specific product, but the manufacturer (her employer) does not pass on the decrease in cost to the consumers. Even though decreasing the cost of the product to the consumers would increase the welfare of the public, it is not at all clear that the engineer has a moral obligation to notify the general public. Furthermore, as engineer Samuel Florman and others have argued eloquently and forcefully since the new ECPD/ ABET code was adopted, even with the explicit priority being given to public safety, health, and welfare, "it is unthinkable that each engineer determine to his own satisfaction what criteria of safety, for example, should be observed in each problem he encounters."[10] While an individual engineer must provide appropriate technical input into the making of various decisions, he or she should not be forced—especially by the professional engineering societies—into unilaterally making the countless complex moral judgments relevant to these decisions. If the engineering societies insist on retaining the paramountcy clause in their codes, then they must think this through all the way and provide *workable* means that enable engineers to *reasonably* fulfil this responsibility. In the almost twenty years that this clause has been in the codes, engineering societies have not seriously considered how this might be implemented in real-world situations, and they have taken no positive action on the few specific proposals that have been made (such as Steven Unger's proposal that the major engineering societies should set up procedures for protecting whistleblowers similar to the American Association of University Professors' procedures for protecting professors against violations of their academic freedom[11]). The most sympathetic interpretation of this failure to act is that the engineering societies discovered that it is extremely difficult if not impossible (1) to come up with a truly workable procedure under which engineers could reliably determine what is in fact in the best interests of the public and (2) to provide protections necessary for engineers who proceed to act on this knowledge in ways they sincerely believe hold the public safety, health, and welfare paramount.

To better understand the difficulty here, it will help to recall a point made earlier: no decision is purely an engineering decision or purely an economic decision or purely an ethical decision; every rational decision is grounded in a set of different kinds of judgments, of which engineering judgments and ethical judgments are but two of many kinds.

With regard to any specific decision related to engineering, it is likely that an individual engineer would be best qualified to make judgments about the engineering aspects of the decision—although in many situations it might take a *team* of engineers to make a reliable judgment. But few engineers would claim the same level of expertise or special insight into most of the other areas (economic, political, aesthetic, etc.) of judgment relevant to the ultimate decision—and certainly it is unlikely that they have any special expertise for assessing what will maximize the public safety, health, or welfare. Moreover, even with regard to the engineering judgments related to a particular decision, different engineers might make different judgments based on differences in their training and experience. In such cases it is not always easy to determine which "expert" is right (e.g., when one engineer has thirty years of professional experience and the other is a recent Ph.D. with impeccable academic credentials). But it is perhaps *most* clear that no single engineer is in a privileged position to make the *moral* judgments relevant to technologically oriented decisions. I must emphasize here that in complex and difficult cases I do not believe that *any* one individual (engineer or nonengineer) is in such a privileged position.

Let us look more closely at several of the specific cases mentioned earlier, and particularly at the Challenger case, to see what the role of the engineer should have been in decisions that were made. There is no doubt that the fiery death of the seven astronauts had a strong emotional impact on all of us. But in assigning responsibility, and particularly blame, for such events we must resist succumbing to the human tendency (often exploited by prosecutors in criminal cases) to convict a defendant because of the horror of the crime rather than because of the weight of the evidence.

The published accounts of the events leading up to the decision to launch the Challenger make it clear that even the "managers" involved in making the decision had all started out as engineers and still considered themselves to be engineers who sometimes wore "managers' hats." Many writers have speculated on exactly what the flaws were in the decision-making procedure that resulted in the fateful decision. It has also been pointed out that the O-rings were just one of literally hundreds of factors that had what was called "criticality"; that is, any one of them could also have caused a disaster—although the probabilities of most of the other events were much lower than the probability of the O-ring failure under the specific temperature conditions.[12]

One fact about the decision process was singled out as particularly significant by other astronauts and most of the Rogers Commission in the subsequent investigation: namely, that none of the Challenger astronauts had been informed specifically of the O-ring problem.[13] Thus, one of the final recommendations of the Rogers Commission was that astronauts and especially members of the crew should be more involved in all aspects of the decision-making process. In particular, it was recommended that "the flight crew commander, or a designated representative, should attend the Flight Readiness Review, [and] participate in acceptance of the vehicle for flight. . . ."[14]

It is widely assumed by commentators that this modification to the process would have led to a different conclusion concerning the launch, but this is not necessarily the case. Even if all of the information about the risks associated with the launch had been adequately communicated to the astronauts, it is still possible that they would have chosen to proceed with the launch. But this does not mean that there is something wrong with this process. As we noted above, a specific negative outcome (the end) of a decision process does not necessarily impugn the moral validity of the process (the means).

If we step back to view decision-making processes in the space program in a broader perspective, we find that other astronauts died in previous accidents. In particular, early in the program (January 1967) three well-known and popular astronauts—Gus Grissom, Ed White, and Roger Chafee—died in a flash fire on the launch pad. The follow-up investigation revealed that "There were numerous warnings [about the hazards that ultimately caused the astronauts' deaths], including a 1964 NASA publication entitled *Space-Cabin Atmospheres, Part II— Fire and Blast Hazards*. The astronauts were aware of all of this information." Moreover, "*the [launch] director . . . wanted to stop, but the astronauts objected.*"[15] Ironically, the Apollo Review Board said that there was a need for better definition of responsibilities, and concluded (in retrospect, of course) that in this case the Project Director should have overridden the wishes of the astronauts.

In other words, despite the psychological fact that astronauts are self-selected adventurers willing to take risks, the primary responsibilities *to the astronauts* of engineers involved in the launch process are to do everything possible to assure that the astronauts

1. are fully informed of the nature of all of the known risks involved in a particular situation; and

2. are not coerced into making a personal decision to proceed with the flight.

(Engineers of course also have other responsibilities to management, which may sometimes appear to conflict with these responsibilities to the astronauts.)

With regard to the Challenger case, if *after* having been given the information about the O-rings and all other significant risks, the astronauts had individually and collectively made the personal decisions that they wanted the launch to proceed, the engineers could still feel comfortable that they had fulfilled all of their responsibilities to the astronauts. Of course, even if the astronauts had expressed their preferences to proceed with the launch, it would still have been quite possible that other participants in the decision-making process would have overruled the astronauts' personal preferences and canceled the launch for other reasons—economic, political, or even ethical. But if the astronauts had decided on the basis of the information provided by the engineers about the O-rings that they did not want the launch to take place, it is difficult to conceive of any argument that would have justified proceeding with the launch.

Although I agree with Samuel Florman that no individual engineer should be put in the position of having unilaterally to make all of the ethical judgments relevant to a complex technology-related decision, many engineers and many members of the general public feel that engineers have no choice but to stick their necks out in real-world situations, particularly given the dictate of the engineering codes to put the health and safety of the public above all else. Roger Boisjoly is still fighting his inner struggle as to whether he should have in some way gone around his superiors to higher authorities or to the press or . . . somewhere to save the astronauts.

In a recent essay,[16] Michael Davis argues that the requirement that engineers hold the public safety, health, and welfare paramount can and should be retained, but that its meaning must be clarified. He suggests that the proper interpretation of the paramountcy principle in the engineering codes should be that "the public" refers to "those persons whose lack of information, technical knowledge, or time for deliberation renders them more or less vulnerable to the powers an engineer wields on behalf of his client or employer." He then goes on to assert that in cases such as the Challenger case, "the engineer's code of ethics would (all else equal) require [an engineer] either to refuse to authorize the launch or to insist instead that the astronauts be briefed in order to get their informed consent to the risk."[17]

I agree with Davis that the engineers involved had a moral obligation to do whatever they could to ensure the parties at risk were informed of the existence of those risks. However, in recommending that "engineers should not only do as their profession's code requires, but should also support it less directly by encouraging others to do as it requires,"[18] Davis is too optimistic in assuming that engineers should (and presumably will) interpret the paramountcy clause along the lines of Davis's own reinterpretation. (It is not even clear that his formulation is consistent with the underlying parentalism that is implicit

throughout the codes and that is part of the basic psychological profile
of the majority of engineers.)

Replacing the Paramountcy Clause

While I fully agree with what Davis offers as an interpretation of the
paramountcy clause, I also believe that such obligations need to be
described as clearly and explicitly as possible in the codes—at least as
an elaboration of the paramountcy clause and preferably as a replace-
ment for it. The strongest argument that engineers and other professionals should play a major and perhaps leading role in making such
changes to their codes is self-interest. The "paramountcy" principle
in their codes imposes an impossible burden of responsibility on
individual engineers (while at the same time usurping the rights of all
other affected parties). Most decisions involving the complex technologies that are ubiquitous in our society cannot be made by any
individual alone, and there is no defensible justification for engineers—
individually or collectively—to take the decision-making responsibility
onto themselves. The only morally justifiable procedure for making
decisions in such complex cases is for all affected parties or their
delegated representatives to be provided with all of the available
information relevant to the decision and for them to have an equitable
say in the final decision.

I published a proposal over a decade ago for changes to the paramountcy clause, the precise wording of which was as follows:

> Engineers have a responsibility to
> 1. recognize the right of each individual potentially affected by a
> project to participate to an appropriate degree in the making of decisions
> concerning that project;
> 2. do everything in their power to provide complete, accurate and
> understandable information to all potentially affected parties. . . .[19]

Although some responses to my proposal involved substantive criticisms and disagreements, by far the majority accepted the concepts
and principles involved but raised questions about practical aspects of
implementation, such as how an engineer could provide information
about risks associated with a particular type of commercial airliner or a
bridge on a heavily traveled interstate highway to *all* of the "potentially
affected parties." My response to such queries was usually a vague

statement to the effect that it was up to the engineering societies to decide the specifics of implementation.[20]

Formulating Implementation Procedures

A number of major works were published in the 1980s that are consistent with and that provide a more elaborate theoretical justification of the obligation of professionals to provide complete information about risks to all potentially affected parties, but I am aware of none that present detailed practical plans for doing so, nor do I know of any discussions of procedures for devising such a plan.[21] I still do not have a detailed solution to the problem of how engineers might be able to provide information to all potentially affected parties, particularly in cases of large-scale technologies for which the at-risk groups are not clearly identifiable and/or readily accessible. However, I *can* suggest one step that engineering societies ought to take that has a good chance of leading to the development of a plan that would facilitate the transmitting of information about risks from engineers to potentially affected parties—whether they be astronauts, airline passengers, or assembly-line workers—hopefully *before* a disaster occurs.[22] This step can be described simply—it is up to the engineering societies to open their doors to interested nonengineers and to participate in a constructive dialogue to devise information-transmittal procedures. But *why* should engineers even consider doing this?

One reason is negative; namely that the status quo is morally untenable. As argued above, engineers (and members of any other profession) should not be assigned (nor should they take upon themselves) the role of being the sole and ultimate definers and protectors of the public safety, health, and welfare. Likewise, neither should they have the unilateral responsibility (nor the right) to devise means of communicating information about risks to potentially affected parties. From a moral point of view, members of professions do not even have the parentalistic responsibility (or right) to unilaterally change their codes (or any other relevant aspects of the larger legal, political, and economic systems in which the codes are embedded) to give the general public access to more information and a greater role in decision-making processes.

Even though the engineering societies have taken a strongly parentalistic stance over the years, they have done relatively little (and some have even exerted a negative force) in the way of developing and lobbying for the establishment of procedures for helping potentially affected members of the public to obtain information from engineers about risks to their safety, health, and welfare. This is doubly significant since such procedures would not only respect the rights of the general public to be informed, but would also lighten the currently heavy burden of moral responsibility that the paramountcy clauses of engineering codes of ethics impose on their members. The eventual development of such procedures and the correlative changes in the codes of ethics will in turn make it possible for engineers to practice in accordance with their codes without having to be omniscient self-sacrificing moral heroes or heroines.

On the positive side, nonengineer members of the general public have a moral obligation to be actively involved in collaborative efforts to have the responsibilities for information processing and decision making spread more evenly across the population. Given that laypersons should neither abdicate nor delegate the responsibility for making such changes exclusively to the members of the professions, one question remains: What specific steps can laypersons realistically be expected to take to increase their access to information in the possession of engineers (and other professionals) concerning risks to which they may be exposed?

It is an axiom of ethical theory that "ought implies can"; that is, it is nonsense to say that someone has a moral responsibility to do something that they are incapable of doing. But it would seem to be a fact that most members of the general public have never even thought about how to increase the availability of information from engineers about risks; even if they had any such ideas, most people would not have the time and/or motivation to do anything with them. In other words, most people *cannot* do anything to make it more likely that engineers will be able to communicate information about potential risks to them. So doesn't it follow that it is nonsense to assert that laypersons have a responsibility to do anything along these lines? Not necessarily.

Although it is true that most laypersons have little or no real ability to do anything to increase the availability of information from engineers about potential risks, there are at least a few who have both the ability and willingness to do so—some on a voluntary basis (e.g., members of environmental and consumer organizations), some for a fee (e.g., free-lance writers and attorneys), and some as part of their regular jobs (e.g., government employees and journalists). The fact of the matter is that even these few people who have the interest, time, and know-how to acquire such information currently have a very difficult time doing so. One major reason for this is the high degree of apathy and even active resistance on the part of engineering societies to interact with laypersons.

Thus, I propose that engineering societies should take the single simple (but not necessarily easy) step of inviting interested nonengineers to participate in a significant way in designing and implementing plans and procedures that would remove some or all of the obstacles and disincentives that currently make it difficult for engineers to communicate information about risks to potentially affected parties. This apparently simple step may not be an easy one; the engineering societies—like most other professional societies—were established and have been operating for almost a century as closed organizations whose internally avowed, primary purpose is to protect the interests of their members.[23] But if they are sincere in their public declarations (in the current versions of their codes) that they hold the public's safety, health, and welfare paramount, then the engineering societies do not seem to have any ethical justification for refusing to take the step of opening up to dialogue with nonengineers on these matters.

Individual engineers like Roger Boisjoly should never have to take the risk of being punished by their employers for going outside of channels to provide potentially affected parties with information relevant to their making of decisions affecting their health and welfare. It is the responsibility of all persons—both engineers and nonengineers— who are concerned about their own well-being to take steps to create attitudes and procedures throughout society that will make the providing of such information a routine matter, rather than hoping for acts of moral heroism and self-sacrifice to prevent disasters and lesser harms.

Notes

1. The only published mention that I have found of the total number of fatalities during the construction of the Sears Tower was in a magazine article written about some of the engineers fifteen years later; "An Empire Scales Back, " *The Chicago Tribune Magazine*, April 30, 1989, p. 16.

2. The point has been commented on by many philosophers. One recent discussion of it is in Thomas Nagel's *Mortal Questions* (Cambridge: Cambridge University Press, 1979), where he asserts (p. 140) that ". . . for most of the questions that need deciding, ethical considerations are multiple, complex, often cloudy and mixed up with many others."

3. Roger M. Boisjoly, "The Challenger Disaster: Moral Responsibility and

the Working Engineer," in *Ethical Issues in Engineering*, ed. Deborah G. Johnson (Englewood Cliffs, N.J.: Prentice Hall, 1991), pp. 6–14.

4. Henry Petroski, *To Engineer is Human* (New York: St. Martin's Press, 1985), pp. 9–10. Petroski acknowledges that engineers are typical of professionals in this regard, not unique. "The medical student worries about losing a patient, the lawyer about losing a crucial case."

5. One of the countless places in which this oath is reprinted is *Principles of Biomedical Ethics*, ed. Tom L. Beauchamp and James F. Childress (New York: Oxford University Press, 1983), pp. 329–30.

6. The definitive history of the early development of the engineering societies and their codes of ethics is Edwin Layton Jr.'s *Revolt of the Engineers* (Baltimore: Johns Hopkins University Press, 1986).

7. This code is reprinted in *Ethical Problems in Engineering* (2nd ed.), ed. Albert Flores (Troy, N.Y.: Rensselaer Polytechnic Institute, 1980), p. 64.

8. This code is also reprinted in Beauchamp and Childress, *Principles of Biomedical Ethics*, pp. 331–32.

9. This code is reprinted with several other major codes (IEEE, APWA, and NSPE) in *Engineering Professionalism and Ethics*, ed. James H. Schaub and Karl Pavlovic (New York: John Wiley & Sons, 1983), pp. 426–33.

10. Samuel C. Florman, "Moral Blueprints," *Harper's*, October 1978, p. 32.

11. For a detailed account of this proposal, see Steven Unger, *Controlling Technology: Ethics and the Responsible Engineer* (New York: Holt, Rinehart & Winston, 1982).

12. Tom Scherberger, "NASA Details 748 Items That Can Destroy Shuttle," *Orlando Sentinel*, March 4, 1986, p. A-1.

13. Tom Scherberger, "Astronauts in Dark About Bad O Rings," *Orlando Sentinel*, March 4, 1986, pp. A-1, A-8.

14. The Presidential Commission on the Space Shuttle Challenger Accident, *Report to the President* (Washington, D.C.: U.S. Government Printing Office, 1986), Recommendation V, p. 200.

15. "The Apollo Mess: Staged for a Rerun?" *Chemical Engineering*, June 19, 1967, p. 92 (emphasis mine).

16. Michael Davis, "Thinking Like an Engineer: The Place of a Code of Ethics in the Practice of a Profession," *Philosophy & Public Affairs*, Vol. 20, No. 2 (Spring 1991), pp. 150–67.

17. Ibid., p. 165.

18. Ibid., p. 166.

19. Robert J. Baum, "The Limits of Professoinal Responsibility," in *Values and the Public Works Professional*, ed. Daniel L. Babcock and Carol Ann Smith (Rolla: University of Missouri Press, 1980) p. 19. Reprinted in Schaub and Pavlovic, *Engineering Professionalism*, p. 293.

20. While I confess to not having provided a practical strategy for implementing this principle, I must indicate that I am not aware of any other proposals more specific than mine.

21. See, for example, Carol C. Gould, *Rethinking Democracy* (Cambridge: Cambridge University Press, 1988), particularly pp. 274–80; Virginia Held, *Rights and Goods* (New York: The Free Press, 1984); and Mike W. Martin and Roland Schinzinger, *Ethics in Engineering* (New York: McGraw-Hill, 1983), especially Part 2.

22. The most recent prod to motivate me to think this situation through further came from Joan Callahan, who made an eloquent and forceful statement about the inadequacy of this aspect of my analysis in an earlier draft of this paper.

23. This statement is probably more questionable for engineering societies than for almost any other professional group. As Edwin Layton, Jr., documented in his *Revolt of the Engineers*, there has been from the beginning a tension within most of the engineering societies between line engineers and corporate executives who started out as engineers. This tension is still strong today, and the major engineering firms exert a strong influence—direct and indirect—within most engineering societies.

7

Legal Ethics: A Paradigm?

Serena Stier

Introduction

Consider the issues facing the three professionals in the following narrative: Aaron Hill is a very troubled man. His wife of fifteen years, Emma, has just left him to live with her lesbian lover. Because of the recession, his business is in difficulty. He is very depressed and unable to sleep because of terrible nightmares. Although no one in his family, so far as he knows, has ever consulted a psychiatrist before, he goes to one for help with his depression and sleep problems. The psychiatrist talks with him for fifty minutes once a week and has started him on an antidepressant, which gives him a little relief. He has told the psychiatrist about his nightmares—vivid scenes in which he goes to the house where his wife and her lover live; he has an axe in his hand; suddenly he is chopping away at them and screaming horrible words and blood and flesh are flying everywhere. Should Aaron's psychiatrist warn Emma and her lover that they may be in danger from Aaron?

Because she did not want to take their twelve-year-old daughter, Pam, out of school in the middle of the semester, Emma left her living in the house with Aaron. However, Emma hopes that since she has been the primary caretaker for Pam all along, she will be given legal and physical custody of Pam after the divorce. Aaron has met with his lawyer and told the lawyer that there is no way Emma is going to take his daughter away from him. After a couple of meetings he also confessed to the lawyer that he feels rather uncomfortable around Pam—she's beginning to develop rather large breasts and Aaron feels as if he'd like to crawl into bed with her after one of his nightmares and just cry on her beautiful, soft chest. Should Aaron's lawyer work to get custody of Pam for Aaron or, instead, consider what arrangement would be in Pam's best interest?

Pam has been sent by the school nurse to a dermatologist because she has developed a strange rash. In talking to the doctor about her eating and living habits and anything unusual going on in her life, Pam suddenly starts to cry and blurts out that she feels scared—her mother has left her; her father acts peculiarly toward her, suddenly kissing and hugging and touching her when he never did so before—and she feels somehow afraid all the time. Should the doctor make a report to the state authorities that Pam may be an abused child?

Here are three different professionals who have come into contact with the Hill family—a psychiatrist, a lawyer, and a medical doctor. What do the stories they have heard from Aaron and Pam require of them? What kind of guidance do the ethical standards of their respective professions give them about what they ought to do? Must they, should they, do anything more than prescribe an antidepressant, file divorce papers seeking custody, provide a medication to cure a rash? Is there a conflict between what they ought to do as good professionals and what they ought to do as good persons?

This paper examines the question whether the law of lawyering provides a paradigm for discussing the ethical obligations of professionals other than attorneys. Can an analysis of the principles underlying the ethical standards of lawyers offer guidance to the therapist and the medical doctor treating the Hill family on how they should interpret the standards of their own professions? In the first part of this paper I will lay out my analysis of how the law of lawyering should be understood. The analysis begins with a discussion of what I call the four elements of an ethics analysis. I show that posing the question as a dilemma between the requirements of personhood and of role is mistaken. I then discuss two principles paradigmatic to understanding the law of lawyering—the Boundaries Principle and the Principle of Normativity—and show how they apply to the law of lawyering. I then argue that a third principle, the Principle of Integrative Positivism, should not be extended to professions other than law. Finally, I suggest how this analysis can be extended to other professions such as psychotherapy and medicine.

Role Differentiation

Role-Differentiation Claim

According to philosopher Richard Wasserstrom, "to be a professional is to be enmeshed in role-differentiated behavior."[1] Moreover, he explains, "it is the nature of role-differentiated behavior that it often makes it both appropriate and desirable for the person in a particular role to put to one side considerations of various sorts—and especially various moral considerations—that would otherwise be relevant if not decisive."[2] Whether it is viewed positively or negatively, role differentiation—the idea that there is a distinction between the ethical requirements of personhood (common morality) and those of professional role—is widely regarded as a salient feature of professionalism. For philosophers such as Wasserstrom, David Luban,[3] and Gerald Postema,[4] it is a source of concern because, among other things, with role differentiation, professionals may have to choose between being good persons and being good professionals. Others, such as Monroe Freedman, have no trouble accepting and defending role differentiation.[5]

According to critics of role-differentiation theory, the need to make choices between acting as a moral person and as an ethical professional has serious detrimental consequences for professionals personally and for society generally. Criticism of role differentiation has been particularly directed toward lawyers and the professional standards that enunciate the ethics of the legal profession (or the law of lawyering). The claim is that the legal profession's ethical standards, as memorialized in either the *Model Code of Professional Responsibility*, passed by the American Bar Association in 1969, or the *Model Rules of Professional Conduct*, approved by the ABA in 1983[6] and now adopted as the legal standard in the great majority of American states, create a "standard conception of lawyering" that fails to promote moral accountability and inspires hyperzealous partisan advocacy. As a consequence, the role-differentiation critics argue that it is not possible for attorneys to be both good persons and good lawyers. Instead, attorneys must compartmentalize various parts of themselves so that the lawyer as person is guided by the requirements of common morality while the lawyer as professional is guided solely by role morality.

An example of such compartmentalization and the resulting conflict is the dilemma posed for the attorney representing Aaron Hill, who has confessed his growing obsession with his daughter, Pam, to his lawyer. Aaron wants and expects his lawyer to do everything legally possible to assure that Aaron becomes the custodial parent for Pam. On one interpretation, the requirements of role morality would forbid the lawyer to do anything other than follow Aaron's wishes and seek custody of Pam for Aaron. In particular, the lawyer would be obligated not to reveal any confidential information from Aaron that would embarrass Aaron or weaken his claim to Pam. Common morality, however, might suggest that the attorney has an obligation to protect the interests of the child Pam rather than follow the wishes of her father Aaron, who is the attorney's client. Thus, a conflict would be created between the dictates of everyday morality and those of professional ethics.

The role-differentiation thesis is less well developed for other professions. The story of the Hill family, however, also provides useful examples of some of the potential issues. Pam's confession to her dermatologist that she feels afraid living with her father is arguably a protected patient confidence. At the same time, however, her doctor may have a legal and ethical responsibility to report instances of suspected child abuse to a state child protection agency.

Aaron has told his psychiatrist in confidence about the terrible nightmares he has had in which he axes his estranged wife Emma and her lover. The potential ethical conflict for the psychiatrist is between an obligation to keep confidential what Aaron has told him and the obligation he may have to report the potential danger Aaron poses to his estranged wife and her lover.

Four-Elements Analysis

As I have argued elsewhere,[7] distinguishing between common and role morality and asking whether one can be both a good person and a good professional—in particular, a good lawyer—is a false distinction and a mistaken question. The question itself assumes an odd disjunction between one's professional and personal life. In both contexts, at different times, one plays a multitude of roles—friend, spouse, parent; legal counselor, adviser, advocate, officer of the court, legal reformer. Critics of role differentiation err in asking whether it is possible to play roles that call for different moral considerations and maintain one's personal integrity. A preferable approach to thinking about ethics provides an analysis based on four elements: (1) persons who (2) act (3) in circumstances (4) for reasons.[8] The first element, agency, assumes that persons are free moral beings.[9] The second element, act, focuses on what actions people might take, not their beliefs. The third element, circumstances, highlights the importance of the context within which persons act. Few physical acts are always right or wrong regardless of their circumstances. And the fourth element, reasons for action, calls for justifications of the actions that are taken on the basis of appropriate standards of conduct invoked by the context.

Whether one has acted ethically depends on the reasons that justify one's actions in the particular circumstances in which the conduct occurs. Performing a professional role is *not* a part of personhood, it is part of the circumstances of practicing one's profession. Thus, it is a mistake to attach the morality of a particular role to the personhood of the actor and then claim that this role morality vitiates the integrity of a professional. The mistake consists in focusing on the first element of the analysis, agency, when attention is properly focused on the third element, circumstances. It would be most peculiar if different circumstances did not properly generate different reasons for action and consequently different moral obligations.

While acting in the circumstance of being a lawyer, a doctor, or a therapist, for example, professionals have special duties to their clients or patients that arise just because they are performing professional rather than nonprofessional functions. Anyone, when acting as a lawyer, doctor, or therapist, would have these ethical duties. When individuals provide legal representation in the circumstance of serving as lawyers, they must consider a number of reasons for action that they would not need to consider when acting in some different context; for example, in the circumstance of being a parent. This is true for other professionals as well.

One's capacity to be both a good person and a good professional is not destroyed by distinguishing among one's reasons for action depending upon the circumstances. A doctor is morally and ethically[10] forbidden to treat the life of some particular patient as less valuable than that of some other preferred patient. Thus, for example, a physician cannot prematurely declare the nonpreferred patient "brain dead" in order to "harvest" his organs to save the life of the preferred patient. However, this same doctor should not be criticized if she chooses to jump into a pond and save the life of her own child who is drowning rather than the life of an unknown child who may also be drowning. We all recognize that the special circumstance of acting as a parent creates a special set of duties, including special obligations to one's own children in preference to other children, whose invocation is perfectly consistent with common, everyday, conventional morality. We need invoke no special role morality to justify choosing to save one's own child rather than some other child.

It simply makes no sense to evaluate the morality of an action in one set of circumstances by comparing it to another set of circumstances in which the facts, including the facts of relationship, are significantly different. Comparing what one does as a professional—labeling this role morality—to what one would do if one were not functioning in a professional capacity—labeling this common morality—is a mistake. The fact of acting as a lawyer, doctor, or therapist makes a moral difference.

Integrity and the Legal Profession's Ethical Standards

The Boundary Principle

Under this four-elements analysis, lawyers can be persons of integrity while performing their professional role as conceived by the standards of the legal profession. I believe that these standards are consistent with personal integrity in part because they respect what I call the Boundaries Principle. Critics of role differentiation would require lawyers to take moral responsibility for their clients' actions. For example, they would require a lawyer to resist a client's request to write a will that disinherits her children simply because they opposed the Vietnam war or to set up a corporate charter for a company that manufactured cigarettes.[11] They criticize the ethical standards of the legal profession for failing to require moral activism of attorneys. They would also hold lawyers morally responsible for the moral harms to third persons and society that result from their representation of a client.[12]

The demand for moral activism may be the most troubling aspect of the role-differentiation critique. Requiring lawyers, or any other professionals, to take moral responsibility for the actions of their clients violates a far more fundamental principle of human relationships. It is the principle that requires lawyers, as well as all other persons, to respect the boundary between themselves as independent moral agents and their clients as separate moral actors. This is the principle I call the Boundaries Principle, which, I believe, should govern the relationships between professionals and the persons they serve. The Boundaries Principle affirms the moral autonomy of *both* the client and the lawyer. Moral independence from clients permits attorneys to acknowledge and respect the boundary between themselves as moral beings and their clients as separate persons with a distinct and equally valid capacity for moral conduct. An attorney, within limits, should refrain from judging the morality and determining the legitimacy of the objectives sought by a client out of regard for that client's own autonomy as a moral agent and as an affirmation of the lawyer's own moral independence within the circumstances of the lawyer-client relationship. The Boundaries Principle should be embedded in the practice of every profession. Because of the special seductions of expertise, professionals may be particularly susceptible to forgetting that clients and professionals are independent moral beings. The evils of paternalism are well known. Michael Bayles argues on behalf of what I call the Boundaries Principle in his critique of paternalism:

> [C]lients go to professionals for their superior knowledge and skills; such knowledge and skill is a defining feature of a profession. However, many decisions require balancing legal or health concerns against other client interests. As many authors have noted, crucial professional decisions involve value choices. They are not simple choices of technical means to ends, and even choices of means have a value component. Professionals have not had training in value choices. Even if they had, they might not know a client's value scheme sufficiently to determine what is best for him when everything is considered. . . . To deny clients authority and responsibility by adopting the paternalistic model is to deny them the freedom to direct their own lives. Clients are not capable of determining the precise nature of their problem, or of knowing the alternative courses of action and predicting their consequences or carrying them out on their own. They need and want the technical expertise of a professional to do so. However, they are capable of making reasonable choices among options on the basis of their total values. They need professionals' information in order to make wise choices to accomplish their purposes.[13]

It should be emphasized that lawyers and other professionals can both respect the boundary between themselves and those they serve as independent moral beings and act in a normative capacity. The Boundaries Principle is not violated when a professional discusses with a client or patient the actions the professional believes would be consistent with the client's own moral interests. The philosopher Joseph Raz provides a way to portray this function with his concept of detached normative statements.[14]

A detached normative statement is made from a point of view that is not the speaker's own; the speaker understands but is not committed to the standards he invokes. Raz provides the example of a Christian who tells an Orthodox Jewish friend who is about to eat something like a pork-filled dumpling unwittingly, "You ought not to eat that."[15]

Such a statement is fully normative, yet the Christian speaks from the point of view of one who understands the kosher laws without endorsing or following them. Lawyers and other professionals similarly may suggest to a client what her reasons for action should be in light of the client's goals without necessarily endorsing those values.

The significance of the Boundaries Principle to professions other than law can be illustrated by returning to the story of the Hill family. Suppose Emma Hill had gone to a counselor for assistance in deciding whether she should continue in her marriage to Aaron or acknowledge that she is a lesbian and seek a divorce in order to live openly with her lover. In working with Emma, does the counselor have a moral obligation to take responsibility for whether divorce is or is not morally wrong? Does the therapist have a moral responsibility for guiding Emma toward heterosexuality or toward making peace with her sexual orientation depending on whether or not the therapist considers homosexuality to be morally right?

Clearly, choosing either the values of commitment and marriage or independence and divorce is a moral decision for Emma but not for her counselor. Choosing whether to live a life consistent with one's sexual orientation despite societal opprobrium is a decision for Emma and not for the therapist to make. In fact, if the counselor has strong feelings one way or the other about the morality of divorce or of homosexuality, she should not engage in counseling on these matters at all, since such strongly held values are likely to lead therapists to intrude on their clients' moral autonomy by breaching the proper boundary between themselves and their clients as independent moral beings.

Lawyers, doctors, therapists, and other professionals are morally responsible for their own acts, including their decision whether or not to represent or treat or serve particular clients and help them achieve their objectives. They are not and should not be responsible for their clients' decisions and acts.

The Normativity Principle

The ethical standards of law or any profession are created by and directed to members of the relevant profession. Most professionals are persons of good character who need some guidance on what the particular circumstances of their profession may require of them. They are good readers of the ethical rules of their profession. Nonetheless, not all professionals are persons of virtue. Thus, professional standards must be understood to be addressed to both good and bad readers.

However, one may still ask, even if the good lawyer is disposed to be virtuous and a good reader of the standards of the legal profession, does the law of lawyering have any special claim of authority for such persons? According to the Normativity Principle, membership in the legal profession provides attorneys with a *prima facie* obligation to obey the law of lawyering for two related reasons. First, such membership gives lawyers access to a state-authorized and regulated monopoly that provides economic, intellectual, and other personal benefits to those persons licensed to practice law. When attorneys accept and enjoy these benefits, they incur concomitant special obligations in fairness. One of these is the duty to obey the law of lawyering. Second, this is a duty undertaken voluntarily. It is not imposed. When lawyers take a special oath upon admission to the bar of a state,[16] they voluntarily and knowingly agree to abide by the regulations of the profession. Of course, this obligation to obey the law of lawyering is a *prima facie* reason for action that can be overridden by an attorney's ultimate obligation to promote just legal institutions when the professional rules are not just and efforts to reform them fail.

Should the Normativity Principle be equally applicable to professionals other than lawyers? Professions from accounting to banking to engineering to journalism and real estate as well as many of the health professions provide their practitioners with codes of professional responsibility.[17]

The American Medical Association (AMA), for example, has adopted a set of "Principles of Medical Ethics" and provides these together with "Current Opinions of the Council on Ethical and Judicial Affairs" to medical practitioners. The AMA provides sanctions including censure, suspension, or expulsion from the AMA for violations of the principles after the opportunity for a hearing before the council.[18] All the major associations of mental health professionals (the American Association for Counseling and Development, the American Psychiatric Association, and the American Psychological Association) as well as the major associations of professional social workers (the National Association of Social Workers and the National Federation of Societies for Clinical Social Work) have ethical codes and provisions for sanctioning those who violate them.

It seems to me that the argument for the applicability of the Normativity Principle to the law of lawyering can and should be applied to the codes of ethics of these other professions. Most, if not all, such professions also enjoy the monopoly benefits of a licensed practice, whose ethical obligations are undertaken voluntarily and knowingly. Consequently, professionals generally have a special duty to obey the commands of their respective ethical codes. However, as with lawyers, this is a *prima facie* obligation that may be overridden. The normative force of professional codes of ethics does not preempt all other moral principles. Nonetheless, as with lawyers, acting contrary to a mandatory norm of the code is still a violation. The moral status of such an act will depend on the reasons for taking the action. The bad reader who seeks personal and impermissible advantage should be subject to moral opprobrium and sanctioning. The good reader, acting out of conscience, may be respected as a conscientious objector but will still be subject to sanctions.[19]

It should be emphasized that any set of professional ethical standards, like law generally, is distinct from morals. Their enactment by an authoritative body, such as the American Bar Association, does not make them moral. Their moral status turns on whether they are morally justified rather than the fact of authoritative enactment. On the other hand, such standards, particularly with respect to lawyers, retain their legal force (normativity) even if demonstrably immoral. When legal rules are mandated, contrary conduct may and should, from a strictly legal perspective, result in sanctions.

The Principle of Integrative Positivism

The ethical standards of law are not only promulgated and adopted by an authoritative body like the American Bar Association. Ethical regulation of attorneys is not solely the province of their professional brethren. For a legal ethical standard to have legal authority, generally it must be adopted by a state court. Lawyers who have been disciplined by a professional body of their peers have recourse to their state courts and ultimately to the Supreme Court of the United States to contest the appropriateness of their discipline. Such legalization is necessary to preserve the legitimacy of the justice system, since attorneys generally control access to the legal process.

I do not believe there should be a law of doctoring or a law of therapy to the same extent as there is a law of lawyering. The standards of the legal profession have a force something like the positive law promulgated by a legislature, which I call the Principle of Integrative Positivism. The circumstances of other professions are different and legalization is neither necessary, proper nor advisable. The Principle of Integrative Positivism is unique to law and should remain so.

Law's Use of Both Mandatory and Permissive Standards

My objections to modeling the ethical standards of other professions on that of law with respect to the Principle of Integrative Positivism are strengthened by examining the approach of the law of lawyering to permitting rather than mandating conduct and to the way the standards function in practice as compared to theory. In important though limited respects the law of lawyering does provide lawyers with opportunities to decide for themselves what actions to take. Most dramatically, the standards invoke an attorney's capacity for moral reasoning with respect to decisions whether or not to reveal confidences in order to prevent serious future harm to others. Both the Code, expansively,[20] and the Rules, more narrowly,[21] permit such revelations at the discretion of the attorney.

Example of Permissive Revelation and Its Value

The confidential relationship between lawyer and client is based on the promise of loyalty that founds the agreement to provide legal representation. Imagine one has agreed to represent a juvenile who is alleged to be involved in illegal drug sales. In the course of talking with the client, the lawyer learns that these sales are continuing and, moreover, that the drug involved is laced with a dangerous substance that can permanently damage the brains of those who use it. What should the lawyer do? On the one hand the attorney has promised loyalty to the person being represented, which includes protecting that individual's secrets. On the other hand, serious and irreversible bodily harm may be done to third persons if the attorney does not act. This is the kind of moral dilemma whose resolution should not be mandated by a political collective and is rightly left to the conscience of each individual lawyer to resolve.

Even within the legal profession itself, what used to be a monolithic approach to ethical standards is breaking down. At one time all attorneys in nearly every state were governed by the Code of Professional Ethics. Today there is a patchwork, with some states following the Code and a majority following the Rules. Within many states, the provisions of the Code or Rules, as promulgated by the American Bar Association, have been amended. In addition, other groups are providing guidance for legal specialties. Thus, the Academy of Matrimonial Lawyers recently approved a set of ethical guidelines for family lawyers that diverge substantially from both the Code and Rules in important respects. The Academy would advise Aaron Hill's attorney, for example, that not only does he have obligations to his client, Aaron, but he should also consider the child Pam's best interests in providing advice on custody arrangements.[22]

Unfortunately, much else is mandatory in the legal standards precisely because they function as positive law and must provide adequate notice to individuals who may be sanctioned through the coercive powers of the state for their violation. Perusal of the codes of other professions reveals a much more open-textured approach that permits greater exercise of an individual's conscience than does the law of lawyering. This is valuable and should be preserved.

A Brief View of the Law of Lawyering in Practice

Legalization, moreover, may reduce a profession to its lowest required level of ethical practice. For example, the preamble of the older Model Code of Professional Responsibility for lawyers points out that much is aspirational and is expressed by means of the ethical considerations that begin each of the nine Canons of Ethics that comprise the Code. Generally, however, the only code violations for which attorneys can be sanctioned are those involving the mandated disciplinary rules, which tend to address the specifics of lawyering rather than implementing a grander ethical vision. Thus, the first ethical consideration of Canon 1 states: "A basic tenet of the professional responsibility of lawyers is that every person in our society should have ready access to the independent professional services of a lawyer of integrity and competence."[23] The second part of the following disciplinary rule then reduces this grand vision to a mundane provision that: "A lawyer shall not further the application for admission to the bar of another person known by him to be unqualified in respect to character, education, or other relevant attribute."[24]

The Code indicates that the "Disciplinary Rules state the minimum level of conduct below which no lawyer can fall without being subject to disciplinary action."[25] In other words, the standards should be treated as a floor and not a ceiling with respect to ethical practice. The preamble to the more recent Model Rules provides: "Within the framework of these Rules many difficult issues of professional discretion can arise. Such issues must be resolved through the exercise of

sensitive professional and *moral* judgement guided by the basic principles underlying the Rules.''[26] Here too the intent is to encourage
lawyers to treat the standards as a framework with the minimal ethical
requirements serving as scaffolding to be amply expanded upon by the
dictates of the consciences of individual attorneys.

One need not listen to many lawyer jokes or read many newspaper
stories about lawyers, however, before concluding that, in fact, the
law of lawyering in practice is treated by many attorneys as a ceiling
rather than a floor for ethical lawyering. Conduct that will be clearly
punished is avoided if discovery is likely and penalties severe; otherwise, many lawyers operate as bad readers looking for loopholes rather
than opportunities to practice ethically. It is likely that legalization of
the professional codes of other professions would suffer the same fate.
In this respect the law of lawyering provides not an example to follow
but one to avoid.

The Law of Lawyering as a Paradigm for Other Professions

The reach of law's paradigmatic guidance depends on the congruity
between the circumstances of lawyering and the special circumstances
attendant on other professional roles, such as being a mental health
therapist or a medical doctor. It might appear that the different goals
of professional service will determine the reasons for action that
should guide different professionals in their practice circumstances.
Insofar as some of these goals may be quite distinct from those that
guide attorneys, law would then fail to provide an appropriate paradigm. However, such a conclusion would be a category mistake
because the appropriate comparison is not the respective goals of the
different professions but the status of the ethical standards as an
authority for reasons for action among the various professions.

In other words, while the substantive aims of professional service
may vary among different professions, the formal, directive function
of each profession's ethical standards does not. This last section
suggests a few illustrations of some salient differences in substance
while demonstrating the pertinence of the Normativity Principle
across disciplines.

The Issue of Confidentiality

Is the core meaning of loyalty different for lawyers, medical doctors,
and therapists? Since loyalty is defined as "faithful adherence to one's

promise,"[27] the answer depends on the content of the promise made by each of these professionals. Does the promise include refusing to reveal any of the information provided by a client or patient which he or she wishes to keep confidential? If Pam Hill's dermatologist goes to the standards of the American Medical Association for assistance in determining what to do about Pam's concerns about her father, what guidance will these standards offer?

The Code of the American Medical Association is essentially half a page stating seven basic principles, followed by discussions of opinions on social policy issues from abortion to withholding or withdrawing life-prolonging medical treatment, together with opinions on other issues from interprofessional relations to professional rights and responsibilities. Part of the promise made by physicians certainly includes maintaining the confidentiality of patient communications since the Code states:

> The information disclosed to a physician during the course of the relationship between physician and patient is confidential to the greatest possible degree. The patient should feel free to make a full disclosure of information to the physician in order that the physician may most effectively provide needed services. The patient should be able to make this disclosure with the knowledge that the physician will respect the confidential nature of the communication. The physician should not reveal confidential communications or information without the express consent of the patient, *unless required to do so by law.*[28]

This provision is nearly indistinguishable from one in the lawyer's Model Code of Professional Responsibility, which provides under Canon 4 that "A Lawyer Should Preserve The Confidences And Secrets Of A Client"[29] and commentary to the comparable Rule 1.6 of the Model Rules explains that by maintaining "confidentiality of information relating to the representation," the lawyer can assure that "[t]he client is thereby encouraged to communicate fully and frankly with the lawyer even as to embarrassing or legally damaging subject matter."[30]

Yet recall that the AMA code for doctors specifically allows for the revelation of confidences when doctors are "required to do so by law." In the opinion section of the physician code that deals with social issues, there is specific discussion of the situation of abuse to children, elderly persons, and others at risk. Here the dilemma created by legal requirements mandating the reporting of such abuse and the pleas of even the victims of abuse to maintain their confidences is described. Yet the section concludes that "[t]he obligation to comply with statutory requirements is clearly stated in the Principles of Medical Ethics."[31] In fact, nearly all states now have laws that mandate the reporting of such abuse by professionals from physicians to teachers to counselors.

The one professional group notably exempt from the reporting requirement is lawyers. In this connection, the paradigmatic value of the prior analysis of the law of lawyering depends on making a two-step analysis. The first step involves recognizing that the substantive content of the professional standards for medicine is different from that of the law of lawyering because the general law incorporated into the medical standards differs from that adopted by the law of lawyering. Doctors are mandatory reporters of possible child abuse while attorneys are not. Whether such a distinction is good or bad is a legislative policy question and does not go to the issue of whether the ethical regulation of each profession should be authoritative for its members. The second step of the analysis would apply the Normativity Principle to the question whether physicians, like lawyers, have a *prima facie* obligation to obey the ethical standards of their profession and report child abuse.

In examining the legislative policy question of whether the exclusion of lawyers as mandatory reporters of child abuse can be justified, one would ask whether the promise of loyalty as manifested in the maintenance of client confidences is significantly different for attorneys than it is for physicians. Any argument that it is different would be based on what is generally called "the adversary system excuse" by critics of legal ethics. To understand the operation of the adversary system excuse, it is necessary to recognize that within law itself there is a paradigmatic approach to all disputing based on litigation and adjudication. According to this model, the legal system functions primarily as a surrogate battlefield with disputants represented by lawyers, with rules of procedure controlling the combatants, and with the referee also having the authority to decide the contest depending on who has made the best and most persuasive legal arguments. This is the adversary system. Arguably, zealous advocacy, including a nearly absolute dedication to maintaining confidentiality, is required to make the adversary system work fairly. This is particularly true in the context of criminal law where individuals at risk of punishment are at the mercy of the overwhelmingly more powerful forces of the state arrayed against them.

Yet, from a legislative policy perspective, I do not believe the adversary system excuse suffices to distinguish attorneys from physicians with respect to client confidences. For attorneys, the decision whether to report a future crime is left to their discretion. It is otherwise for physicians. Why? Because society has made the judgment that, on balance, the importance of reporting abuse to children and the elderly is so great that it trumps the need to protect the confidentiality of the physician-patient relationship.

One wonders, however, whether this is an exception that will eventually swallow the promise of confidentiality itself. For instance, it is now the practice in many hospitals to report to criminal authorities when pregnant patients seek prenatal care and illegal drug use is admitted or suspected. Those who support such a practice argue that the patients are, after all, engaged in using drugs already declared illegal by the society and somehow such reporting will protect fetuses. But substantially more harm is done to fetuses each year by pregnant women who consume alcohol, a legal drug. Should confidences about alcohol consumption be reported to some authority who will seek to criminally penalize pregnant women who do not abstain from the use of alcohol or smoking or overeating during their pregnancies?

Nonetheless, the legislative wisdom of making doctors mandatory reporters of child abuse while protecting the confidentiality of the attorney-client relationship is a separate issue from the question of whether the ethical standards of the American Medical Association are authoritative for doctors. To determine whether the law of lawyering is paradigmatic for other professionals such as physicians, one must ask whether, given the normativity principle, doctors have a *prima facie* obligation to obey the law of doctoring in virtue of their membership in their profession.

Does such membership provide physicians with access to a state authorized and regulated monopoly that provides economic, intellectual, and other personal benefits to persons licensed to practice medicine? If so, then, like attorneys, doctors incur concomitant obligations. These would include the duty to obey the ethical standards of medicine. Moreover, as with lawyers, this duty is undertaken by consent— it is voluntary and informed. However, as with attorneys, the obligation provides only a *prima facie* reason to obey the profession's ethical standards. This reason can be overridden by a doctor's ultimate obligation to his or her patients and to the integrity of the profession of medicine. Doctors are free and obligated to work to change both the general law and the standards of their profession when they consider the law and those standards to be morally wrong. Nonetheless, when they disobey the profession's ethical standards, even for the very best of reasons, they are civil disobedients and properly subject to sanctioning by their peers.

Let us now examine the paradigmatic value of the law of lawyering to the third profession used illustratively in this presentation—psychotherapy, in particular, psychiatry. The Code of the American Psychiatric Association provides: "Psychiatrists at times may find it necessary, in order to protect the patient or the community from imminent danger, to reveal confidential information disclosed by the patient."[32] This exception to confidentiality is based on the famous *Tarasoff* case decided by the California Supreme Court in 1976.[33] In that case, a group of therapists were held civilly liable for failing to warn a young woman, Tatiana Tarasoff, of possible danger from a patient being treated in their facility as an outpatient. Tatiana was eventually murdered by the patient and her parents sued the doctors involved. The court held that therapists not only have a duty to "warn" but, depending upon the nature of the case, may be required "to warn the intended victim or others likely to apprise the victim of the danger, to notify the police, or to take whatever other steps are reasonably necessary under the circumstances."[34] There have been numerous cases since *Tarasoff* that recognize that psychiatrists and psychologists can be held liable under the law of torts for failing to warn potential victims that their clients intend to harm them or to take other appropriate steps. There do not appear to be comparable cases imposing liability on attorneys for failing to warn that their clients intend to engage in dangerous conduct toward others.

The American Psychiatric Association takes a very interesting step in providing for an exception to confidentiality, however, when appearing in court. Their guidelines provide:

When the psychiatrist is ordered by the court to reveal the confidences entrusted to him/her by patients he/she may comply or he/she may ethically hold the right to dissent within the framework of the law. When the psychiatrist is in doubt, the right of the patient to confidentiality and, by extension, to unimpaired treatment, should be given priority.[35]

This provision seems to authorize resistance to general law under the standards of the profession. However, such an interpretation may be controverted by the insertion of the phrase authorizing the "right to dissent *within the framework of the law.*" At the very least, however, the exception would, by extension, appear to suggest that mere fear of civil liability should not lead to *Tarasoff* precautions if the psychiatrist believes this to be ethically wrong. Attention to the need for psychiatrists to exercise their own discretion as illustrated here is consistent with the Normativity Principle, but would be less likely to exist were the Principle of Integrative Positivism to be treated as paradigmatic as well.

Conclusion

Let us return to the Hill family—Aaron Hill with his depression and nightmares about harming his wife, his growing obsession with his twelve-year-old daughter Pam, and Pam with her peculiar rash. Let us think again about the possible obligations of the various professionals who are working with Aaron and Pam—the lawyer Aaron wants to help him get custody of Pam in the divorce, the psychiatrist treating Aaron for his depression, and the medical doctor whom Pam has seen about her rash. What, if anything, does the law of lawyering permit Aaron's attorney to do with the information, shared in confidence, about Aaron's obsession with his daughter? According to the Model Rules generally, the lawyer, if he or she believes Aaron is likely to commit a criminal act against his daughter that will lead to substantial bodily harm, is permitted but not mandated to report such a future crime to the legal authorities. However, the possibility of such serious future harm is so speculative at this point that the lawyer has little if any professional authority to so proceed. Can the lawyer speak to Aaron's wife? Absolutely not, according to the Principle of Integrative Positivism and the law of lawyering. Is this an ethical result? Yes, in a society with an adversarial legal system and a division of responsibility in which the person Aaron can best rely on is his attorney. Is this the system I would design if it were up to me? Absolutely not. However, even under the requirements of the present system, Aaron's lawyer has both a professional and a moral obligation to properly counsel his client about Pam's custody. Such counseling should include encouraging Aaron to talk with his psychiatrist about his motivations for wanting to have physical custody of Pam. Standards like those of the Academy of Matrimonial Lawyers should inform the lawyer's practice. They affirm the attorney's obligation to consider Pam's interests as part of the legal counseling process with Aaron.

Ethically, Aaron's psychiatrist and his daughter Pam's dermatologist have far more discretion to decide what they ought to do than does the attorney under the circumstances. Legally, they may be constrained if the doctor is a mandated reporter of child abuse and the psychiatrist is worried about tort liability for future harm to Aaron's wife Emma and her lover. But from a professional point of view, both the psychotherapist and the medical doctor have and should have as much leeway as possible to consider the specifics of their respective clients' situations and to respond as creatively as possible to assist them.

Notes

1. Richard Wasserstrom, "Lawyers as Professionals: Some Moral Issues," *Human Rights*, 5 (1975): 5.
2. Ibid., 3.
3. David Luban, *Lawyers And Justice: An Ethical Study* (Princeton: Princeton University Press, 1988).
4. Gerald Postema, "Moral Responsibility in Professional Ethics," *New York University Law Review* 55 (1980).
5. See, for example, Monore H. Freedman, *Lawyer's Ethics in an Adversary System* (Indianapolis, Ind.: Bobbs-Merrill, 1975).
6. For the text of the Code or Rules, see Stephen Gillers and Roy D. Simon, Jr., *Regulation of Lawyers: Statutes And Standards* (Boston: Little, Brown and Company, 1991).
7. Serena Stier, "Legal Ethics: The Integrity Thesis," *Ohio State Law Journal* 52 (1991): at 560–61.
8. The author is grateful to Professor Steven J. Burton, her spouse, for bringing this analytical framework to her attention. See Steven J. Burton, *Judging In Good Faith* (Cambridge: Cambridge University Press, 1992), Sec. 2.2.1.
9. It should be emphasized that in this framework there is a single integrated being who weighs the various reasons for action derived from her different circumstances. One major reason for action is always one's character, which provides dispositions to act on certain reasons in all circumstances. For an understanding of the interaction between character and life, see Martha Nussbaum, *The Fragility of Goodness* (New York: Cambridge University Press, 1986). For an excellent discussion of character and lawyering, see Anthony Kronman, "Living in the Law," *University of Chicago Law Review* 54 (1987): 835.
10. I have made no consistent effort to distinguish between "morality" and "ethics" in this paper. However, when I use both words, as here, I am taking the view that morals refers to common morality while ethics refers to standards adopted by a professional collective to guide their practice.
11. The examples are taken from Wasserstrom, "Lawyers as Professionals," 7–8. For a critical discussion of the first example, see Ted Schneyer,

"Moral Philosophy's Standard Misconception of Legal Ethics," *Wisconsin Law Review* 1984 (1984): at 1562–64.

12. See Luban, *Lawyers And Justice*, at 160; William Simon, "The Ideology of Advocacy: Procedural Justice and Professional Ethics," *Wisconsin Law Review* 1976 (1976): at 133.

13. Michael Bayles, "The Professional-Client Relationship," in *Ethical Issues In Professional Life*, ed. Joan C. Callahan (New York: Oxford University Press, 1988): 117–18.

14. Joseph Raz, *Practical Reason And Norms* (London: Hutchinson, 1975): 175–77.

15. Cited in H. L. A. Hart, *Essays On Bentham* (Oxford: Oxford University Press, 1982): 154. As Hart notes:

Raz's distinction between committed and detached normative statements focuses attention on a little-noticed but important feature of moral discourse. It is a feature of such discourse that normative statements may be made both by those who themselves accept the relevant principles as guides to conduct and standards of evaluation and those who do not so accept them. Statements made by the former are committed statements and are to be contrasted with statements made by those who speak from the point of view of those who accept the principles and so speak as if they themselves accepted them though they do not in fact do so. Such statements are detached. . . . Similar normative statements [referring to example in text] of law (not merely statements about the law) may be made from the point of view of one who accepts the laws of some system as guides to conduct, but though made from that point of view are in fact made by one who may be an anarchist and so does not share it.

16. Charles Wolfram, *Modern Legal Ethics* (St. Paul: West Publishing, 1986): 849.

17. For a collection of these see *Codes of Professional Responsibility*, ed. Rena A. Gorlin (Washington, D.C.: Bureau of National Affairs, 1990).

18. Gorlin, *Codes of Professional Responsibility*, at 185–86.

19. Stier, "Legal Ethics: The Integrity Thesis," at 593.

20. DR 4–101(C)(3) provides that a lawyer "*may* reveal . . . [t]he intention of his client to commit a crime and the information necessary to prevent the crime" (emphasis added). Gillers and Simon, *Regulation of Lawyers: Statutes And Standards*, 277. Notice that the option of revelation exists regardless of the seriousness of the proposed crime.

21. Rule 1.6(b)(1) provides that a "lawyer *may* reveal [confidential] information to the extent the lawyer reasonably believes necessary . . . to prevent the client from committing a criminal act that the lawyer believes is likely to result in imminent death or substantial bodily harm." Gillers and Simon, *Regulation of Lawyers: Statutes And Standards*, 40 (emphasis added).

22. *Balance of Advocacy: Standards of Conduct* (Chicago: Academy of Matrimonial Lawyers, 1991): at 27.

23. Gillers and Simon, *Regulation of Lawyers: Statutes And Standards*, at 243.

24. Ibid., 245.

25. Ibid., 242.

26. Ibid., 7.

27. *The Compact Edition of the Oxford University Dictionary* (Oxford: Oxford University Press, 1971): 480.

28. Gorlin, *Codes of Professional Responsibility* at 207, emphasis added.

29. Gillers and Simon, *Regulation of Lawyers: Statutes And Standards* at 274.

30. Ibid., 40.

31. Gorlin, *Codes of Professional Responsibility* at 192–93.

32. Ibid., 242.

33. *Tarasoff v. Regents of University of California*, 17 Cal.3d at 431, 131 Cal.Rptr. 14, 551 P.2d at 340 (*Tarasoff II*).

34. *Tarasoff II*, 131 Cal. Rptr. at 20.

35. Gorlin, *Codes of Professional Responsibility* at 242, emphasis added.

8

Selling Drugs in the Physician's Office: A Problem of Medical Ethics

David N. James

Prescription drugs are the most common and effective weapons in medicine's fight against disease. Not until the sulfa drugs and antibiotics were synthesized early in this century did visits to the doctor's office become clearly less risky and more beneficial than self-care. The social prestige and income of physicians began rising at the same time—surely not just a coincidence. A division of roles, erected in U.S. law during the decades when these spectacular drugs began to appear, gave licensed physicians the exclusive right to prescribe drugs and licensed pharmacists the right to sell prescription drugs to the public.

Since the early 1980s physicians have increasingly begun to dispense drugs for profit directly to patients. Aggressive marketing by the pharmaceutical repackaging industry—about thirty firms, mostly started from scratch within the past few years—stresses patient convenience and the profit potential of contemporary physician dispensing.[1] Most family-practice physicians prescribe fewer than fifty drugs: birth control pills, antibiotics, hypertensive drugs, minor tranquilizers, and so forth. Pharmaceutical repackagers buy drugs and medicines in bulk to repackage in unit doses, creating for physicians, in essence, a mini-pharmacy: typically, a cabinet with thirty to fifty small drawers, each containing standard dosages and amounts of a prepackaged drug ready to be handed to a patient leaving the doctor's office.

One executive of a drug-repackaging firm predicts that by the mid-1990s half of all physicians will routinely sell drugs.[2] Pharmacists, naturally, are screaming foul. They are concerned about loss of income and authority from redrawing the border between two neighboring professions. This opposition of pharmacists to physician dispensing has its counterpart in physician opposition to giving pharmacists even

161

the most narrow legal authority to prescribe medications, such as has been done in Florida. But more is at issue than a turf battle between pharmacy and medicine. For one thing, many physicians are also opposed to physician dispensing on moral grounds, including Dr. Arnold Relman, until recently editor of the *New England Journal of Medicine*.[3] The federal stress on competition and deregulation is also part of the matrix of issues. The Federal Trade Commission sees physician dispensing as beneficial competition. In 1987 the FTC warned Georgia that state efforts to regulate physician dispensing would reduce competition and probably be in violation of federal laws forbidding monopolies.[4] Federal legislation was proposed during 1987 to forbid physician dispensing for profit of orally administered drugs except for special circumstances such as emergencies and isolated rural areas without retail pharmacies. The proposed federal prohibition was not enacted, and little activity on the issue is visible so far in the 1990s.[5] Currently, most states allow physician dispensing for profit, many regulate it, and a few forbid it. But the debate is far from over, and it will undoubtedly heat up again as physician dispensing becomes more common.

As often happens with health policy, conceptual, factual, moral, and political issues are enmeshed with economic concerns. Except for three articles in *Biomedical Ethics Reviews 1989*, bioethicists have said little about this issue.[6] This paper frames the debate over physician dispensing in terms of several fundamental moral principles: beneficence, nonmaleficence, autonomy, justice, and fidelity. This method of bioethical problem solving, which has also been adopted by many who work with issues in nonmedical applied and professional ethics, is given a theoretical statement and defense by Tom Beauchamp and James Childress in *Principles of Biomedical Ethics*.[7] The appeal to *prima facie* moral principles may be defended, Beauchamp and Childress argue, from both rule-utilitarian and rule-deontological perspectives. This is undoubtedly a major source of its continuing popularity and philosophical appeal.

Although physician dispensing lacks the passion and high drama of physician-assisted suicide and surrogate motherhood, it poses an interesting test for this standard problem-solving methodology. We shall see that the light that autonomy, beneficence, and nonmaleficence shed on physician dispensing is decidedly dim. These abstract principles of individualist ethics are obviously useful and important in many clinical contexts and in institutional contexts such as review of research involving human subjects. Yet they turn out to be less than impressive tools for social engineering at the systemic level. In comparison, it is much easier to be clear about what a good therapeutic relationship requires. To make headway on the problem of physician dispensing, the old-fashioned ethic of trust in the physician/patient relationship gives more solid mooring than the shifting sands of *prima facie* moral principles. The principle of fidelity to patients' best interest provides firm enough support to conclude that physician dispensing is ethically a poor idea, or so, at least, I shall argue.

Providing Benefits

According to the principle of beneficence, we ought to benefit others. Defenders of physician dispensing point to two benefits. First, physician dispensing is a convenience to the patient, eliminating an additional stop at a pharmacy and the wait, sometimes twenty or thirty minutes, needed to fill a traditional written prescription. Parents with crying children in tow, workers losing time on the job, and ill and injured patients heading home to bed all benefit from having drugs conveniently available at the doctor's office. Second, it is argued, physician dispensing enhances price competition among providers of drugs, leading to lower prices. Lower-cost drugs and medications are particularly beneficial to patients, because, unlike other areas of health care where third-party reimbursement is now the norm, prescription drugs most often are a direct, out-of-pocket expense for the patient.[8]

Critics of physician dispensing challenge both arguments. First, they point out, almost fifty percent of all prescriptions are refills.[9] Unlike doctor's offices, pharmacies generally are open weekends and evenings. For refill prescriptions, therefore, returning to the physician's office is less convenient. Furthermore, most drugstores offer delivery service, so the claim that an extra stop is needed is mistaken.[10]

Proper assessment of this "convenience" debate seems to hinge on awareness of certain facts. No doubt many people refilling prescriptions would benefit from the longer hours of business at a retail pharmacy. But not all pharmacies deliver. Many charge for it. Even without a delivery charge, this still means extra time is required for patients to get their medicine. Moreover, ambulatory care centers are a growing part of the health care system. These freestanding "urgent care" centers, as they are often called, are less costly than emergency rooms but are open on a walk-in basis during evening and weekend hours, just like drugstores. Even in more traditional physician offices drug dispensaries could remain open for refills after the doctor goes home. That an ill or injured person who needs medicine will get it faster through physician dispensing seems a particularly significant benefit for those patients. Taking all these factors into account, if we look only at convenience, beneficence would favor physician dispensing.

Defenders of physician dispensing also point to the more frequent use of lower-cost generic drugs in physician dispensing. Some claim further that a long-term reduction in prices will inevitably follow more vigorous competition. In reply, pharmacists and their economic consultants have challenged the claim that physician dispensing would lead to lower-cost drugs. The economic issues cannot be fully discussed here. But enough will be said to suggest why the "lower cost" argument for physician dispensing remains unconvincing.

For one thing, an empirical study of prices revealed that prices of drugs dispensed by physicians are higher than prices for the same items in chain drugstores.[11] Though this study only covered the District of Columbia it is enough to prove the point, particularly since during congressional hearings on physician dispensing representatives of the repackagers were explicitly challenged to offer empirical evidence of lower prices and were unable to offer any independent studies whatever to support their claims about lower costs.[12] Armchair economic reflection leads to the same conclusion. Having two middlemen marking up prices—repackagers and physicians—would seem more likely to lead to more expensive drugs than when drugs only pass through the hands of a single pharmacist middleman.

Finally, if the Glassman-Oliver report is correct in asserting that the retail drug industry is already quite competitive, physician dispensing would be unlikely to lead to further price reduction. Competition leads to lower prices only if buyers are free to seek out less costly alternatives. But as Lewis Engman argues:

> Physicians who dispense generally do not list or advertise their drug prices or give the patient a written prescription order. Patients are unlikely to even ask the physician the price of a drug, much less challenge him as to whether it might be available elsewhere at a lower price, or ask him for a written prescription order, so that patients have the option of having it filled by a pharmacy. Thus, encouraging broad-scale physician dispensing means that less price information is available to patients and undercuts long-standing FTC policy that encourages drug price advertising by pharmacies.[13]

Engman's point is well taken. Many patients are intimidated by physicians, too intimidated to ask about pricing or to decline the medications the physician has just prescribed in order to compare prices at a pharmacy. Since many patients are not in a position freely to compare prices, the "lower-cost" argument collapses.

One benefit—lower costs—favors pharmacy dispensing. Another benefit—greater convenience of ill or injured patients—favors physician dispensing. Since convenience and cost point in opposite directions, appealing to the principle of beneficence here has mixed and inconclusive results.

Avoiding Harms

According to the principle of nonmaleficence, we should avoid harming others. Pharmacists and other critics of physician dispensing appeal to nonmaleficence by referring to the "checks and balances" in the present system of drugstore dispensing. Pharmacists, trained from five to seven years, have a greater understanding of the composition, effects, proper dosages, and interactions of drugs than do physicians, who have only one year of training in pharmacology. Pharmacists can advise patients on how and when to take their medications, spot potentially harmful drug interactions, and double-check questionable prescriptions. Since physicians sometimes make mistakes and have less pharmacological knowledge, requiring an additional check by pharmacists reduces the risk of harm to patients.[14] Proponents of physician dispensing, on the other hand, point to harms avoided through better patient compliance with physician recommendations.[15]

How should we assess these appeals to nonmaleficence? The "checks and balances" argument sounds plausible. The pharmacy literature is full of examples of physician error. But advocates of the "checks and balances" argument usually fail to acknowledge two crucial points: First, the key factor here is *total* harm; and second, pharmacists also make mistakes and cause unintended harms.[16] The most plausible procedure for cases involving several harms is to compare the number and seriousness of each sort of harm to determine which system is most likely to minimize harms overall. The least harmful system would then be preferable according to the principle of nonmaleficence. To assess systemic total harms it would be necessary to know how often the "checks and balances" in the present system's division of roles prevent serious harms to patients and also to know how many serious harms are caused by preventable patient noncompliance, by pharmacist error, and by miscommunication between physician and pharmacist.

Some philosophers are skeptical about whether social research can provide any reliable and specific predictions of future consequences in such complex situations. Other philosophers allow that rough predictions about the future serve well enough to know what will happen, but are skeptical about attempting to compare diverse harms and benefits on a common scale. Assume that answers to such skeptics are available—something I make no attempt to prove here but which must be assumed to appeal to beneficence and nonmaleficence at all. Quite apart from more general skepticism about consequentialist prediction and measurement, in the present instance it is difficult to imagine how any empirical study could determine error rates accurately enough to compare systemic total harms. Nobody likes to admit making mistakes, and when mistakes may amount to culpable negligence or some other legal tort, health care providers have additional reason not to admit to them, even on some purportedly anonymous survey instrument. The accurate information needed to compare physician error and pharmacist error is, accordingly, unobtainable. Since the data will not be forthcoming, the "checks and balances" argument is doomed to remain inconclusive.

The moral significance of harms to noncompliant patients who fail to fill their prescriptions is also more difficult to assess than may at first be supposed. In the existing system there is a gap between prescription and dispensing of medicine, a gap that results in between 5 and 10 percent of all written prescriptions not being filled.[17] Such noncompliance results in longer illnesses, increased risks to health, and preventable suffering. Defenders of the "increased compliance" argument for physician dispensing—indeed, most health care providers—usually assume that all cases of noncompliance represent an obvious evil for the noncompliant patient. If this is granted, then nonmaleficence would apparently favor physician dispensing. Of course even patients who have filled prescriptions may still forget to take their pills or throw them away. But more of them are more likely to initiate and continue drug therapy if they have their medications in hand as they leave the physician's office. Though some patients who get their medicine at the doctor's office would still fail to take it, the incidence of patient noncompliance under a system with substantial physician dispensing would surely be less than under a system where 5 to 10 percent of all patients fail to obtain their prescriptions in the first place. Accordingly, it seems we should conclude, net harm to patients would be less with substantial physician dispensing.

The Moral Complexity of Noncompliance

All of this follows if we assume that noncompliance is a clear and obvious evil. But it is not. Contrary to this common assumption, noncompliance with prescription drug recommendations sometimes is beneficial and sometimes enhances autonomy.[18] A Pfizer Pharmaceutical survey conducted by Louis Harris and Associates asked a representative sample of Americans who reported taking less medicine, or taking it less often, than their doctor prescribed which of six reasons described why they were noncompliant. The reasons and the percentage of undercompliers who said this reason is "very close" to their reason is as follows.[19]

You felt better:	44%
You just forgot:	35%
You're concerned about negative side effects:	19%
You're concerned about how this medicine will interact with other medicines you're taking:	16%
You're not sure the medicine is actually working:	13%
Your doctor didn't emphasize the importance of taking this medicine exactly as he or she asked:	12%

According to the principle of autonomy we should respect the free choices of rational adults. This data strongly suggests that some noncompliance is autonomous and some is not. A person who forgets to buy a drug or does not understand the importance of doing so most likely is acting on desires she would not endorse or identify with when fully informed. Assuming that this is a plausible test for autonomous actions, such cases of noncompliance are not autonomous.[20]

Someone who chooses not to fill a prescription because she felt better or because she is concerned about negative side effects or interactions with other drugs, however, may sometimes have a reason not to fill her prescription that she—or any rational person—would endorse or identify with when fully informed. Two different aspects of autonomy are relevant here, autonomy as free action and autonomy as effective deliberation.[21] Autonomy as free action concerns the *consent* part of informed consent. Actions are autonomous in this sense when they are voluntary and intentional rather than the result of coercion, duress, or undue influence. A patient who feels pressured to purchase a drug from her physician has lost autonomy as free action insofar as her action is the result of duress or undue influence.

Autonomy as effective deliberation concerns the *informed* part of informed consent. Autonomy as effective deliberation requires that a person making a decision is aware of the alternatives and the consequences of the alternatives, evaluates both, and chooses an action based on that evaluation.[22] Patients who have less than adequate time to fully consider whether or not to fill a prescription have lost autonomy as effective deliberation. So have those who override nagging but sometimes legitimate doubts about their medications later on at home by reasoning, "Since I already paid for these pills, I'd better take them." Once the role of autonomy in these two senses is made evident, the ethical complexity of prescription drug noncompliance increases considerably. Noncompliance involves both nonautonomous and autonomous choices. While undoubtedly eliminating some harms to some people, a system with significant physician dispensing would also restrict the autonomous choices of other people.

Many classic bioethical issues involve conflicts between nonmaleficence and autonomy in situations where both principles apply to the same person. The problem here, however, involves different people making similar choices for different reasons, some autonomous and some not. Joel Feinberg distinguishes "weak paternalism," where harms are prevented by restricting nonautonomous choices, from "strong paternalism," where harms are prevented by restricting autonomous choices.[23] In these terms the question is how many individual cases of justified weak paternalism does it take to justify a system that also results in some other cases of strong paternalism?

Answering this question would require determining the nature and frequency of harms noncompliant patients are seeking to avoid—a very tall order. Authorities have long asserted that prescription drugs are overprescribed, that Americans are overmedicated, and that there are serious risks of harm from drug toxicity and interaction. Here are three examples:

First, in January 1976 the *New York Times* published a five-part series on "Medical Incompetency" in the United States and said that, in addition to the 30,000 fatalities each year, "perhaps ten times as many patients suffer life-threatening and sometimes permanent bleeding, and loss of hearing or vision" as a result of wrong or unnecessary prescriptions.[24]

Second, D'Arcy and Griffin's more systematic summary of twenty-one studies into the epidemiology of adverse drug reactions between 1964 and 1977 suggests that "between 2 and 7.8 percent of patients require admission to hospital because they react to their medication."[25]

Third, a 1989 report by the Inspector General of the U.S. Department of Health and Human Services concluded that "a growing body of evidence accumulated over the past ten years indicates that mismedication of the elderly has become a critical health care issue, labeled by some as the 'nation's other drug problem.'"[26] One factor mentioned in the HHS report was faulty prescribing patterns among doctors, which reflect inadequate medical training and education in pharmacology.

Even assuming that such statements are accurate, it still seems beyond dispute that most prescription drug noncompliance is harmful to patients. Yet we must also recognize that some prescription drug noncompliance is autonomous and that it may sometimes prevent serious harms caused by prescription drug toxicity or interactions. Once we see the complex relationships among harm, autonomy, and justice involved in making a moral choice about systems of prescription drug dispensing, no single, simple argument from nonmaleficence by itself will be conclusive.

So far I have shown that comparing different systems of dispensing medications involves complex trade-offs of largely unknown degrees of autonomy, benefit, and harm among many different, unidentified people. Inevitably, therefore, questions of justice also arise. We do not have sufficient empirical data to determine who would be affected and how much, and, barring some now unimagined methodological breakthrough in social research, we shall never have it. Even if we had the data, we would need a theory of how to ethically resolve such complex trade-offs. We do not have this, either. No such theory has gained wide agreement among philosophers. For such systemic questions, appeals to the *prima facie* moral principles of beneficence, nonmaleficence, justice, and autonomy yield indeterminate and conflicting indications rather than a solid moral diagnosis.

Keeping Faith with Patients

The last argument I shall discuss also involves harm but is best framed in terms of the principle of fidelity in the physician/patient relationship. Fidelity is the principle that we ought to honor explicit and implicit promises made to others. Fidelity to patients, though often criticized today for sanctioning paternalistic excesses, has historically been the central norm in medical practice. Patients implicitly trust physicians to be committed to furthering the patient's best interest. Contemporary codes of medical ethics mention this duty explicitly, as does the law in speaking of the "fiduciary relationship" between physicians and patients. When a physician stands to profit from selling drugs, however, commitment to the patient's best interests is compromised, weakening trust and risking harm to patients. A system with substantial physician dispensing would lead to less than optimal care in several ways. Physicians would be tempted to sell drugs to patients when over-the-counter medications or none at all would be just as useful. They would be tempted to prescribe drugs stocked in their own dispensary, even if another dosage or formula or similar drug available at a retail pharmacy would be better in a particular patient's case. Such temptations, according to critics of physician dispensing, risk harm and weaken trust by building an inherent conflict of interest into the physician/patient relationship.[27]

Defenders of physician dispensing reply to this "conflict of interest" argument from fidelity by pointing out that such situations are common. We frequently consult professionals whose advice to us is to do something that will benefit us and at the same time earn them additional money. Through the end of 1986 the American Medical Association made this argument. The AMA maintained that disclosure is ethically required when physicians recommend services from which they stand to benefit financially. Provided these financial interests are disclosed, physician dispensing is no different from physician ownership of ambulance companies, diagnostic services, or a pharmacy across the street. According to this AMA position, all of these practices are ethical provided patients are informed and allowed to select alternative providers if they wish.[28]

There is increasing dissatisfaction with this view within organized medicine. In December of 1986 the Council on Ethical and Judicial Affairs of the American Medical Association identified physician dispensing as a situation with a potential for creating a conflict of interest. The council recommended that

Although there are circumstances in which physicians may ethically engage in the dispensing of drugs, devices or other products, physicians are urged to avoid regular dispensing and retail sale of drugs, devices or other products when the needs of patients can be met adequately by local ethical pharmacies or suppliers.[29]

The ethical justification for discouraging physician dispensing is not difficult to appreciate. In the past two decades a whole literature has arisen concerning unnecessary surgery, unnecessary testing, and excessive prescribing by physicians. Where physicians have had a financial interest some have been able to induce demand for unnecessary further treatment and diagnosis.[30] Even if some physician ownership practices would survive ethical scrutiny, an appeal to such precedents as physician ownership of a pharmacy or a diagnostic services company to legitimate physicians dispensing is naive and simplistic. When new risks are added to old ones, together they are more likely to culminate in an unacceptable result. There is a big difference between the appeal to precedent, which ignores threshold effects and cumulative risks, and appeal to consistency, a basic requirement of all good reasoning. One may, accordingly, consistently oppose some appeals to precedent.

The question here is which system of drug dispensing should we have? It is not really to the point to argue that honest practitioners will not exploit patients even if there are financial incentives to do so, for two reasons: First, a few doctors are not honest; and second, many honest doctors are not aware of the subtle determinants of their own behavior. Although physicians like to believe that they arrive at therapeutic decisions according to the scientific effectiveness of the medication for a particular patient, careful studies have shown that their actions are often influenced by drug advertisements.[31] Critics of physician dispensing rightly worry about the cumulative effect of increasing the financial incentives to compromise patient welfare. Putting new temptations into a social practice leads to more people giving in to them, with many who give in not even realizing they are compromising patient welfare. In short, the "conflict of interest" argument from fidelity survives criticism. It is the best argument against physician dispensing.

Two more general philosophical morals have emerged from this inquiry. First, many *prima facie* moral principles are not terribly useful tools for social engineering at the systemic level. Second, in comparison, it is much easier to be clear about what a good therapeutic relationship requires. The force of the fidelity argument stems from its emphasis on the physician/patient relationship rather than from systemic features of drug dispensing. Uncertainties about what will hap-

pen and priority disputes about conflicting moral principles begin to
seem beside the point after turning to norms and ideals within the
physician/patient relationship. Though no consensus on resolving priority disputes among beneficence, nonmaleficence, autonomy, and
justice is in sight, in the end appealing to fidelity in the therapeutic
relationship is a good reason to conclude that physician dispensing is
ethically a poor idea.[32]

Notes

Copyright 1992 by David N. James. A version of this article appeared in
Business and Professional Ethics Journal 11 (Summer 1992): 73–88.

1. Glassman-Oliver Economic Consultants, "Physician Dispensing of Prescription Drugs: An Economic and Policy Analysis." Prepared for the American Pharmaceutical Association, 1987, 3–7.
2. U.S. Congress, House Committee on Energy and Commerce, *Physician
Dispensing of Drugs: Hearing before a Subcommittee on Health and the
Environment on H.R. 2093*, 100th Cong., 1st sess., 1987, 2.
3. Arnold S. Relman, "Doctors and the Dispensing of Drugs," Editorial,
New England Journal of Medicine 317 (1987): 311–12.
4. "Physician Dispensing of Prescription Drugs," 2.
5. The original bill introduced by Representative Ron Wyden, HR 2093,
was modified slightly and reintroduced with nine additional sponsors as HR
2168 on November 18, 1987. HR 2168 was reported to the floor of the House,
where it languished. More recently the bill has attracted additional sponsorship
in the House and renewed interest in the Senate. "MD Dispensing Bill Picks
Up Support," *American Druggist* (April 1988): 24. For a survey of regulations
and legislative activity at the state level, see Glassman-Oliver, 7–10.
6. William B. Irvine, "The Case for Physician-Dispensed Drugs," in
Biomedical Ethics Reviews 1989, ed. James M. Humber and Robert F. Almeder
(Clifton, N.J.: Humana Press, 1990), 59–73; Calvin H. Knowlton et al.,
"Physicians as Pharmacists," in ibid., 75–93; and Michael P. Weinstein,
"Should Physicians Dispense Drugs for a Profit?" in ibid., 95–112.
Physician self-referral arrangements, in which physicians have an ownership or investment interest in laboratories and ancillary service providers to
which they refer patients, have many parallels with physician dispensing. A
comprehensive discussion of the ethics of physician self-referral is Dan W.
Brock, "Medicine and Business: An Unhealthy Mix," *Business and Professional Ethics Journal* 9 (Fall–Winter 1990): 21–37. One key difference is the
sharpness of interprofessional conflict over physician dispensing. In part this
reflects the fact that pharmacists have an older and more clearly delineated

tradition of independent professional practice than do X-ray technicians or medical technologists.

7. This by now familiar "principles" approach is given a theoretical statement and defense in Tom L. Beauchamp and James Childress, *Principles of Biomedical Ethics*, 2d ed. (New York: Oxford University Press, 1983).

8. W. Scott James, "The Physician's Experience," *Journal of the Medical Association of Georgia* 77 (1988): 30–36.

9. *Drug Topics* (18 March 1985): 33.

10. John T. Sherrer and Larry Braden, "The Pharmacist's Experience," *Journal of the Medical Association of Georgia* 77 (1988): 30–36.

11. "Physician Dispensing of Prescription Drugs," 18, 30–31.

12. "Physician Dispensing of Prescription Drugs," 150.

13. "Policy Forum: An Interview with Lewis A. Engman," *American Pharmacy* 27, no. 11 (November 1987): 26.

14. This is by far the most frequently repeated argument in the pharmacy literature, found in nearly every issue since 1985 of *American Pharmacy*, the journal of the American Pharmaceutical Association (APhA). See also "Physician Dispensing of Prescription Drugs," 56–78 and passim.

15. For example, Mark Tabak, head of Clinical Pharmaceuticals in Nashville, speaking for the Coalition for Competitive Health Care (an organization of repackagers) at a conference on "The Future of Prescribing in America." Reported in "AMA Official OK's MD-Dispensing but Rejects RPh-Prescribing," *American Druggist* (December 1987): 32.

16. An example of the neglect of these points is Michael T. Rupp, "Evaluation of Prescribing Errors and Pharmacist Interventions in Community Practice: An Estimate of 'Value Added,' " *American Pharmacy* 28NS (December 1988): 22–26. This study of physician error purports to calculate the "value added" by pharmacist's double check down to the penny per prescription. But the existence of miscommunication and pharmacist error is nowhere acknowledged, making such research useless for estimating total systemic harms.

17. Pfizer Pharmaceuticals, "Americans and Their Doctors," conducted by Louis Harris and Associates (1985): 54–56.

18. Virtually alone in recognizing this is Peter Conrad, "The Non-Compliant Patient in Search of Autonomy," *Hastings Center Report* (August 1987): 15–17.

19. "Americans and Their Doctors," 38–39. These were the *only* choices mentioned in the survey. Noteworthy by its absence is "You cannot afford the medicine," an omission that renders invisible the degree to which poverty contributes to noncompliance.

20. Gerald Dworkin, "Autonomy and Behavior Control," *Hastings Center Report* (February 1976): 23–28.

21. Bruce Miller, "Autonomy and the Refusal of Lifesaving Treatment," *Hastings Center Report* (August 1981): 22–28.

22. "Autonomy and the Refusal of Lifesaving Treatment," 24.

23. Joel Feinberg, "Legal Paternalism," *Canadian Journal of Philosophy* 1 (1971): 105–24. Paternalism has attracted enormous philosophical attention, but nothing on the question asked here.

24. Griffin, *Drug-Induced Emergencies* (Bristol, UK: John Wright and Sons, 1980), 4.

25. *Drug-Induced Emergencies*, 1–2.

26. Quoted in "Widespread Drug Lapses Found Among Elderly," *New York Times*, 15 February 1989, A1, A17. The study was based on information gathered from a survey of forty-eight state agencies that provide prescription drug benefits to Medicaid patients, review of previous research on drug use and the elderly, and a series of interviews.

27. See, for example, Relman, "Doctors and the Dispensing of Drugs."

28. American Medical Association, "Current Opinions of the Council on Ethical and Judicial Affairs": 8.03, "Conflicts of Interest: Guidelines" and 8.06 "Drugs and Devices: Prescribing" (1986), 30–31.

29. Quoted in David I. Olch, "Conflict of Interest and Physician Dispensing," *The Internist* 28 (October 1987): 16. This is by no means common practice, however: In 1991 the state of Virginia decided to regulate physician sales of medication, a "regulation" consisting entirely of a requirement to pay a $200 license fee.

30. Victor R. Fuchs, "The Supply of Surgeons and the Demand for Operations," *Journal of Human Resources* 13 (1978): 21–34; Richard Auster and Ronald L. Oaxaca, "Identification of Supplier Induced Demand in the Health Care Sector," *Journal of Human Resources* 16 (1981): 327–42; and Dan W. Brock, "Medicine and Business: An Unhealthy Mix?" *Journal of Human Resources* 16 (1981): 26–29.

31. Jerry Avorn, Milton Chen, and Robert Hartley, "Scientific versus Commercial Sources of Influence on the Prescribing Behavior of Physicians," *The American Journal of Medicine* 73 (July 1982): 4–8.

32. I am grateful to Judith Andre, Robert Baum, Glenn Erickson, Ruth Ann Frank, Jeanne Thomson James, Ingemar Lindahl, Mark Nelson, George Rainbolt, Robert Redmon, Daniel Wueste, and audiences in Los Angeles, California, Hampton-Sydney, Virginia, and Clemson, South Carolina, for comments and suggestions on this paper.

9

Professional Responsibility, Reproductive Choice, and the Limits of Appropriate Intervention: The Battle Over RU 486

Kathleen Marie Dixon

Introduction

RU 486 is one of the most controversial reproductive pharmaceuticals to be developed in the past two decades. This paper approaches the moral issues involved in its use and availability from the vantage point of professional ethics. Its first section presents RU 486's corporate and political history. Features influencing the drug's development and distribution are emphasized. The second section of the paper carefully describes RU 486's chemical function, its clinical use, and effectiveness. The third section presents three types of arguments examining physicians' and patients' entitlements to access and use of RU 486. The first argument tests physicians' *prima facie* obligation to provide patients with the safest, most effective mode of medical treatment. The second argument affirms health care providers' obligations to sustain and promote patients' responsibility for specific treatment decisions and general health maintenance. The third argument utilizes the notion of professional privilege.

The final section of the paper offers four arguments addressing corporate obligations to commercially distribute abortifacients. Each of the four presents a different characterization and application of corporations' social responsibilities. The first claims that if corporations are to act in a socially responsible manner, they must carefully calculate and review a product's net social utility. A second, related argument describes corporations' social responsibility in terms of obligations to produce and distribute goods and services that sustain and enhance human life (Camenisch, 1986: 149). The third argument limits concerns of social responsibility to maximization of corporate profit. The fourth articulates a relationship between corporate and professional obligations. It asserts that corporations that manufacture prescription drugs have special duties to physicians as their immediate constituency. These arguments support the conclusion that Roussel-Uclaf and Hoechst cannot justify their policies by appeals to corporate social responsibility.

History: The Development and Marketing of RU 486

In April 1980, a compound called RU38486 was synthesized in the laboratories of Roussel-Uclaf (Lader, 1991: 48). This product, an antiprogesterone steroid, was the culmination of ten years of research conducted at a number of facilities. Research progressed from the initial identification of the uterine progesterone receptor in 1970 through numerous studies of hormone receptor sites to attempts to synthesize compounds interfering with hormonal availability or function (Baulieu, 1989b: 1809). After seventeen months of multispecies animal studies, it received its first clinical trial in women (Raymond et al., 1991: 9). This compound came to be known as RU 486 or mifepristone.[1]

Mifepristone blocks progesterone receptors presenting a chemical impediment to the function of progesterone. Progesterone causes decidualization of the endometrium, a process that thickens the lining of the uterus and increases its blood supply. Progesterone sustains this thick lining of the uterus, preparing it for implantation of the blastocyst approximately two weeks after fertilization (Palca, 1989: 1320). By blocking progesterone receptor sites, mifepristone produces a uterine environment hostile to preembryos and embryos, resulting in bleeding and contractions with termination of pregnancy or failure to implant. Initial trials conducted in 1982 on eleven volunteers desiring pregnancy termination established mifepristone's efficacy as an abortifacient (Baulieu, 1989b: 1811). Nine pregnancies were terminated in eight women after five days; another woman terminated on the ninth day (Raymond et al., 1991: 10). Subsequent studies demonstrated that when RU 486 is combined with prostaglandin, the treatment is 96 percent effective in obtaining a complete termination of pregnancy. Expulsion of the blastocyst occurs within four hours of the administration of prostaglandin in 69 percent of patients (Baulieu, 1989: 1354). Thus, in a combined therapeutic regimen, mifepristone's efficacy is comparable to that of an aspiration abortion and appears to have no adverse side effects on women's subsequent ability to conceive and gestate healthy offspring.

The commercial history of RU 486 emphasizes the hazards of marketing products of reproductive research. Roussel-Uclaf, the large French pharmaceutical company that developed RU 486, had been acquired by a German company, Hoechst AG, in 1974. In 1982 the French government bought 36.25 percent of the company, leaving Hoechst with a 54.5 percent interest and a few shares remaining on the public market (Lader, 1991: 41). On September 23, 1988, French health officials gave Roussel permission to send RU 486 to registered French abortion facilities. Roussel and Hoechst came under immediate fire from religious conservatives. Cardinal Jean-Marie Lustiger of Paris denounced RU 486 as "savage liberalism" and a "chemical weapon against the unborn" (Lader, 1991: 50). The health ministry and Roussel offices were picketed. Roussel also received bomb threats (Palca, 1989: 1319). Both Roussel and Hoechst proved susceptible to a threat of boycott by Catholic hospitals in the United States (Palca, 1989: 1319). Catholic hospitals control approximately one-third of all U.S. hospital beds (Lader, 1991: 132); their cooperation in a boycott could have significantly reduced Hoechst's $4 billion annual U.S. sales (MacFarquhar, 1989: 54).

Lader suggests that Roussel may have experienced intramural pressure from Hoechst's president, Wolfgang Hilger. Hilger was apparently unprepared for the compound's success as an abortifacient. He is a devout Roman Catholic with strong personal objections to abortion. Hoechst's corporate history may have also undermined the companies' commitment to the drug. Hoechst AG is the successor company to I. G. Farben which produced the gas used in the death chambers of Nazi concentration camps (Lader, 1991: 50). An "abortion pill" could prompt too many unsettling and tragic analogies. Overriding strong objections by its own management and researchers, Roussel announced on October 26, 1988, that it was taking RU 486 off the market.[2] Roussel director of medical relations, Arlette Geslin, explained the decision, "We didn't want to get into a moral debate" (Lader, 1991: 50).

Roussel and Hoechst found that the decision to remove RU 486 from use subjected them to public scorn and professional furor. The announcement was made during the annual meeting of the World Congress of Obstetrics and Gynecology. The audience was stunned, and petitions were immediately prepared and signed by most participants (Lader, 1991: 50). They threatened to boycott Hoechst products if Roussel failed to distribute the drug in France (Palca, 1989: 1320). In a dramatic show of force, French health minister Claude Evin threatened to use a 1968 law that permits the French government to revoke and reassign the license of a company that withdraws a safe and effective drug from public use (Lader, 1991: 51). Evin said he "could not permit the abortion debate to deprive women of a product that represents medical progress. From the moment government approval for the drug was granted, RU 486 became the moral property of women, not just the property of the drug company" (Palca, 1989: 1320). This strategy proved effective, and Roussel restored the drug on the same day. However, twenty-seven months after this dramatic threat, the Conseil d'Etat reprimanded Evin for exceeding his authority in ordering the restoration of the drug (Raymond et al., 1991: 13). In the most bizarre twist in the story to date, Evin "now claims that he had not issued such an order because 'discussions and exchange of arguments with representatives from Roussel Uclaf had made recourse to this procedure unnecessary' " (Raymond et al., 1991: 13–14).

RU 486 has enjoyed a strong market presence. Since January 1989, French facilities have administered the drug to over 2,000 women per month (Baulieu, 1989b: 1812). Between one-quarter and one-third of French women choosing to terminate pregnancies use RU 486 (Palca, 1989: 1320). Lader indicates that 77 percent of French women who have used both vacuum aspiration and RU 486 to terminate a pregnancy preferred the pill. Additionally, of the first 103 women studied by Dr. Mackenzie in Britain, more than 80 percent said they would use RU 486 if they required another abortion (Lader, 1991: 18–19).

Roussel-Uclaf has been under considerable pressure to allow the distribution of RU 486 in the United States. Delegations from the National Organization for Women and Planned Parenthood have flown to France in attempts to persuade Roussel to market the drug here. Eleanor Smeal, president of the Fund for a Feminist Majority, presented company executives with a petition signed by 125,000 Americans who urged immediate introduction of the drug (Lader, 1991: 131). In March 1990, the California Medical Association "voted overwhelmingly" for the pill's admission, arguing that "It is in keeping with basic medical standards to avoid surgical procedures whenever an equally effective non-invasive alternative is available." This conclusion was ratified in a unanimous voice vote at the June 1990 meeting of the American Medical Association's House of Delegates (Lader, 1991: 113). The companies' obduracy in the face of these appeals was expressed in a statement made in March 1990 by Edward Norton, a spokesman for Hoechst-Roussel Pharmaceuticals of New Jersey. "We've been petitioned, we've been yelled at, and we've been telephoned by everybody. But our formal position hasn't changed in two years, and I don't expect it to change." Arielle Moutet, head of international marketing at Roussel in Paris, reiterated the point in July 1990: "Selling in the United States is out of the question at the moment" (Lader, 1991: 132).

Corporate obstinacy is not the only obstacle to be surmounted in efforts to obtain RU 486 in the United States. In 1989, the FDA issued an import alert, adding RU 486 to the list of drugs whose import it bans. The FDA denied that this ban impeded the process of U.S. research on the drug, charging that its exclusive intent was to prevent harm that might arise from unsupervised personal use. However, even those physicians and researchers whose work would not test RU 486's efficacy as an abortifacient have indicated that the ban "thwarted" and "whiplashed" their efforts to obtain it for experimentation (Noah, 1990: C 19).

American researchers realized that they faced twin perils when considering clinical testing on RU 486: the hostile ideology and regulatory environment of the Bush administration and threatened boycotts by religious fundamentalists. The repressive measures that the first failed to formalize were more casually achieved by the second. Researchers and prospective patients suffered substantially under the weight of the combined blows. The ill effects were nowhere more visible than the National Institutes of Health (NIH). Regulations barred NIH from supporting any abortifacient research on RU 486. Although RU 486 could be tested for other uses, researchers were forced to undertake bizarre and extreme methods to avoid all possible taint by abortion. NIH investigators attempting to determine the amount of RU 486 that would be safe for a pregnant woman to use for its anti-glucocorticoid effects were prevented from using the most efficient methodology because it could induce abortions on test monkeys. Scientists had to use hormones on castrated monkeys to simulate pregnancy instead (Lader, 1991: 103–4). Sheldon J. Segal of the Rockefeller Foundation summarized NIH scientists' reactions saying, "They've suffered a kind of chilling effect. . . . They're scared to death of the threats against anybody who does anything with this drug" (Palca, 1989: 1321).

While the investigators in the NIH anti-glucocorticoid study were able to identify alternative, though more difficult, means to obtain the necessary information, others were not so fortunate. Regelson et al. indicate that two important studies were cancelled in April 1989 as a result of antiabortion groups' threatened boycotts of Hoechst and Roussel products.[3] A U.S. multicenter clinical study of breast cancer and a study of mifepristone's potential in treatment of AIDS were both abandoned. The only U.S. facility testing RU 486 as an abortifacient was harassed into secrecy and silence. Although the University of Southern California (USC) gave the drug to some 400 women in different doses at various stages of pregnancy, representatives refused to discuss what USC was doing. As Marcia Lacarra, a nurse and family planning counselor at USC's Women's Hospital stated, "We're tired of getting threatening letters" (Palca, 1989: 1321).

The Bush administration could not credibly limit its responsibility for these research barriers. It consciously and tenaciously sustained and expanded the conservative reproductive agenda. Indeed, the original FDA import ban appears to have been the product of political pressure. Little federal interest in a potential ban appeared before key conservatives wrote to Frank Young, then commissioner of the FDA, to complain about U.S. citizens' possible access to the drug (Noah, 1990: C 19).[4]

On his second day in office, which, as it happened, was the twentieth anniversary of *Roe* v. *Wade*, President Clinton signed five abortion-related memoranda ordering the reversal of the restrictions established by the Reagan–Bush administrations. He also ordered a review of the import ban on RU 486 (Toner, 1993: A 1). Thus, President Clinton has begun the process of dismantling the research barriers erected by his predecessors. Moreover, he has indicated that he will invite Roussel-Uclaf to apply for permission to market RU 486 in the United States, and Dr. David A. Kessler, commissioner of the FDA, has said that such an application would be welcome. Nevertheless, it seems unlikely that the drug will be marketed here any time soon (Hilts, 1992: A 38).

RU 486: Clinical Use and Effectiveness

RU 486 is an antiprogesterone, a chemical that blocks the normal action of the hormone progesterone. Progesterone causes decidualization of the endometrium by binding with progesterone receptors, which are themselves attached to specific proteins called "heat-shock proteins." When progesterone joins this complex chemical dance it creates a reconfiguration of the larger pattern and jettisons the heat-shock proteins. This creates a free space in the pattern. The progesterone-progesterone receptor complex attaches itself to a new "partner" (i.e., the hormone response elements in the nucleus' DNA), and the genes controlled by progesterone are transcribed. As a result, the lush lining of the uterus is maintained, ready for implantation by a blastocyst. Progesterone also suppresses the hormones in the brain that trigger the next cycle of ovulation (Cherfas, 1989: 1320). Other important functions of progesterone include decreasing the responsiveness of the smooth muscle of the uterus, firming the cervix, and encouraging the formation of a mucous plug over the cervix. These are all important conditions for the maintenance of a pregnancy (Baulieu, 1989: 1351).

RU 486 acts as a controlling partner in this chemical dance. It occupies the same site that progesterone would, but it does not "spin off" the heat-shock proteins. Instead it holds them more tightly. Progesterone can't enter the site and as the compound is not reconfigured, no transcription of genes can occur. Consequently, all physiological processes that depend on progesterone fail or cannot occur (Cherfas, 1989: 1320).

Baulieu describes the function of RU 486 as "contragestion," a term he developed as a contraction of contragestation. For RU 486 works primarily on the decidua, the rich lining of the uterus, causing edema, necrosis, and capillary damage. This would either preclude implantation of the blastocyst or cause the chorionic tissue of the blastocyst to detach from the uterine wall. The prostaglandin that is administered thirty-six to forty-eight hours after RU 486 stimulates myometrial contractions and facilitates dilatation and softening of the cervix (Baulieu, 1989b: 1812–13). Thus, a woman receiving the combined treatment experiences bleeding much like a normal period shortly after the prostaglandin is administered. Bleeding continues for four to forty days, with a mean of ten days. Average blood loss is between 70 and 80 ml. and is similar to the blood loss associated with aspiration abortion or heavy menstruation (Baulieu 1989: 1354). However, studies also suggest that between 18 and 23 percent of women experience heavy bleeding. The scientific community is divided on the question of the effectiveness of the combined RU 486 prostaglandin treatment in limiting the severity and duration of bleeding. Prolonged and heavy bleeding could reduce hemoglobin levels, requiring iron treatment or transfusion. It could also necessitate curettage. Some studies indicate that prolonged and serious bleeding is the most significant clinical problem associated with the treatment (Raymond et al., 1991: 40–41, 17). However, other scientists and physicians have voiced strong concerns about the safety of prostaglandins. Roussel urged physicians to use alternative means of abortion with patients who were obese, heavy smokers, and those who had elevated serum lipids, diabetes, or high blood pressure. Two serious cardiovascular accidents were subsequently associated with prostaglandins when combined with RU 486. A thirty-one-year-old woman died from cardiovascular shock shortly after an injection of the prostaglandin Nalador (Raymond et al., 1991: 17, 23, 40).

Baulieu summarizes the specific treatment received by French women who select RU 486 as an abortifacient. A 600 mg. dose of RU 486 is administered orally, followed thirty-six to forty-eight hours later by a small dose of a synthetic prostaglandin analog either in an intramuscular injection or a vaginal pessary (Baulieu, 1989: 1354).[5] Patients are monitored for a short time and then may be released. The process has been completely successful for over 95 percent of the seven-week pregnancies terminated in France and the nine-week pregnancies terminated in Great Britain. Expulsion of the blastocyst occurs within four hours of the administration of prostaglandin in 69 percent of patients. Patients tolerate the procedure very well. Side effects include nausea, vomiting, diarrhea, and menstrual-type cramps, but are typically reported as mild (Silvestre et al., 1990). Baulieu indicates that only 10 percent of patients receiving RU 486 require strong analgesics (Baulieu, 1989: 1355). In a British study of 1,000 women, 48 percent reported no pain, 29 percent reported enough discomfort to warrant taking an analgesic, and 23 percent needed a stronger pain killer (Lader, 1991: 58).

Baulieu argues that administration of RU 486 in an outpatient setting requires strict medical supervision to monitor cases of excessive blood loss requiring dilation and curettage (D&C) or transfusion. One percent or less of the women who receive RU 486 will require a D&C; 0.1 percent require a blood transfusion (Baulieu, 1989b: 1812). Baulieu indicates that follow-up care will also be required in cases of incomplete abortion and tubal pregnancy. Between 3 percent and 4 percent of the women receiving the combined treatment will experience incomplete abortions that require surgical intervention. In 1 percent of the patients, pregnancy continued. Although physicians recommend instrumental termination of pregnancy, there is no evidence of a teratogenic or fetotoxic effect of RU 486 (Baulieu, 1989b: 1812).

RU 486 shows additional promise as a method of birth control. Baulieu has described three different ways in which the drug could fulfill this function. The first is as a "menses inducer." If a woman takes RU 486 in the second half of her ovulatory cycle in the days preceding the expected menstruation, there is an 80 percent chance that she will begin to bleed. The actual failure rate of this method of birth control would be 4 percent (Baulieu, 1989b: 1812). Similar results can also be achieved by taking RU 486 in the last three to four days of the cycle, the late luteal period. The second method involves using RU 486 as a chemical intrauterine device (IUD). Baulieu speculates that very small amounts of RU 486 administered during the first half or middle of the luteal phase would prevent implantation by causing changes in the endometrium. To achieve this effect RU 486 would be administered for the last ten to twelve days of the woman's cycle, until menstruation occurred (Baulieu, 1989b: 1812–13). The final method uses RU 486 to suspend ovulation, offering significant promise of an estrogen-free mode of contraception (Baulieu, 1989b: 1813).

RU 486's function as an antiprogesterone gives it a remarkably broad clinical range. Gupta and Johnson report that RU 486 can be used independently to dilatate and soften the cervix, reducing the risk of cervical trauma associated with D&C, insertion and removal of IUDs, endometrial biopsy, and laser eradication of cervical lesions (Gupta and Johnson, 1990: 1239). RU 486 shows promise in treating breast cancer. Some breast tumors require both estrogen and progesterone to grow. While antiestrogens are available to stop the growth of these tumors, studies indicate that RU 486 improves the effectiveness of the antiestrogens (Palca, 1989: 1320). Regelson et al. describe the administration of RU 486 to patients with advanced breast cancer in a phase 1 study. Eighteen percent of one group of patients showed "significant measurable tumor regression in this preliminary trial" (Regelson et al., 1990: 1026). RU 486 may also prove to be effective in the treatment of other types of cancer. Markwalder, Waelti, and Grunberg et al. have all reported that the drug is valuable in the treatment of inoperable meningiomas, primary tumors of the membranes surrounding the brain (Regelson et al., 1990: 1026). RU 486 also inhibits the progesterone-stimulated production of epidermal growth factor. This suggests that the drug might be helpful in the treatment of bowel and kidney tumors (Regelson et al., 1990: 1026). RU 486 may also be used to treat endometriosis, fibrocystic breast disease, and some forms of ovarian cancer (Lader, 1991: 84).

Another entire range of important clinical benefits derive from RU 486's function as an anti-glucocorticoid. Cushing's syndrome is a disease resulting from an excess production of cortisone. It can be caused by a tumor in the adrenal cortex that is initially too small to detect. RU 486 can be used to keep patients alive until the tumor becomes large enough to be isolated and surgically removed (Palca, 1989: 1320). As glucocorticoids enhance viral proliferation and decrease host resistance to infection or viral tumors, RU 486 offers hope in the treatment of a variety of viral infections including Epstein-Barr virus and AIDS (Regelson et al., 1990: 1026). Finally, since corticosteriods delay healing, RU 486 may enhance local treatment of skin wounds such as burns and abrasions (Palca, 1989: 1320).

Benefit, Responsibility, and Professional Privilege: RU 486 and Professional Ethics

Medical Benefit

The principle of beneficence, a cornerstone of medical ethics, requires health care providers to maximize patients' net benefit (Veatch, 1987: 18–20, 92, 93). This exacting moral standard requires physicians to provide the safest, most effective modes of medical treatment. The principle of beneficence also serves as a goad against medical complacency. It urges clinicians and researchers to press the boundaries of established technique when innovative approaches offer the most favorable outcomes at the lowest costs. Indeed, if patients are entitled to the best care that health professionals can provide, they have a right to receive innovative treatments when these represent the epitome of professional knowledge and skill (Dixon, 1991: 171). The obligations created by this principle are usually expressed as *prima facie* moral duties. This limitation should be cast in terms of recognition of patients' and providers' moral agency. This requires physicians to concede that patient autonomy establishes the parameters of the concept of beneficence. Similarly, patients must recognize that their entitlements to determine their care do not require providers to abnegate important professional or personal values and principles.

If health care providers and patients are successfully to prosecute a claim to access and use of RU 486 as an abortifacient, they will have to ground their claims in a right to pursue and enjoy the benefits of medical innovation. One cannot credibly assert that there are no other effective or safe means to terminate pregnancy. Suction or sharp curettage offer women safe and very reliable methods of pregnancy termination. They present very little risk of mortality, 1.2 and 2.8 deaths per 100,000 abortions respectively (Legge, 1985: 19). Major complications only occur at a rate of 0.4 per 100 for suction curettage and 0.9 per 100 for sharp curettage (Legge, 1985: 19–20).

What can be successfully argued is that RU 486 is an innovation that obviates existing categories of medical risk. When mifepristone is combined with prostaglandin in carefully titrated dosages, most women can avoid hazards associated with instrumental termination and anesthetic use. Successful treatment with the combined regimen allows women to avoid completely the risks of infection, cervical injury, uterine perforation, and adhesion (Baulieu, 1989b: 1812). As RU 486 does not require administration of any form of anesthetic, women can avoid both the risks of convulsions and fever associated with local anesthesia (Legge, 1985: 25) and the risks of general anesthesia including arrhythmia and drug reaction (Eiseman, 1980: 193).

It is important to note that while mifepristone allows most patients to avoid important categories of medical risk, it is not risk free. As indicated previously, most women experience no pain in the course of the treatment; side effects are generally described as mild and include cramping, nausea, vomiting, and diarrhea (Silvestre et al., 1990). However, some feminists reject literal interpretation of these medical assessments, reminding us that "medicine . . . often minimizes women's pain, reporting it as 'insignificant,' 'acceptable,' and/or 'tolerable' " (Raymond et al., 1991: 42). We cannot afford to ignore these concerns, but women themselves are the most adequate judges of their tolerance. Seventy-seven percent of French women who have used both vacuum aspiration and RU 486 to terminate a pregnancy preferred the latter. Eighty percent of a group of British patients indicated that they would use RU 486 if they required another abortion (Lader, 1991: 18–19). Although most women who use mifepristone to terminate pregnancy experience blood loss similar to that associated with a heavy menstruation, between 18 and 23 percent of women experience heavy bleeding (Raymond et al., 1991: 40–41). The cardiovascular risks associated with prostaglandin require scrupulous observance of contraindications. Additional clinical tests should be conducted to creatively and carefully pursue alternatives that reduce women's levels of risk. RU 486 is not a panacea. Some women's risk profiles will be minimized by suction aspiration.

Mifepristone may also confer important psychological benefits to patients. Postabortion trauma and abortion stress are typically plotted on two vectors: one measures the extent to which women feel their decisions are the product of their own choices as opposed to being determined by external factors, while the other axis describes gestational age or duration of pregnancy. Emotional or psychological harm is inversely related to self-reported reproductive choice. Interestingly enough, these same harms seem to increase with gestational age and to affect both providers and patients (Legge, 1985: 31). Mifepristone minimizes psychological or emotional harms to women by maximizing perceived reproductive control. Dr. Elisabeth Aubeny interviewed seventy-five women who terminated their pregnancies with this method. She indicates that almost every woman expressed satisfaction with her choice and emphasized her own responsibility for the termination of her pregnancy. She writes,

> Instead of being passive as they are in vacuum aspiration, they manage their own abortions. By taking the tablet, the woman acts to trigger the process and supervises evacuation at home. In the vacuum technique a doctor is in sole control. A woman can be virtually absent if she chooses general anesthesia. But RU 486 fits the needs of responsible patients who can cope by themselves, as many women want to do. (Lader, 1991: 54)

Women indicate that unlike other methods of abortion, mifepristone is not traumatic, offers no intrusion on the integrity of the body, and generally enhances the quality of their experience by liberating them from institutional constraints and the medicalization of reproductive choice (Lader, 1991: 53–55).

Mifepristone also minimizes psychological and emotional stress by allowing women to implement their decisions to terminate their pregnancies without any undue delays. Suction curettage is less reliable in the first six weeks of pregnancy when the embryo is small and can easily be missed. Consequently, hospitals and clinics generally urge their clients to postpone a suction curettage until after eight weeks of pregnancy (Lader, 1991: 57). As an abortifacient, RU 486 can be used as soon as pregnancy can be reliably confirmed. As a contragestive, it can be used to induce menstruation.

To complete the discussions of psychological and emotional stress associated with abortion, two additional dimensions must be added. First, although 69 percent of the patients in one study terminated their pregnancies within four hours of the administration of prostaglandin, they also waited between forty and fifty-two hours from the administration of mifepristone for these abortions to occur (Silvestre et al., 1990). Researchers and prospective recipients will have to consider the psychological and emotional ramifications of this aspect of treatment and compare them with aspiration abortions, which terminate pregnancies in a matter of minutes.

RU 486 has also been promoted for its ability to "guarantee the right to privacy by placing abortion in a doctor's office, with no one but the woman and her doctor aware of the procedure" (Lader, 1991: 14). This is an important claim as American women exercising their constitutional rights to pregnancy termination have increasingly been subjected to physical violence, public abuse, and shame. With RU 486, abortion need no longer be a public trauma for women, but could again be a privately negotiated reproductive decision. However, for these hopes to be fulfilled, RU 486-induced abortions must move beyond reproductive clinics and a few private offices that can be selectively targeted by antichoice forces. While professional response to this form of abortion has been very favorable, it remains to be seen whether access to this method would induce a greater number of health professionals to offer abortion services. We must also consider the limitations of privacy arguments when applied to RU 486. This drug does not offer women a nonmedicalized termination option. Mifepristone and prostaglandin require close professional supervision. Risks and contraindications of these drugs present reasonable impediments to their over-the-counter distribution. Their use may also be associated with more visits to health care providers than aspiration abortions.

When health care providers and patients consider RU 486's contragestive function, they can more credibly claim that there are no comparably safe methods of treatment. Many physicians and patients argue that IUDs present an unacceptable risk-benefit profile. Most women using IUDs experience adverse changes in their menstrual cycles: menses last longer, are heavier, and are accompanied by more severe and prolonged menstrual cramps (Knight and Callahan, 1989: 156). IUDs subject women to a tenfold increase in their risk of ectopic pregnancy (Knight and Callahan, 1989: 157). A quarter of all pregnancies that occur while an IUD is in place become septic. This results in uterine infection and high fever, and can produce systemic infection and death (Knight and Callahan, 1989: 158). Use of an IUD subjects women to a fivefold increase in their risk of contracting pelvic inflammatory disease (PID), which can be life-threatening (Knight and Callahan, 1989: 159–60). Other contragestives, including diethylstilbestrol (DES), produce intense nausea, vomiting, headaches, and breast tenderness. Antiestrogens can result in a woman taking an unsafe dosage of steroids (Knight and Callahan, 1989: 166–69). Mifepristone may offer the most favorable risk-benefit profile to many women. However, additional and long-term clinical testing may be required before women and their doctors can be assured of the reliability of this relative risk assessment.

Responsibility

The second type of argument that can be formulated supporting physicians' and patients' entitlements to obtain and use mifepristone draws on notions of moral responsibility for choices and treatments. These arguments affirm health professionals' obligations to sustain and promote patients' responsibility for treatment decisions and health maintenance. In reproductive medicine, this involves acting as facilitators for women, encouraging them to function as effective regulators of their own fertility.

Abortion opponents fought the introduction of RU 486 to the United States on the grounds that it would result in an explosive increase in the number of abortions and discourage effective and sustained use of contraceptives. As David Neff wrote, "Removing early-term abortions from the clinic to the boudoir would make the abortion option seem just too easy" (Neff, 1988: 16). Others suggest that the drug's ease and availability might discourage critical self-reflection about reproduction by making abortion "as easy as taking two aspirin" (Greenhouse, 1989: E 18).

There is an important punitive underpinning to these arguments that reveals fundamentalists' perception of abortion as a sexual crime. The pain, stigma, terrorization, and profound stress that American women currently face in their efforts to obtain an abortion represent consciously inflicted punishments for "inappropriate" or unsanctioned female sexuality (McDonnell, 1984: ii–iii). Kathleen McDonnell explores similar dimensions of conservative abortion statutes writing,

> The "exceptions" that exist (in parental consent laws as well as in other abortion legislation) for cases of rape and incest can only be rationalized within an understanding of unwanted pregnancy as the female wages of sin. Only in those rare cases where women clearly do not control sex, therefore, can abortion be allowed. The right's true moral position lies in restricting female ability to willingly initiate sex without severe, punitive consequences. Getting pregnant still means getting caught. And getting caught still means having to pay. (McDonnell, 1984: xi–xii)

Although we should reject conservatives' punitive reproductive agenda, we ought to take their charges about RU 486 seriously.

Thoughtful physicians who reflect on medicine's painful history of paternalism and authoritarianism should be strongly motivated to avoid limiting patients' autonomy and personal responsibility for health and health care. Will RU 486 erode effective reproductive deliberation and choice? Will it exponentially increase "fetal wastage"?

Available data from France and the United States indicate that conservatives' fears are ungrounded. The number of abortions in France has hardly risen since 1982 when the French social security system began to cover most abortion costs. In 1986, according to the ministry of health there were 166,797 abortions performed in France. In 1988, after RU 486 was approved for national use, there were 162,598 abortions performed (Lader, 1991: 56). French women argue that they are indeed fully conscious of termination when using mifepristone. Rather than discouraging full reflection and careful choice, RU 486 may facilitate them, for RU 486 enhances women's responsibility and control of abortion. Women help implement their choice themselves and monitor the effects of their choice in their homes (Lader, 1991: 53). Women who flee or seek to lessen their responsibility for abortion tend to be dissatisfied with RU 486. Dr. Elisabeth Aubeny, speaking of her work at Broussais Hospital, described this kind of patient reaction to RU 486. One woman indicated, "You see everything that takes place and that's difficult." Another concluded, "I would have preferred the doctor to have taken complete charge of everything." However, women who want to exercise reproductive autonomy express their profound appreciation for RU 486. An American who obtained RU 486 in a test program at USC described her experience,

> I heard about RU 486 through friends. I wasn't worried about bleeding—I had faith in my body. I took the pill on a Tuesday and started spotting a little. I had the prostaglandin shot on Friday and rested about forty-five minutes. There was only mild cramping and nausea. My husband drove me home. It was just heavy bleeding for three days like a miscarriage, tapering off in a week or so. I couldn't see any tissue or solid matter. What I liked was taking care of myself, not being in the hands of doctors. It brought a sense of knowledge and control, a positive existential experience. (Lader, 1991: 54)

Professional Privilege

The third type of argument supporting physicians' and patients' entitlements to obtain and use mifepristone utilizes the concept of professional privilege. These arguments assert that physicians' unique obligation and entitlement to determine what constitutes adequate medical care should be restricted only when exercise of this privilege offers clear threat to patients' health or other interests.[6] As an abortifacient, RU 486 is reliable and safe for most women. Because mifepristone obviates important categories of medical risk, it should be made available for informed and willing providers and patients. As the California Medical Association argued, mifepristone allows physicians to act in accordance with a basic medical norm: surgical procedures should be avoided when equally effective, noninvasive means are available (Lader, 1991: 113). Mifepristone also offers significant hope of amelioration of some serious medical problems, including Cushing's syndrome, meningioma, breast cancer, and AIDS. For this reason alone, American scientists have argued that it ought to be made immediately available for study in the "crisis constituency." Patients with limited life expectancy or serious compromise to their quality of life whose medical needs are unrelated to abortion or contraception ought to be able to utilize this important new drug (Regelson et al., 1990: 1027).

Denial of access to RU 486 in a context of legal abortion represents an unnecessary and unwarranted intrusion into medical practice, impeding physicians' attempts to provide efficacious medical care. It violates professional obligations by requiring physicians to subject some of their patients to higher levels of medical risk and psychological harm without clear evidence that the intrusion is warranted to protect these patients' interests or health. Denial of access also threatens the adequacy of medical decision making by shifting determinations of what constitutes appropriate medical care away from the medical community and prospective patients to political pressure groups. However, when these groups make health care recommendations based on alternative and perhaps even professionally suppressed readings of the medical risks associated with an intervention, we should pause and give their medical data a full and careful professional and public hearing.

The fundamentalist and extremely conservative political groups that challenge RU 486 have not done so on medical grounds.[7] Some feminists also oppose RU 486, arguing that "there is no chemical, least of all the RU 486/PG-containing chemical cocktail, which is a viable alternative to conventional abortion" (Raymond et al., 1991: 106). They suspect professional minimization of specific side effects including pain, diarrhea, cramping, and nausea. They fear inadequate professional response to cardiovascular accidents associated with prostaglandins. These concerns merit careful and sustained professional and public attention and extended clinical study. However, analysis requires both open dialogue and multicenter, longitudinal studies of the drug's various uses. This would require removal of existing barriers to sustained, appropriate, and effective clinical research. Women and seriously ill patients must not be sacrificed to religious fundamentalism and political or professional expediency. Patients and their physicians must be free to choose effective modes of treatment without undue intervention by political pressure groups, corporations, or the state. This is a battle for scientific integrity, professional autonomy, reproductive freedom, and the right to innovative medical care. If zealotry wins the day, all drugs with abortive or contraceptive potential that have other important applications can also be jeopardized (Regelson et al., 1990: 1027).

Access to RU 486: Corporate Responsibility and the Limits of Appropriate Intervention

If you were to ask a consumer, health care provider, or business executive whether a pharmaceutical company has a moral obligation to market a safe, clinically effective, innovative drug that it has developed, most would answer in the affirmative. If you were to indicate that the drug in question is an abortifacient, the situation would immediately become more complex. At least four different arguments could be formulated regarding corporations' social responsibilities to commercially distribute abortifacients.[8] The first claims that if corporations are to act in a socially responsible manner, they must carefully calculate and review a product's net social utility (Davis, 1986: 157). A second, related argument describes corporations' social responsibility in terms of their obligations to produce and distribute goods and services that sustain and enhance human existence (Camenisch, 1986: 149). The third argument takes the narrowest possible sense of corporate social responsibility and asserts that it can only be expressed in terms of obligations to maximize profit. The fourth argument articulates a relationship between corporate and professional obligations. It asserts that corporations that manufacture prescription drugs have special duties to physicians as their immediate constituency. If warranted claims about Roussel-Uclaf's and Hoechst's responsibilities to market RU 486 are to be made, each of these arguments will have to be examined in turn.

Social Responsibility as Net Social Utility

If blastocysts, embryos, or fetuses were persons or if Roussel and Hoechst were to view these entities as persons, one might readily understand a corporate decision not to develop, produce, or market an abortifacient. The Alan Guttmacher Institute has claimed that the total range of abortions performed annually is between 40 and 60 million. If the French preference patterns were mirrored globally, that would suggest that RU 486 could produce between 13 and 20 million abortions annually. Careful and complete calculations of net social utility would include the number of lives potentially saved through the drug's secondary effects. The welfare and interests of those whose symptoms and disease states would be ameliorated by the drug would also have to be weighed. If abortions were viewed by Roussel and Hoechst as deaths of persons, then the sheer number that could be associated with their product, when coupled with the prematurity and speculative nature of talk of lives saved through mifepristone's broad range of clinical applications, would support the conclusion that RU 486 has a deleterious net social effect.

However, this position cannot credibly be ascribed to Roussel or Hoechst. These corporations are willing to market RU 486 as an abortifacient in France, Great Britain, and other European countries. This suggests that they do not define or describe abortion in terms of a culpable death of persons. Instead, it suggests that they view abortion as either a legitimate medical treatment or a potentially appropriate personal reproductive choice. Some might argue that Hoechst and Roussel were not free to develop a socially responsible corporate policy on abortion. They would point to the French government's 36.25 percent interest in Roussel and its alleged threat to use a 1968 law to revoke and reassign Roussel's license to the drug as evidence of governmental coercion restricting exercise of corporate social responsibility. While this argument offers some explanation of the corporations' decisions to market the drug in France, it cannot be successfully applied to their uncoerced decision to market RU 486 in other European countries. Further, it is not clear that such an argument adequately supports the resolution to market the drug in France.

If Roussel and Hoechst defined abortion in terms of a serious and morally culpable killing of persons, then they had two morally preferable options that they failed to pursue. If abortion is a serious moral crime, Roussel could have limited corporate responsibility for abortions by attempting to buy out the French government. If such a buyout had been successful, Roussel could have subsequently attempted to protect its patent rights and refused absolutely to market the drug anywhere. As providers are free to prescribe or utilize a drug for a range of different objectives, absolute refusal to market the drug might be required to prevent Roussel from being directly or indirectly responsible for any abortions.

Given the wide discussion of the drug's function and clinical effectiveness and other companies or groups' willingness and ability to manufacture generics or "clones," Roussel and Hoechst would not be able effectively and completely to limit access to mifepristone by maintaining the integrity of their patent rights. Neither could they "unmake" the drug. The technology is available to be copied or simulated. However, their decision to withdraw the drug could have delayed, by several years, millions of patients' access to such a product (MacFarquhar, 1989: 54). In this environment, the sound option for a corporation with moral objections to abortion would be to remove itself from the abortifacient business. If state law mandated transfer of the corporation's patent to another institution or entity, Roussel and Hoechst could have sought legal remedies and relief. If a corporation halted research and development on any future abortifacients and exhausted legal options to preclude access to its product, it would have done all it reasonably could once the product was developed to prevent it from being used for abortions.

Again, this situation does not seem to obtain with Roussel and Hoechst. There is no evidence that they attempted to buy out the French government. Similarly, they neither offered legal challenge to the 1968 law nor attempted to "call Evin's bluff." They did not permit the French government to reassign their patent rights to the product. Groups in the United States have approached Roussel and Hoechst, attempting to obtain a license to distribute the drug or to purchase manufacturing rights. All attempts to transfer ownership of RU 486 have been refused. Decisions made by Roussel and Hoechst to retain their rights and market the drug in France, Great Britain, and other European countries suggest a corporate willingness to profit by abortion. This in turn suggests that alleged corporate reluctance to market the product in France and corporate refusals to do so in the United States are strategies to minimize exposure to financial risk by potential boycott rather than refusals to become implicated in morally culpable killings (Raymond et al., 1991: 21).

Some might argue that Roussel's culpability for abortion is unavoidable given its role in the research and development of the drug. RU

486 was developed in Roussel laboratories, where corporate policy tolerated and sustained this research. Is Roussel not responsible then for any deleterious social effects? The best way to resolve this question is to recognize that reasonable entities and individuals can come to divergent good-faith calculations of the social utility of abortifacients. Roussel's early activities suggest a corporate policy of toleration toward abortion, perhaps ultimately resting on women's privacy or autonomy rights. The corporate policy emerging at Hoechst was incompatible with Roussel's position. When a unified intercorporate abortion policy emerged, it seemed to be antiabortion. Roussel and Hoechst could well be faulted for failing to develop a single, coherent reproductive policy prior to the introduction of one of their most controversial products. They could also be blamed for failing to demonstrate the courage of any alleged corporate moral convictions by authorizing the distribution of RU 486.

The most plausible explanation of corporate behavior, however, suggests that this was not a thoroughly considered policy to which both corporations were committed. Had there been genuine corporate moral aversion to abortion, Roussel and Hoechst would have tried to remove the drug from the market completely or minimize its potential distribution. If abortion is not a morally culpable killing of persons or if fetal rights and interests can be subordinated to other rights and claims, then an argument for the net social utility of RU 486 could readily be made. The medical and psychological benefits it offers many women, its potential promotion of their privacy rights, and its enhancement of their reproductive responsibility would all urge Roussel and Hoechst to support and extend clinical testing and use.

This argument would be strengthened by the substantial promise the drug shows as a contraceptive and its status as a safe and effective contragestive. Discussion of the drug's potential benefits in amelioration of a broad range of disease processes and disorders would further enhance the argument for extensive clinical testing. To these claims of patient benefit, one would have to add the professionally based arguments discussed in detail in the third section of this paper. Social utility would be furthered by affirming health professionals' obligations to provide patients with the safest, most effective mode of medical treatment. Social utility would be promoted by defending physicians' unique obligation and entitlement to determine what constitutes adequate medical care and restricting this privilege only when its exercise offers clear threat to patients' health or other interests. Finally, social utility would be enhanced by encouraging physicians to sustain and promote patients' responsibility for treatment decisions and health maintenance.

If boycotts and controversy were considered from the vantage point of social utility rather than the narrower frame of corporate interests, available data would support broad distribution of the drug. Those who might protest its availability or adopt, support, and sustain an antiabortion boycott of Roussel or Hoechst products represent a small but vocal minority in American public opinion. A Louis Harris poll conducted in 1988 showed that 59 percent of Americans polled supported U.S. distribution of RU 486 (Lader, 1991: 111). Corporate executives attempting to assess the social utility of American distribution of RU 486 would also have to weigh the considerable controversy associated with previous decisions not to admit the drug to the U.S. market. Some feminists, health care providers, and abortion-rights advocates have all threatened a boycott of Hoechst and Roussel products if RU 486 continues to be withheld. A boycott of pharmaceuticals by these groups would be more disruptive of social utility than a boycott by nonprofessional members of the extreme right. The only other group likely to mount an effective campaign and boycott would be Catholic hospitals in the United States. These groups might also experience external pressure to limit the scope or duration of any boycott, as it could be argued that they would be subordinating the medical welfare and liberties of a diverse class of patients in an effort to obtain universal application of their own religious beliefs.

Corporate Social Responsibility and the Quality of Life

A second, related argument could be formulated regarding corporate obligations to distribute abortifacients. This argument describes corporations' social responsibility in terms of obligations to produce and distribute goods and services that sustain and enhance human existence (Camenisch, 1986: 149). Health care products are more important than many other corporate commodities as they have a more direct and immediate relationship to sustaining and enhancing the quality of human life. A highly effective, safe, novel drug would rank highly in any prioritized list of health care products. A corporation producing a safe pharmaceutical innovation with the wide range of applicability of RU 486 would seem to have a moral obligation based in this view of social responsibility to pursue aggressively the broadest, clinically warranted distribution of its product.

If safe and clinically efficacious drugs improve the quality and length of human life, and corporations have responsibilities to sustain and enhance human existence, pharmaceutical corporations would have a moral responsibility to maintain a corporate environment that is conducive to sound pharmaceutical research. If staff scientists develop a safe, highly effective drug that serves an important medical need and the corporation chooses to limit or prohibit distribution of this product, effective pharmaceutical and clinical research would be repressed. This could reduce or destroy the morale of the scientific staff. It could lessen their commitment to effective research and it could ultimately deprive the corporation of the expertise it requires to fulfill its social obligations.

Roussel and Hoechst also have reasons to refuse to market RU 486 that rest on corporate social responsibility to protect and enhance human existence. If their concern with Hoechst's corporate history and ties to I. G. Farben are more than worries about corporate image, this particular corporation might have compelling reasons not to be associated with any product responsible for human deaths. Regardless of views of its moral propriety, an abortifacient terminates human fetal life. Given Hoechst's corporate history and the structure and effects of Nazi ideology, this corporation could have strong moral reasons to find contemporary discussions of the conditions of moral or legal personhood and the juridical or moral foundations of rights to life to be insufficient bases for the formation of corporate reproductive policy. If the absence of coercion and the importance of women's reproductive autonomy and responsibility do not prove to be morally compelling arguments from the corporation's point of view, we could expect to see corporate decisions to implement restrictive strategies identical to those described in the preceding subsection.

An additional option would be available. Hoechst could sell its interests in Roussel. As it is Hoechst's corporate history and past corporate culpability that is at issue, it might choose to limit its subsequent responsibility by selling off the offending company. This might preserve corporate moral interests while respecting the entitlements of women to reproductive autonomy and choice. If Hoechst subsequently wanted to implement antiabortion corporate policies or to use its philanthropic or research and development resources to encourage or provide nonlethal options to problem pregnancies, it would be free to do so. However, as was the case with the restrictive policies previously described, Hoechst has shown no inclination to sell its interests in its profitable subsidiary, Roussel. This again undermines the strength and integrity of this version of the argument for corporate social responsibility.

Corporate Social Responsibility and Profit

If concerns with maximizing corporate profit exhaust legitimate expressions of corporate social responsibility (Friedman, 1986: 144), then two options are available to Roussel and Hoechst executives. If responsible management requires minimization of potential financial risk, then Hoechst and Roussel should not only extract themselves from the research and development, production, and distribution of abortifacients, but should also abandon any work with contraceptives. Drug companies legitimately fear both potential loss of sales and damage to their reputation as purveyors of high-quality health products. Contraceptives and abortifacients subject companies to boycotts that threaten both revenue and reputation.[9] However, mifepristone may be one of the most profitable drugs ever to suffer corporate restrictions on its availability. It could significantly improve Roussel's and Hoechst's profitability. The Population Crisis Committee has stated that RU 486 could become one of only a handful of billion-dollar drugs (MacFarquhar, 1989: 54). If the drug were used for even a third of the total number of abortions performed annually, it would generate well over a billion dollars in revenue each year.[10]

If potential risk to Hoechst's estimated annual revenue of $20 billion is not offset by estimated annual returns of $1 billion (MacFarquhar, 1989: 54), then Hoechst and Roussel again should have tenaciously pursued the restrictive strategies described above. If the culpability of intentional fetal death is the banner under which the far right marches, then one might expect that the fiscally conservative characterization of corporate social responsibility would have precluded all efforts to market the drug. Conservatives are no less likely to rue the termination of French blastocysts on moral grounds than they would American ones. Expansion of the market beyond France should have been bitterly contested as it could only increase the corporations' exposure to boycott and other financial threats.

If Roussel and Hoechst were going to articulate a moral argument for restriction based on a fiscally conservative characterization of corporate social responsibility, then they should have expanded their policies to include contraceptives. These products also prompt consistent and sustained boycotts by religious fundamentalists and extreme conservatives. Indeed, the decisions by nineteen other corporations to limit their potential financial exposure by withdrawing completely from research, development, and manufacture of contraceptives in the United States speaks to the pervasiveness and seriousness of corporate assessments of this source of risk (Lader, 1991: 109). Roussel and Hoechst have demonstrated no such willingness to expand their restrictions.

On the other hand, if responsibility requires a reasoned and measured response to financial risk, and if a $1 billion increase in annual revenue is too substantial to forgo, one might expect Roussel and Hoechst to pursue broad international distribution of the drug. These corporations might attempt to minimize the risk of effective boycott by negotiating with institutions that provide abortion services or support professionals' entitlements to provide a full range of legal services to clients who wish to utilize them. Hoechst and Roussel could negotiate with professional organizations. The American Medical Association and the California Medical Association have already expressed their support for access to the drug. Corporate executives must also realize that failure to enter specific national markets, particularly that of the United States, exposes them to substantially increased financial risks associated with a sustained professional boycott of their products.

Corporate Social Responsibility and the Professional Constituency

The fourth and final argument regarding corporate obligations to distribute abortifacients or contragestives commercially expresses a relationship between corporate and professional obligations. It asserts that corporations that manufacture prescription drugs have special duties to physicians as their immediate constituency. When corporations fail to respond to the legitimate requests of this constituency, they can be held accountable (Benoit, 1989: 35).

Roussel and Hoechst have received petitions and requests to lift distribution restrictions on RU 486 to the United States from our most powerful and prestigious medical organizations. Physicians from all over the world have also requested or demanded access to RU 486 in order to fulfill their professional obligations to their patients. Roussel and Hoechst were petitioned by physicians attending the World Congress of Obstetrics and Gynecology (Palca, 1989: 1320). The California Medical Association voted "overwhelmingly" for the introduction of RU 486 to the American market. The same question was unanimously supported by the American Medical Association's House of Delegates

(Lader, 1991: 113) A campaign to introduce RU 486 to the United States was cosponsored by the American College of Obstetricians and Gynecologists (Lader, 1991: 111). It is hard to imagine more compelling, pervasive, or sustained professional requests being made to any pharmaceutical company.

Roussel and Hoechst have violated their corporate social responsibilities by ignoring these medically well-founded requests. If these corporations had good reasons to doubt the solidity of professional reasoning or the reliability of professional claims of medical and psychological benefit, they might appropriately reject professional requests. Corporations could deny professionals' access to the drug in order to protect the interests of their other constituency: potential patients. Roussel and Hoechst cannot effectively utilize this line of argument. They have no reason to believe that the drug presents a hazard to patients' medical interests or well-being as long as medical contraindications to its use are observed. Indeed, there are significant medical and psychological reasons to prefer RU 486 in some patient populations to other forms of abortion. The contraceptive potential of the drug and its wide range of secondary applications support professionals' arguments for access to the drug. At the very least, patients' interests would ultimately be promoted through expansion of longitudinal clinical trials. Finally, if these corporations thought that their product posed substantial risk to patients' lives or health, they would be morally compelled to remove it from all markets. Roussel's and Hoechst's willingness to market the drug in Europe suggests that they do not believe it presents a substantial threat of harm to patients' lives, health, or well-being.

Conclusion

This paper has explored the foundations and tested the strength of claims to enhanced clinical investigation, access, and use of RU 486. These claims are warranted by arguments from medical benefit. RU 486 is an innovative mode of treatment that offers an improved risk profile for many patients. It may confer important psychological benefits to women terminating pregnancies. RU 486 holds out the promise of broader and less caustic access to abortion services that enhances patient autonomy and privacy. Claims to extended access to and use of RU 486 were also justified through careful examination of arguments affirming health professionals' obligations to promote patients' responsibility for treatment decisions and health maintenance. Arguments from professional privilege were shown to support removal of existing barriers to appropriate and effective clinical research on RU 486. Concerns about mifepristone's comparative risk-benefit profile as an abortifacient support sustained professional and public attention to the drug and scrupulous clinical study rather than a ban.

Four arguments from corporate social responsibility were presented that analyzed Hoechst's and Roussel-Uclaf's moral obligations to distribute RU 486 commercially. The first argument focused on net social utility. The second, which is related to the first, spoke in terms of obligations to produce and distribute goods and services that sustain and enhance human existence. The third argument limited concerns of social responsibility to the maximizaton of corporate profit. And the fourth spoke of an obligation to support a professional constitutency. In each case, the argument upheld the view that Roussel-Uclaf and Hoechst have moral obligations to extend commercial distribution of mifepristone. Hoechst's and Roussel-Uclaf 's corporate practices cannot be credibly presented as supporting product restriction in order to prevent or limit serious and morally culpable killing.

The fact that two such important pillars—professional ethics and corporate responsibility—defend enhanced clinical investigation, access, and use of RU 486 lends strength and depth to patients', health care providers', and activists' demands for the drug. RU 486 is neither a panacea nor a "demon drug." Instead it represents another link in a chain of medical technology requiring careful, rational reflection if it is to be used wisely and well.

Notes

1. Mifepristone is the generic name of the chemical developed by Roussel-Uclaf.

2. Lader reports that Roussel's managing committee voted three to two for the withdrawal (Lader, 1991: 50). MacFarquhar suggests that Roussel researchers were frustrated by Hoechst's corporate policy not to market abortifacients. One researcher states, in apparent reference to the contradiction between the company's willingness to research and develop an abortifacient and its reluctance to market it, "What we need is a company psychiatrist" (MacFarquhar, 1989: 54).

3. The International Right to Life Federation called for a boycott in March of 1989 of Groupe Roussel-Uclaf and Hoechst A. G. The Canadian affiliate of this group broadened its threatened boycott to include all French products.

Right-to-life groups in this country have threatened to boycott the products of any company that even seeks FDA approval for the drug (Noah, 1990: C 19).

4. The Bush administration even attempted to limit RU 486 research conducted by the World Health Organization (WHO). Assistant Secretary of State John R. Bolton wrote a letter to Dr. Hiroshi Nakajima, WHO Director General, requesting information on the organization's projects using RU 486 and its policies governing distribution of the drug. The letter required WHO to determine whether any American funds were going to promote the use of RU 486, and demanded copies of any contracts the organization made with Groupe Roussel-Uclaf (Altman, 1991: Y 10). While WHO was willing to allay the Department of State's fears that it would become an aggressive promoter of the drug, it would not grant its request for contract review. Apparently, this pressure from the Department of State was prompted by private political groups and a conservative congressman, Christopher H. Smith of New Jersey. Reproductive biologists subsequently expressed concern that the Department of State's inquiry offered a threat to WHO's RU 486 research program, which represents 1.7 percent of the organization's $20.7 million annual budget for human reproduction programs (Altman, 1991: Y 10).

5. The World Health Organization has tested a 200 mg. dose that has proved to be both safe and effective (Lader, 1991: 134).

6. A physician who advised a pregnant patient to use diethylstilbestrol (DES) in the mid to late 1970s as a prophylactic against spontaneous abortion and premature labor could have had his or her treatment decisions legitimately overruled on these grounds. Knight and Callahan indicate that numerous reports appeared in the mid-1970s suggesting that the daughters of pregnant women using DES may have suffered various teratogenic effects (Knight and Callahan, 1989: 247). If these pregnant women had strong interests in maintaining the life and health of these fetuses, which they presumably did, seeking treatment to prevent premature labor and miscarriage, then their interests were harmed by the administration of these drugs. Prospective parents also have interests in protecting the health of the fetuses they expect to carry to term as they may be called upon to provide medical support and meet the special care needs of sick or disabled offspring.

7. Conservatives' exclusive interest is to prosecute their religious and moral beliefs. They do not limit their interventions to arguably safe abortifacients but attempt to prohibit access to very safe or risk-free contraceptives (Lader, 1991: 96). Contraceptive research and marketing have already suffered dramatically from governmental neglect and corporate fear of fundamentalists' ire. In 1970, twenty major companies were active in American contraceptive research and development. Only one remains today (Lader, 1991: 109).

8. The arguments in this section do not presume that corporations are moral persons in the fullest possible sense described by Peter French (French, 1988: 265). Such a strong and metaphysically unwarranted position is not a necessary condition for holding corporations responsible for their actions. I agree with the thesis carefully articulated by Larry May.

For corporate behavior to be assessed in moral terms, there must be intentional behavior which can be attributed to the corporation, but it need not be shown that the corporation is a moral entity in its own right. In order to show that intentions can be attributed in a limited sense to the corporation it is sufficient to show that the members of a corporation jointly engaged in purposive conduct. In addition, this purposiveness must be explained in terms of the structure of the corporation and cannot be reduced to the aggregated intentions of the individuals who compose the corporation. (May, 1987: 65)

May continues, arguing that corporate decision procedures combine and change the intentional states of human members of the organization and produce purposive corporate behavior (May, 1987: 65).

9. Hoechst and Roussel are not the only companies to limit their own sales or withdraw completely from markets that could taint corporate image or reduce general sales. Upjohn discontinued research on contraceptives some time ago, and after a boycott of its prostaglandins by the National Right to Life Committee, it withdrew them from the general market and restricted their use to a small number of hospitals (Lader, 1991: 106). Hoechst, fearing both White House opposition and conservative boycott, has demurred entering the U.S. market with RU 486. Hoechst enjoys $4 billion in annual sales in the United States (MacFarquhar, 1989: 54). It has decided to pursue safer, more stable markets in Europe (Lader, 1991: 108).

10. This is based on annual abortion estimates from the Alan Guttmacher Institute and a predicted consumer cost of $100 for the drug (Benoit, 1989: 35).

References

Altman, Lawrence K. 1991. "U.S. Quizzes World Health Organization on Abortion Pill Research." *New York Times*, 7 April, Y 10.

Baulieu, Etienne-Emile. 1989. "Contragestion and Other Clinical Applications of RU 486, an Antiprogesterone at the Receptor." *Science* 245, 1351–57.

Baulieu, Etienne-Emile. 1989b. "RU–486 as an Antiprogesterone Steroid: From Receptor to Contragestion and Beyond." *Journal of the American Medical Association* 262, No. 13, 1808–14.

Benoit, Ellen. 1989. "Why Nobody Wants $1 Billion: How a Small Band Has Intimidated Some of the World's Biggest Companies." *Financial World* 158, June 27, 34–35.

Camenisch, Paul. 1986. "Business Ethics: On Getting to the Heart of the Matter." In *Moral Issues in Business*. 3rd ed. Ed. Vincent Barry. Belmont, Calif.: Wadsworth, 148–55.

Cherfas, Jeremy. 1989. "Stopping the Progress of Pregnancy." *Science* 245, 1320.

Davis, Keith. 1986. "Five Propositions for Social Responsibility." In *Moral Issues in Business*. 3rd ed. Ed. Vincent Barry. Belmont, Calif.: Wadsworth, 155–60.

Dixon, Kathleen Marie. 1991. "Ethical Issues in Pediatric Populations." In *Tracheal Reconstruction in Infancy*. Ed. Thom E. Lobe. Philadelphia: W. B. Saunders, 161–75.

Eiseman, Ben. 1980. *What Are My Chances? What You Need to Know about the Surgical and Medical Odds of Getting Well*. Philadelphia: W. B. Saunders.

Forrest, Jacqueline Darroch. 1988. "The Delivery of Family Planning Services in the United States." *Family Planning Perspectives* 20, No. 2, 88–95.

French, Peter. 1988. "Corporate Moral Agency." In *Ethical Issues in Professional Life*. Ed. Joan C. Callahan. New York: Oxford University Press, 265–69.

Friedman, Milton. 1986. "The Social Responsibility of Business is to Increase Its Profits." In *Moral Issues in Business*. 3rd ed. Ed. Vincent Barry. Belmont, Calif.: Wadsworth, 144–48.

Greenhouse, Steven. 1989. "Fears Confine Abortion Pill to France." *New York Times*, 3 March, E 18.

Gupta, Janesh K., and Nicholas Johnson. 1990. "Effect of Mifepristone on Dilatation of the Pregnant and Non-Pregnant Cervix." *The Lancet* 335, 1238–39.

Hatcher, Robert A., et al. 1990. *Contraceptive Technology: 1990–1992*. 15th rev. ed. New York: Irvington Publishers.

Hilts, Philip J. 1992. "Abortion Pill's Sale Unlikely Soon Despite Change of Administration." *New York Times*, 15 November, A 38.

Knight, James W., and Joan C. Callahan. 1989. *Preventing Birth: Contemporary Methods and Related Moral Controversy*. Salt Lake City: University of Utah Press.

Lader, Lawrence. 1991. *RU 486: The Pill That Could End the Abortion Wars and Why American Women Don't Have It*. Reading, Mass.: Addison-Wesley.

Legge, Jerome S., Jr. 1985. *Abortion Policy: An Evaluation of the Consequences for Maternal and Infant Health*. Albany: State University of New York Press.

MacFarquhar, Emily. 1989. "The Case of the Reluctant Drug Maker: An Abortion Pill that's Not for Sale." *U.S. News and World Report*, 23 January, 54.

May, Larry. 1987. *The Morality of Groups*. Notre Dame: University of Notre Dame Press.

McDonnell, Kathleen. 1984. *Not an Easy Choice: A Feminist Reexamines Abortion*. Boston: South End Press.

Neff, David. 1988. "The Human Pesticide: Controversial Abortion Pills Are a Form of Chemical Warfare Against Our Own Species." *Christianity Today* 32, 16–17.

Noah, Timothy. 1990. "Import Curbs Said to Stall Research on Abortion Pill." *Wall Street Journal*, 20 November, C 19.

Palca, Joseph. 1989. "The Pill of Choice?" *Science* 245, 1319–23.

Raymond, Janice G., Renate Klien, and Lynette J. Dumble. 1991. *RU 486: Misconceptions, Myths and Morals*. Cambridge, Mass.: Institute on Women and Technology.

Regelson, William, Roger Loria, and Mohammed Kalimi. 1990. "Beyond 'Abortion': RU-486 and the Needs of the Crisis Constituency." *Journal of the American Medical Association* 264, No. 8, 1026–27.

Silvestre, Louise, et al. 1990. "Voluntary Interruption of Pregnancy with Mifepristone (RU 486) and a Prostaglandin Analogue." *New England Journal of Medicine* 322, 645–48.

Toner, Robin. 1993. "Clinton Orders Reversal of Abortion Restrictions Left by Reagan and Bush." *New York Times*, 23 January, A 1.

Veatch, Robert M. 1987. *The Patient as Partner*. Bloomington: Indiana University Press.

10

Human Genetic Engineering and the Ethics of Knowledge

Robert Wachbroit

"Discoveries in human genetic engineering will have an enormous impact, dramatically changing our lives." That sentence, although perhaps a bit too wordy to be an actual headline, captures well the significance often attributed to human genetic engineering. Unfortunately, some of this significance can be lost or misunderstood because remarks of this sort are common to every branch of science. Indeed, they are familiar in the social history of science. We need only think back to the 1940s and 1950s to find similar remarks made about atomic and nuclear physics. And, of course, in many cases these remarks are true; our lives have been dramatically changed because of discoveries in nuclear physics. Nevertheless, when we turn to the case of human genetic engineering, its profound impact will take a distinctive form.

Scientific discoveries typically affect us in two ways. The most obvious way is through the application of the discoveries through their associated technologies. The obvious impact of nuclear physics has been in its applications, specifically in military technologies and energy technologies. The second way discoveries can affect us is through a concern about risk.[1] The risks associated with the applications of discoveries, as well as with their establishment and testing, have become more and more a matter of social concern. It is now one of the standard costs considered when the acceptability of different technologies is debated. Again, nuclear technology can provide vivid illustrations of this point.

Human genetic engineering will certainly affect us in these two ways, through its applications and through its risks, and I will have more to say on those two aspects later. But it will also affect us deeply in a third way. The scientific discoveries themselves—independently of their applications or risks—will have a social significance. The knowledge that we will gain from these discoveries will alter how we see ourselves.

This is in sharp contrast to many other kinds of scientific discoveries. The Theory of Relativity, for example, revolutionized physics and many other areas of science, but its effect on nonscientists was for the most part confined to how the new physics was applied and, later, in the risks identified in those applications. The scientific discoveries themselves did not have a comparable social significance.

This paper is divided into two parts. I begin by describing the impact of human genetic engineering. After briefly describing the typical areas of concern regarding scientific developments, I look more carefully at what I have called the third area of concern, a concern about knowledge. Since scientific discoveries do not often raise such a concern, there has been little discussion about it, either in general or in particular. How will human genetic engineering change how we see ourselves? In the second part I raise the question of what this might mean for the responsibility of scientists. A common way of formulating the question of the responsibility of scientists is, "To what extent are scientists (morally) responsible for how their discoveries are used?" Does it make sense to ask whether scientists have a moral responsibility concerning the discoveries themselves?

The Discoveries of Genetic Engineering

Let me begin by describing some of the impact of human genetic engineering. Of the three areas of concern that I've mentioned— concerns about its applications, concerns about its risks, and concerns about what we will discover about ourselves—concerns about its risks are the easiest concerns to understand. They were also the most urgent concerns in the beginning.

When recombinant DNA techniques were first developed as tools for laboratory research, there was a great deal of anxiety about their safety and environmental risk. Critics described in lurid detail a "gruesome parade of horribles" that the new technologies might unleash: epidemics, ecological disasters, and "killer tomatoes." While some of the scenarios were not impossible, none of the possible disasters were unique to genetic engineering or biotechnology in general: the roster is much the same for the discharge of industrial wastes or toxic chemicals, the introduction of exotic species into new environments, and the more mundane run of medical research. Nor did there appear to be anything novel in evaluating biotechnological risks; as several commentators argued, genetic engineering does not require any special techniques for assessing overall risk.[2]

Nevertheless a moratorium, proposed by scientists, went into effect while these issues were discussed. Regulatory guidelines were soon proposed by the National Institutes of Health. And the Recombinant DNA Advisory Committee, or RAC, was formed to review and amend the guidelines when necessary.

When we turn to concerns over the application of human genetic engineering, the situation becomes much more complicated. As a medical tool, genetic engineering has great promise. Since many diseases have a significant genetic component, appropriate modifications of the genes of diseased people could become an effective cure for many diseases. The list of diseases would include not only rare disorders such as Lesch-Nyham disease but also common ones such as cancer and heart disease. Nevertheless, as a medical technology, genetic engineering raises the standard but important issues regarding the access, distribution, and priority of such treatments or services. It also raises special issues about obtaining informed consent for these procedures. A genetic modification may be done in such a way that the modification becomes inherited—so-called germline gene therapy. Germline therapy might seem to be appropriate if the disease is hereditary; not only could we be ridding the individual of the disease but we could also be ridding his or her possible progeny of the disease as well. But then, what becomes of the standard requirement of having the informed consent of those being treated? In the case of germline therapy, possible progeny would seem to be patients without a choice.

Human genetic engineering could also have nonmedical uses. Commentators have speculated about our being able to design people with certain traits insofar as these traits are genetically determined. We might find ourselves in a position where we have to decide, as one writer put it, what sort of people there should be.[3] This, of course, raises the specter of eugenics, but with important differences. First of all, the contrast between medical and nonmedical uses of genetic engineering recalls the distinction made early in this century between negative and positive eugenics, between correcting defects and creating enhancements. This distinction rests on a prior understanding of human health or normality. That understanding, and with it the distinction between correction and enhancement, is seriously challenged by discoveries in human genetic engineering, as I will try to suggest a little later. Second, eugenics, as traditionally understood, often referred to a set of policies that involve procedures such as forced sterilization, compulsory abortions, forced matings, etc., none of which need be part of human genetic engineering. Prospective parents may be able to choose not only when to have a child but also what kind of child to have.

There is a growing debate over what moral constraints should be placed on this new eugenics. Is it a matter of weighing the costs against the benefits in each case or are there special or intrinsic limits to genetic manipulation that we should respect? In any case, nearly everyone agrees that this new eugenics constitutes the most exciting or most disturbing application of human genetic engineering.

These two areas of concern—about risks and about applications—can easily overshadow the third area of concern over human genetic engineering: a concern about knowledge. And yet some of the most striking changes will come from this area. Through genetic engineering we will come to discover things that could profoundly affect us. This impact would not be a question of possible risks resulting from this knowledge or of possible applications of this knowledge. Its impact would be in how we see ourselves, an impact that, arguably, is morally significant. Since this area of concern is the least talked about and, possibly, the hardest to understand, let me turn to some examples to clarify what I have in mind.

Diagnoses without Abilities

The first kind of case I want to talk about concerns our increasing ability to diagnose disorders. As I noted earlier, many diseases have a distinctive genetic component. In many cases, the technology needed for identifying and detecting the genetic components of a disease will be in place well before we are able through gene therapy or any other sort of therapy to treat or cure that disease. For a growing list of diseases, we will be able to know whether someone has that disease, but we will not be able to do much to treat the disease.

Consider, for example, Huntington's disease. This is a disease that generally does not manifest itself until the individual is over thirty, at which time he or she suffers a rapid neurological deterioration ending in death. The disease is hereditary: the child of someone suffering from Huntington's disease has a 50 percent probability of having it as well. At the present time we can determine whether someone has Huntington's disease well before any symptoms would appear—we can identify the lethal gene—but we are not able to treat such individuals even with advance warning. We can know but we cannot do anything. Given this state of technology, many people who know that they have a 50 percent chance of having the disease nevertheless choose not to settle the matter definitely one way or the other. They would rather not know.

As unfortunate and frustrating as this situation may be, it might not appear to present any special problem. Knowledge, it might be argued, is a component of health care. People have a right to refuse treatment, and that should include a right to refuse to know. But this response oversimplifies the situation. When someone does not want to know whether he has an incurable, lethal disease, his desire may be more than that he doesn't want to know. He may want it not to be known. His desire not to know may be a desire that others not know about his condition as well.

This possibility might suggest that the proper way of viewing the matter isn't that of a patient's refusing treatment; the matter is one of privacy. A person's medical condition is a private matter. As long as it doesn't harm anyone, he can decide whether anyone knows about it or not. This response, however, does not quite fit the situation. A concern about privacy would be a concern about information becoming public. In this case, however, the patient doesn't want anyone to know, including himself. The patient's concern is not over the information becoming public; the concern is over the information becoming known, regardless of whether it is known publicly or privately.

We can make this point vivid by considering a case of identical twins, one of whose parents has Huntington's disease. Although each twin has a 50 percent probability of having the lethal gene, if one twin has the gene, then the probability is 100 percent that the other has it as well. Now suppose that one of the twins wants to know but the other twin does not want it to be known. They cannot both be satisfied. Here we have one person's presumed right to know pitted against another person's presumed right not to know.

This problem about knowledge—a problem about what to do with it—is fairly clear. What drives the problem is how knowledge can affect how we see ourselves. Nevertheless, this example may seem peculiar and temporary. It may seem peculiar because there are not that many diseases about which we can do nothing, even with advanced warning. It may seem temporary because our repertoire of therapies is increasing so that we might expect this list of diseases to shrink. Consequently, let me turn to an example that is broader and more systematic.

Refining the Normal

As we learn more and more about the genetic component (or genetic causal factors) of various diseases, there will in many cases be a shift to explaining diseases in terms of genetic factors. One of the features of this explanatory shift will be a corresponding reassessment of what constitutes normality or health. For example, as we learn more and more about the genetic components of heart disease, we may come increasingly to explain why someone has suffered a cardiac infarction in terms of his genetic constitution rather than in terms of his lifestyle or diet. And the conception of a person with a normal or healthy heart might correspondingly shift from one characterized in terms of lifestyle or diet to one characterized in terms of genes. Thus, discoveries in human genetic engineering can alter our understanding of normality, and therefore alter how we see ourselves.

In order to develop this point further, let me first explain what I mean by "normal" or "normality."[4] There are, broadly speaking, three distinct ways of understanding normality: the concept of normality can be understood as a mathematical concept, as an evaluative concept, or as a biological concept.

When the concept of normality is understood as a mathematical concept, it may be defined as the average—as the mean, median, or mode—or in terms of some portion of a distribution of items (e.g., the "normal curve"). Normality in this sense—$normal_{math}$—can have a precise definition. What is $normal_{math}$ may vary with changes in the population. If most people were to become taller, and if the "normal height" of a person were understood as the mean height, then, plainly, the "normal height" (the $normal_{math}$ height) would increase. Normality as a mathematical function is the simplest and clearest understanding of normality.[5]

The second way of understanding normality is as an evaluative concept. Examples of this would be conventional norms, cultural norms, institutional norms, and ethical norms. Normality in this sense—$normal_{val}$—is admittedly a crude classification, since a number of quite different articulations are being grouped together here. There are of course important disputes over the differences and relationships among these various understandings of this concept of normality, but for this discussion, we can put them to one side. Normality$_{math}$ is clearly different from normality$_{val}$ in that something could be normal in one sense but not in the other. The normal procedure need not be the usual procedure.

The third understanding of normality—the biological concept of normality—is often invoked when a biologist talks about a normal heart, a normal reaction, a normal environment. This understanding of normality is nicely brought out when we consider biological functions. When a biologist ascribes a function to an organ, to what, exactly, is he or she ascribing the function? Consider one of the favorite examples of the philosopher of biology—"The function of the heart is to circulate the blood." That statement is clearly not about any *particular* heart. No particular heart is named or intended. Nor is it a statement about *all* hearts, since some hearts (sometimes) fail to circulate blood. Indeed, the statement isn't about *most* hearts or about the (statistically) average heart. Suppose a calamity occurred in which most people's hearts failed to circulate blood so that they needed some implanted medical device for blood circulation. This would hardly undermine the statement about the heart's function. And the statement is not about the ideal heart. Why limit the ideal heart to merely pumping blood? What the statement is about is the *normal* or *healthy* heart, and a particular heart or all hearts or most hearts or the average heart or the ideal heart may not be normal.

With this clarification, my earlier remarks should be understood as being about the biological concept of normality: Genetic discoveries will affect our understanding of the biological concept of normality. Our concept of normality$_{bio}$ will become so refined that people who previously appeared to themselves and others as normal may become reclassified as abnormal in various ways.

Consider, for example, the discovery of genetic susceptibilities. Having a genetic susceptibility to a disease does not mean that one will contract that disease or even that one has a high probability of contracting it. It should be understood as a subjunctive, or "counterfactual," conditional: if you were exposed to such-and-such environments (or maintained such-and-such a lifestyle), you would contract (within a range of probabilities) such-and-such diseases. In other words, having a genetic susceptibility means that you have a special genetic vulnerability. Thus, for example, having a genetic susceptibility to a certain form of cancer or heart disease would mean having a special vulnerability to that disease.

The advent of these new classifications—these new, more refined determinations of normality and abnormality—will be ethically and socially significant. On the one hand, genetic susceptibilities do not constitute disease classifications; having a genetic susceptibility to heart disease does not mean that you have heart disease. On the other hand, genetic susceptibilities do seem to be disabilities of a sort. Someone with a genetic susceptibility to cancer will be limited in what he or she can do when compared to someone without that susceptibility. There may be certain materials that person can't work with or be near; there may be certain environments that person can't live in. Thus, people with a genetic susceptibility could be seen by themselves and by society as handicapped.

The significance of this change in perception can take many forms. For example, Section 504 of the Federal Rehabilitation Act of 1973 protects those with perceived handicaps from certain kinds of discrimination. Should those with genetic susceptibilities enjoy the same protection? If so, then the percentage of the U.S. population covered by the Rehabilitation Act would be far greater than it is now. Indeed, so many people may be covered by it that its goal of offering special protection may be lost.

Responsible Science

Let me summarize this paper thus far. I have tried to show that in addition to concerns about risk and applications, the discoveries associated with human genetic engineering raise concerns about the knowledge itself. I have sketched two examples: the detection of diseases in asymptomatic individuals without the ability to treat those individuals, and the discoveries of new kinds of abnormalities or disabilities. Rather than examine these cases further, I want to turn to the theme of this conference and ask, Do these kinds of cases raise an issue about the responsibility of scientists? Many people, scientists included, believe that scientists have a distinct responsibility in communicating the risks associated with their discoveries and in shaping how their discoveries are applied. Does their responsibility extend to the discoveries themselves?

It would seem that it does, especially if we consider what I believe is the common view of the scientist's responsibility. According to that view, the moral responsibility of scientists rests on their causal responsibility: one argues from the scientist's causal responsibility or involvement in the risk or application to his or her moral responsibility.

Of course, I do not wish to suggest that there is a direct connection between involvement and moral responsibility. The connection is quite complex, turning on the details of the case, the nature of the alleged involvement, the choices people have, what they know, and so forth. The point, however, is a general one: the scientist's moral responsibility in how their discoveries are applied or in the risks they generate arises from the scientist's involvement in those discoveries. Whether this involvement is sufficient in any particular case to warrant imputing moral responsibility is a different and difficult matter.

Seen in this light, we could argue that the discoveries themselves, along with the applications and risks, were elements about which the questions regarding the scientist's responsibility should be raised. There is, however, a metaphysical objection to this inclusion. The applications of discoveries and the associated risks can be morally assessed, but, so one might argue, it does not make sense to talk about the moral assessment of the discoveries themselves. The applications of discoveries can be good or bad and the risks incurred in making discoveries can be good or bad, but the discoveries, because they constitute knowledge, are, if anything, good.

We seem to have a tension here. The application of discoveries or knowledge may well raise questions about moral responsibility, but how could the knowledge itself raise such questions? Part of our puzzlement rests in our having the view that knowledge is neither good nor bad or in our having the view that knowledge is always good. On either view, knowledge is not the sort of thing about which one could have a moral responsibility. Nevertheless, I have described two cases where the discoveries in genetics, as opposed to the applications of these discoveries, appear to be morally significant. Thus, on the one hand we have scientists involved in morally significant discoveries, but, on the other hand, the question of the scientist's moral responsibility concerning his or her discoveries doesn't seem to make sense. How can this tension be resolved?

Let me begin by responding to the metaphysical objection. That objection rests on a narrow conception of how scientific discoveries themselves can be morally significant. It assumes that in order to morally assess knowledge itself, it must have intrinsic moral value; indeed, it must be possible for some knowledge to be intrinsically morally suspect. This ignores an important way in which knowledge is morally significant. Knowledge can alter our moral responsibilities. What you know or what you could be expected to know can affect your moral responsibilities.

The point is sufficiently plain that it does not need much in the way of argument. In many cases, ignorance is an excuse. For example, a physician who prescribes what turns out to be an extremely harmful drug may not be morally responsible for the harm if he didn't know and couldn't be expected to know that the drug was so harmful. Or, to take an entirely different example, what transforms Oedipus's moral responsibilities, according to Sophocles' play, is not anything he does but rather what he discovers.

Thus, knowledge itself can alter our responsibilities. The next point we need to realize in responding to the metaphysical objection is that the very having of a responsibility can be open to moral assessment regardless of what actions are taken. It can make sense to ask of a particular responsibility whether there are moral objections to having it.

In order to establish this last point, we should first remind ourselves that there certainly are responsibilities that we don't *want* to have. We might not want a particular responsibility because we don't have—or, for some reason, we don't want to commit—the appropriate abilities or resources. Some people might not want to have the responsibilities of raising a handicapped child because they don't want to devote the time and energy that acting responsibly would demand. Some people might not want the responsibilities of political office because they don't have the negotiating skills to make effective use of that office. These are cases where we have nonmoral reasons for not wanting a particular responsibility.

There can also be moral reasons for not wanting a particular responsibility. Consider paternalism. Paternalistic behavior can be seen as the assumption of another person's responsibility for making her own decisions. A paradigm example is that of the physician who decides whether her patient should have surgery without seeking that patient's consent. The physician takes the responsibility for a decision that should be the patient's. Insofar as there are moral objections to paternalism, there are moral objections to having certain responsibilities in particular contexts. The moral objections can be about assuming certain responsibilities and not just about acting in certain ways. A physician might, for moral reasons, not want certain responsibilities.

These examples—parenthood, politics, and paternalism—indicate some of the range of attitudes we may have toward responsibilities. They also show that we can sometimes refuse responsibilities that we don't want. But we can sometimes be stuck with responsibilities we don't want. Can we be stuck with responsibilities to which we have moral objections?

Consider the case of trait-selection—using our knowledge of genetics to design children. As I mentioned earlier, this is the most controversial area in genetic engineering, and there is much we do not know. We do not know what traits can be controlled or determined by genes or how various genes can be manipulated. Depending upon what the facts are, we might have to face ethical problems of deciding not only what traits are good but also whether or which traits should be a matter of design. To what extent should children be made rather than born?[6] Questions arise not only about how to exercise this responsibility, should we have it, but also about whether it would be good for us to have this responsibility.

How might one get this responsibility? Some science fiction will help to make the case vivid. Suppose we discovered that a particular trait is determined simply by the circumstances of conception. If conception occurred in the daylight, the fetus would have the trait; if conception occurred otherwise, the fetus would lack the trait. Prior to this discovery, a couple could conceive without being responsible for whether their child had the trait in question. Once the discovery is known, however, the couple now becomes responsible for whether their child has the trait regardless of how they act regarding conception. Depending upon the trait, this piece of knowledge gives people a responsibility that they might have moral objections to having. Knowledge in this case would not be morally neutral.

In a fuller study one would need to identify and assess these alleged moral objections. My present task, however, is much more modest. I have tried to identify a moral significance to knowledge that does not simply boil down to a matter of how that knowledge is applied. I have argued that knowledge can affect what our responsibilities are and that we can have moral objections to having certain responsibilities regardless of what our actions might be.

One might try to defend the metaphysical objection by claiming that all the considerations I've raised thus far can be understood to reflect moral concerns about the applications of knowledge rather than the knowledge itself. Knowledge can affect our actions even when it doesn't affect our behavior because it can affect how we describe our actions to ourselves. For example, knowledge may in some cases determine whether a piece of behavior is an act of conceiving a child or an act of conceiving a child with a particular trait. If the new action is such that we have moral objections both to performing it and to performing its alternative—for example, we have moral objections against selecting for as well as selecting against a trait—the knowledge that gave rise to these new possibilities has put us in a moral bind. On this way of describing the matter, we do not talk about how knowledge affects our responsibilities, but rather about how knowledge changes our actions even when there is no change in our behavior. These changes in our actions are understood to reflect applications of knowledge.

The problem with this attempt to preserve the metaphysical objection is that it undermines the idea of "an application." The term "application" is now expanded so that not only might there be an application of a piece of knowledge without any change in our behavior, but also there might be no choice whether to apply a piece of knowledge—knowing would be tantamount to applying. Since the point of talking about the applications of knowledge is to contrast it with the knowledge itself, this expansion preserves talk about applications of knowledge by undermining its point.

Let me conclude with some remarks about the scientist's responsibility in the light of the points I've just made. Because scientific discoveries can alter our moral responsibilities—indeed, perhaps some discoveries could generate responsibilities that we have moral objections to having—the scientist's moral responsibility in this regard is a responsibility concerning this alteration. It is, if you will, a second-order responsibility, a responsibility about changes in our responsibilities. Second-order responsibilities appear to be somewhat different from first-order responsibilities. First-order responsibilities are about actions and their consequences, which in turn are open to moral assessment. Second-order responsibilities are about changes in first-order responsibilities, but the moral assessment of such changes is not obviously the same sort of thing as the moral assessment of actions and their consequences. Hence, there is a *prima facie* moral difference between first- and second-order responsibilities.

I should, however, repeat my earlier qualification. Not every application of a scientist's discovery can be laid at the scientist's feet as his or her moral responsibility. Similarly, not every change in our view of ourselves or in our moral responsibilities that results from a scientist's discovery can be laid at the scientist's feet. That turns on the details. My point is a general one. It makes sense to raise the question of the scientist's moral responsibility for the discoveries themselves because this responsibility arises from the change these discoveries may make in our moral responsibilities.

In any case, it is by no means clear how the scientist should act on these responsibilities. On the one hand, if a scientist makes a discovery that gives rise to a morally objectionable responsibility, that would seem to be a reason for the scientist to suppress that discovery. On the other hand, such suppression goes against the most entrenched values of the scientific profession. In that case the scientist faces an unhappy situation whose resolution, satisfactory or otherwise, will depend upon the details.

Of course, a good deal more needs to be said to clarify what these responsibilities amount to, but that is the work of another occasion. My aim has been a much more general one. I have tried to show that there is a question about the scientist's responsibility regarding his or her discoveries that does not arise simply because of how these discoveries are applied or from the associated risks. That is to say, even though one might think that knowledge in itself is always good or neither good nor bad, there are moral responsibilities attached to its discovery. I have also suggested that this responsibility should be understood as a second-order responsibility. But all this is at a regrettably high level of generality. Part of the problem here is that we need more philosophical research. While there is a substantial philosophical literature on moral responsibility, the topic of second-order responsibility has been largely neglected. Part of this neglect might be due to the thought that second-order responsibilities are rare and of little importance. Nevertheless, as I hope I have shown in my earlier remarks about human genetic engineering, we need to understand this area better. The impact of genetic discoveries on our moral responsibilities will only increase.

Notes

Research for this paper was supported by a grant (R01 HG00419) from the National Institutes of Health Center for Human Genome Research.

1. Some might regard risk not as a separate category but as a result of applications of discoveries. Nothing that follows depends upon whether we regard risk as a separate category or not.

2. Cf. Joseph Fiksel and Vincent T. Covello, *Biotechnology Risk Assessment: Issues and Methods for Enviromental Introduction* (New York: Pergamon Press, 1986).

3. Jonathan Glover, *What Sort of People Should There Be?* (New York: Penguin Books, 1984).

4. The following points are developed in more detail in my "Normality as a Biological Concept" (forthcoming).

5. I should emphasize that while the mathematical function characterizing normal$_{math}$ may be clear and precise, the *choice* of the function will be a much more complicated matter, as the study of statistics reveals.

6. Cf. E. E. Cummings, "pity this busy monster mankind," in *Collected Poems* (London: Granada Publishing, 1981), vol. 2, p. 554.

11

Scientific Autonomy, Scientific Responsibility

William Maker

Science's right to a relatively high degree of freedom from external interference in its operations has been long recognized and consistently defended as fundamentally valuable.[1] The autonomy of science is traditionally regarded as one of modernity's unproblematic achievements, and a society's granting of this autonomy is commonly perceived as an indicator of its maturity and civility. Attempts to compromise it, whether on religious grounds, as with Galileo and Darwin, or political grounds, as in the case of Lysenkoism, are uniformly denounced as dangerous assaults on truth, objectivity, and the well-being of the human condition. In the words of the biologist Robert L. Sinsheimer:

> If one believes that the highest purpose available to humanity is the acquisition of knowledge (and in particular of scientific knowledge, knowledge of the natural universe) then one will regard any attempt to limit or direct the search for knowledge as deplorable—or worse.[2]

I shall argue here that science's continued claim to autonomy is based on an increasingly outdated perception of how science functions in society. The contemporary reality of scientific activity cannot provide an unqualified justification for science's traditional freedom from social interference. As scientific knowledge has become increasing essential to the functioning and the well-being of society, science has become increasingly dependent on public and private support.[3] Scientific knowledge itself is now a valuable commodity and its production has come under the control of particular interests in a variety of ways that compromise science's traditional independence from such interests and undercut its claim to autonomy from social regulation. By way of illustrating this situation I will indicate how the traditional

professional ethos of science, crucial to maintaining scientific autonomy, has been challenged and sometimes disregarded in contemporary
scientific practice. (My approach here, and my conclusions about
scientific practice, complement those of Joan Callahan. See her essay,
"Professions, Institutions, and Moral Risk," in this volume.) Concluding that a return to the conditions that could legitimate autonomy is
unlikely, I shall contend that we need to rethink the nature of science's
relation to society and its social responsibility.

The Legitimacy of Scientific Autonomy

First, what is the traditional understanding of the conditions legitimat-
ing scientific autonomy?

The right to scientific autonomy, like all rights, is not unconditional.
Rights are always accompanied by responsibilities. The traditional
understanding of the legitimacy of scientific autonomy recognizes that
the scientific community has certain basic obligations whose fulfillment
is needed to justify science's self-regulation.[4] According to this traditional view, there is an implicit social contract between science and
society.[5] Society grants science considerable autonomy not afforded
to comparable institutions because it is believed that science serves a
socially valuable end of a special sort, and because science's autonomy
is seen as essential to attaining that end.[6] What does science provide
for society that earns it a right to autonomy?

The goal of science is objective truth, knowledge of the workings of
nature that is *universal* in scope and validity: science accounts for
phenomena accessible (in principle) to all in a manner all can agree
upon. The pursuit of such universal knowledge is seen as deserving
society's support both because it is inherently valuable in its own right
and because the application of this knowledge can serve particular
public and private interests.[7] Although scientific knowledge has proven
utility, defenders of science's autonomy insist that scientists' first and
overriding concern must be with attaining knowledge irrespective of a
calculation of its possible utility, not only because such knowledge is
inherently valuable, but in order that the practical fruits of this knowledge can be harvested: Truth is an end in itself and must be seen and
sought as such in order to ensure that it may be a means to other ends.[8]

Thus society's support of science and the special autonomy it
grants to it are conditioned upon science fulfilling its responsibility of
promoting the end of universal truth. According to Bernard Barber,

"only the pursuit of truth for its own sake can develop and maintain the standards which are necessary to ensure the objectivity and the value of research, pure or applied."[9] Of course, science is not the only institution that serves society. How does science differ from other institutions such that it is accorded a special autonomy?

Other institutions that receive a considerable measure of public support, (e.g., the military) and that markedly affect society (e.g., banking) are subject to external supervision and control in the name of the public good. We do not allow the experts in these disciplines the same measure of unregulated authority, inside and outside their fields, that we accord to scientific experts.[10] We treat other special disciplines differently in part because we believe that by their very nature they are always in danger of becoming captive to particular interests that may conflict with the common interest society expects them to serve. This insistence on public regulation extends even to the discipline most closely related to science, technology. (I will comment on why this is the case below.) In contrast to these other institutions science is, for the most part, free from external regulation in the name of the public interest, not because its practitioners are more virtuous, but because we believe that it has internal, institutionally maintained procedures that keep it from falling prey to influences that would cause it to deviate from the public interest. What is it about science that is supposed to justify this difference in treatment? Why is science, in spite of its importance for, support by, and influence on society, not in need of democratic supervision and regulation? The story goes like this:

In seeking universal truth science aims to uncover natural phenomena that are objective in the sense of being accessible, in principle, to all knowers, regardless of the particular differences of circumstance and background that distinguish us one from another in a variety of ways and shape the plurality of our divergent individual interests. Science is thought to be unique in its ability to adopt universal means in order to discover universal truths that transcend social, cultural, and political differences, just those differences that the system of checks and balances in democratic society is supposed to control. But science need not be subjected to such balancing or regulation. We are assured that neither a scientist's economic, national, political, racial, religious, or cultural background, nor her personal beliefs can—in the long run—enter in a substantive fashion into what come to be recognized as accepted scientific procedures and results.[11] Believing that other fields do not possess the independent, objective criteria of judgment that make this universality possible, we regard them with suspicion; we fear that, to one degree or another, they will allow a subjective influence into their judgments. Consequently, we either deny them the unmediated *public* authority—the right to speak for all—that we accord science, or, if a measure of such public authority is accorded, it is under strict external supervision in the name of the common good. An early advocate of scientific autonomy, Galileo, drew quite forcefully the key distinction between science and other fields upon which according autonomy and authority to science alone is based:

> If this point of which we dispute were some point of law, or other part of the studies called the humanities, wherein there is neither truth nor falsehood, we might give sufficient credit to the acuteness of wit, readiness of answers, and the greater accomplishments of writers, and hope that he who is most proficient in these will make his reason more probable and plausible. But the conclusions of natural science are true and necessary and the judgement [arbitrio] of man has nothing to do with them.[12]

In Galileo's vision, science alone transcends the merely human level of judgment, where irresolvable disputes abound, even though science too is undertaken by humans.

So it is not simply that science has universal truth as its aim. The same might be said for religion, philosophy, history, or the arts. What marks the difference in the accord and treatment we give to science as opposed to these other disciplines is our conviction that science alone has the successful means to arrive at demonstrably universal truths. In matters of nature we take the view that only one self-selected community of experts ought to determine, without external supervision or intervention, how truth is established, what this truth is, and who may speak in its name, and we socially recognize the pronouncements of this autonomous community as public truths. (Witness the uproar at attempts to present an alternative, religious, view in science classes.) Such special status is not accorded to any religious, philosophical, or artistic group, not because these topics have no public significance, but in large measure because (in social agreement with Galileo) we do not believe that any such group can rightly claim to be able to speak for all. While our recognition of freedom of speech and assembly allows such groups autonomy, they lack the public authority of science. (Or when one of them does speak in the public name—as in the case of the National Endowment for the Arts—they do so under public supervision and scrutiny and without the public conviction that this group of experts has a final say.)

The same Galilean epistemology underlies the different treatment accorded to the technological disciplines: there is a perceived distinction drawn between attaining scientific knowledge and applying it. Attainment is solely a matter for the experts selected by their community of peers to determine, whereas by contrast the application rightly concerns us all. The former is a matter of truth that can only be determined by experts; the latter importantly involves opinions or value judgments in which all affected parties are entitled to a say. Defenders of scientific autonomy consistently draw this distinction and point out that science deserves and requires social autonomy, while technology does not.[13]

According to the traditional view, the fact that science alone possesses the means to transcend particular private interests and biases and attain universal knowledge not only justifies but also *requires* science's autonomy from social regulation in the name of the common good. What the nature of the common good is, is open to diverse interpretations; it's a matter of opinion, not a demonstrable universal Truth. This view holds that, strictly speaking, there is no universal common good, only particular, varying perceptions of it, and thus such particular perceptions must be excluded from the universal domain of science. If science is to be able to serve its socially valuable universal ends, we are told, it must be autonomous from *all* forms of external influence, both private and public.

So the pursuit of scientific truth cannot be particularized, in the sense of making the substantive content of scientific procedures and their results subservient to beliefs, whether those of some particular individual or of some particular culture, political system, or society. External particular influences of all sorts must be excluded from science and the only means to do this lies in science's internally established and maintained procedures for assessing truth claims.

Insofar as this view is correct, science's primary social responsibility ought not to be determined from outside of science. The key point is that science's basic social responsibility is not something other than furthering its own ends: science best serves society by defining and pursuing its own goals. Scientific autonomy is a social good.

The scientific community has, in essence, bargained for substantial autonomy by claiming the inherent efficiency and, indeed, necessity of an unregulated scientific enterprise, and by promising practical contributions

to economic progress in return for funding without intervention. Its
bargaining strength comes from belief in the intrinsic value of knowledge,
and from the promise of its contribution to the public good. Underlying
the negotiation is the implicit threat that society will lose out on the
benefits of science if excessive intervention accompanies government
support. If the acquisition of basic knowledge is restrained by externally
imposed limits, it is society which will bear the costs.[14]

The Ethics of Science

What is the traditional ethic connected with this view of science? In
his classic 1942 study, "The Normative Structure of Science," the
sociologist of science Robert K. Merton analyzed an uncodified scientific ethic that he found operative in the scientific community.[15] Basic
to this ethic is the scientist's self-understanding of science's autonomy
and its correlative commitment to an end which is valuable for its own
sake. In Merton's words, scientists see themselves "as independent of
society" and they also see science as autonomous in the positive sense
of being "a self-validating enterprise which is in society but not of it."
Rooted in this vision of scientific autonomy (and of the transcendent
value of science associated with it) is a scientific ethic defined by four
"institutional imperatives": universalism, communism, disinterestedness, and organized skepticism. These imperatives follow from science's goal of objective knowledge and the techniques employed to
attain that goal, but according to Merton they are followed not merely
because they are efficient means to science's end but also because
they are seen to be inherently ethical: "they are believed right and
good. They are moral as well as technical prescriptions."[16] The philosopher of science Israel Scheffler agrees with this perception of the
scientific endeavor as an inherently moral enterprise; he traces this
feature of science precisely to its commitment to objective truth.
Scientific procedures "embodied in and transmitted by the institutions
of science" ensure that our subjective beliefs are submitted to independent controls; it is not the authority of individuals but "independent
and impartial criteria" that are determinative.[17]

This insistence on subjecting all claims to "preestablished impersonal criteria" is what Merton describes as the first, core component
of the scientific ethos, the imperative of universalism. It calls upon the
scientist to transcend all particularistic features of "race, nationality,
religion, class and personal qualities."[18] And this feature of science

endows it with a value that transcends the utility of the knowledge it produces; its unswerving commitment to objectivity gives it a "moral import" in that it is a model of "responsible belief."[19] The commitment to universal knowledge is reflected in two of the other imperatives Merton designates—communism and disinterestedness—and a brief consideration of them will disclose how they bear on science's autonomy.

By "communism" Merton refers to the openness of communication and the sharing of scientific discoveries. "Communalism" may be a less confusing term. This is not a feature of science reflecting a high-minded altruism or generosity on the part of scientists; indeed the competition for priority of recognition is extensive and does not compromise the sharing of results. Rather, communalism is an institutional feature of scientific practice that is integral to the attainment of universal knowledge, as is the imperative of distinterestedness. I shall later contend that communalism (the nonprivatization of scientific knowledge and the communal process of its validation) and disinterestedness (the renunciation of personal self-seeking or self-aggrandizement in the name of truth, where this is certified by peer accountability) are increasingly threatened and compromised by the commodification of science, so their relation to the universal goal integral to scientific autonomy needs to be carefully delineated.

Remember that science's attainment of universal knowledge hinges on the impartiality of the criteria against which particular subjective claims are judged. It is said that impartiality—objectivity—of judgment is not a feature of the personality or authority or particular beliefs of individual scientists; it pertains—in practice—to institutional features: to practices shared in common and communally supervised. Before a scientific claim is recognized as valid it must be subjected to the judgment of the community; results must be replicable in order to ensure that the individual producer of scientific knowledge has not made a merely subjective, particular claim.[20] William Lowrance stresses the necessity of peer accountability as a guarantee of the integrity of scientific work. He notes that scientists always act in particular contexts as particular individuals whose actions are influenced by a variety of value judgments. These influences are inescapable; the only effective control on them lies in "proceeding by the internal quality control norms of one's particular scientific community."[21] And according to Lowrance, part of science's responsibility to society involves maintaining scientific integrity by sharing information and adhering to standards established and enforced by the community.[22] Thus peer review is at the core of the scientific claim to offer universal knowledge. According to Merton, it is this internal feature of scientists policing one another that grounds the claim that scientists are, in fact, disinterested when they pursue knowledge. "The translation of the norm of disinterestedness into practice is effectively supported by the ultimate accountability of scientists to their compeers."[23] Thus, results must be shared.

The significance of communalism for the maintenance of science's claim to offer objective, universal knowledge should perhaps be stressed. It is a feature of scientific autonomy that the scientific community recognizes no criteria for science save those endorsed by the community. Thus the *effective determination* of what counts as the *operative* standards of objective judgment and their application falls to the community and to the community alone. Now, we may adopt the philosophical view that the scientific community has, by and large, endorsed criteria which, as a matter of fact, *are* objective and whose objectivity can be determined independently of the judgment of the scientific community. Or we may adopt the view that what we mean by "objective criteria" is whatever criteria the scientific community endorses. Which of these philosophical positions we endorse is irrelevant as long as we recognize two facts of scientific practice: (1) the traditional endorsement, by the scientific community, of communalism, especially as it involves peer review, is an essential feature of what grounds science's claim to offer objective knowledge; and (2) that, in actuality, it is just those more specific standards of objectivity endorsed by the community that are effective in scientific practice.[24] In short, whatever our philosophical views are about the ultimate nature of scientific objectivity, in practice it falls to the community of scientists, operating as an autonomous community, to determine and apply its procedures and standards.

Scientific results are also the product of the whole community of science in another way. The communal character of scientific knowledge also pertains to the fact that any individual's ability to carry on research is tied to access to the results of others.[25] In the words of Isaac Newton, "If I have seen so far it is because I stood on the shoulders of giants." Merton links these features of openness in observing that scientific achievement is "essentially cooperative and selectively cumulative."[26] The need to share discoveries both in order to pursue research and to test its results is completely compatible with the competitive character of science, as Merton observes and as the events related in James D. Watson's *The Double Helix* amply illustrate.

What is private property is the priority of discovery. "The products of competition are communized, and esteem accrues to the producer." Communalism, then, is really "the imperative of the communication of findings" and it is antithetical with secrecy.[27]

Merton also sees the willingness to share results as a feature of the distinctively moral character of science. The imperative of openness is not followed solely because it is a technical necessity; there is "a moral compulsion for sharing the results of science." "Even though it serves no ulterior motive, the suppression of scientific discovery is condemned."[28] While Merton does not further analyze communalism's link with the moral dimension of science, I would suggest that it is an important feature of science's claim to be acting, without external supervision, in and for a common good. Science establishes that it is in pursuit of a universal end, and not particular, private ends, and that it is acting for the good of all, by openly communicating and sharing its findings. Communalism is also part of what distinguishes science from technology, according to Merton, for technology is recognized as private property while scientific knowledge is not.[29]

This unqualified image of an autonomous science, in but not of society, effectively free from all interests save an interest in universal knowledge, is no longer defensible. At least two avenues of criticism can be brought to bear on it, one internal and theoretical, the other external and practical. The first, which I shall only mention in passing, would consist in reiterating the criticisms of the very possibility of universal objective knowledge that have been commonplace, if controversial, in anglophone philosophy of science since Kuhn. The contention here is that one can establish in principle that all knowledge is relative to contexts and shaped by interests. The second, external and practical critique of the image of autonomous science, which I shall pursue, is independent of the first. It is based on two sets of empirical observations. The first questions the traditional claim that the pursuit of scientific knowledge can be meaningfully disentangled from its application. The second contends that science has for all intents and purposes become a business. Taken together they point to the conclusion that scientific practice has come under the control and supervision of particular public and private interests that in many instances conflict with the interest in universal knowledge. This conflict is not a matter of how such knowledge, once attained, is used, but concerns the very processes by which the scientific community is supposed to ensure the "scientific"—universal—character of its knowledge.

Traditionally, the character of the particular socioeconomic context in which scientific knowledge is produced has been regarded, along with all particular features of context, as an external matter, pertaining to the "context of discovery" and not the "context of justification." Insofar as scientific procedures are properly followed, how the research happens to be funded is a matter of indifference as regards the scientific character of the results. Whether the bill is being paid by a private corporation interested in profit, or a public university, or a national research institute may well make some difference in overall direction (in the kind of research undertaken, and in what uses are made of the results) but the scientific—universal—character of the knowledge will not be affected. This autonomy of science from economic interests presupposes two (related) conditions that have gradually but steadily changed since the middle of this century. The change in these conditions bears markedly on the notion of scientific autonomy. What I have in mind is (1) the continued erosion of a meaningful distinction between science and technology or between basic or pure science and applied science and (2) the steady transformation of scientific knowledge itself into a valuable commodity, like technology. The former consideration is relevant to the issue of scientific autonomy since, as noted above, defenders of science's autonomy usually presuppose that a far-reaching and meaningful distinction can (still) be drawn between science, as the search for truth guided only by the interest in truth (focusing exclusively on theoretical concerns), and its application (focusing on practical concerns), where the consideration of other ends and other interests becomes effective and where social regulation is appropriate.[30] Because of space limitations I shall not pursue this issue here, except to note that many critics of the distinction have contended that today science and technology are intimately and inseparably interconnected and interdependent. Some have further concluded that because of this interpenetration science is properly described as a form of action guided by a variety of interests (and open to public regulation as all modes of action are) rather than as a mode of contemplative thought serving only the interest in truth (where it would be deserving of autonomy on grounds of the freedom of thought and speech.)[31]

A Conflict of Ethics

What I shall focus on is the challenge to scientific autonomy presented by the fact that, in virtue of its utility, scientific knowledge itself has become a valuable commodity. According to Dorothy Nelkin:

[T]he knowledge generated by research is growing in economic and policy importance. . . . In the past, commercial interests looked primarily to the goods and services produced through applied research; today, more fundamental knowledge is recognized as having intrinsic value.[32]

Because knowledge itself now has this kind of value, the activity of its pursuit has come under the influence, or the control, of those, publicly and privately, who have an interest in its usefulness and marketability. They bear the costs of research, and are convinced of their right to control the process of production and the product itself. Why should this be seen as threatening science's claim to be serving universal truth and thus its right to social autonomy? What I shall contend is that as the scientific enterprise is becoming increasingly commodified, a rival set of values and a rival ethics—those of the marketplace—are coming into conflict with the traditional values and the traditional ethics of science. In some instances the conflict is such that, when the market ethic prevails, science's ability to serve its universal end is compromised.

The issue of the commodification or industrialization of science is broad, and I can only focus on certain aspects of it. (Joan Callahan's essay "Professions, Institutions, and Moral Risk" presents a further consideration of the challenge to traditional norms of practice which the commodification of science has presented.)

What is the nature and extent of commodification and what are its effects? First, commodification pertains to the fact that knowledge is regarded as proprietary, belonging to or strictly controlled by either the individual scientific entrepreneur (itself a new and still relatively rare phenomenon), or those who employ her. Second, commodification pertains to the fact that the process of the production of scientific knowledge comes under the control of those who are paying for it. Defined in this fashion, commodification is not restricted to what occurs in the private sphere, but also pertains to the government, one of the most important employers of scientists and financiers of scientific research. (That much publicly funded research is directly or indirectly available for private exploitation, that businesses and universities are increasingly engaging in joint research ventures—a phenomenon with its own potentially insidious implications—points to the need to define commodification broadly.)

The extent of commodification is broad. For a variety of reasons, chief among them the costs of doing research, the self-supporting scientist who answers to no one but himself and his peers, is a thing of the past. The majority (two-thirds) of scientists today work under contract for, or are employed by, industries or consulting firms. And even those doing work for government agencies or at universities are only relatively insulated from the effects of commodification.[33] What are these effects as they pertain to the ethics of science?

If knowledge is proprietary, and commercially valuable, by the ethic of the marketplace I am under no obligation whatsoever to share it freely, since doing so would run counter to my interest in selling it for a profit. Correlatively, if this knowledge not only has an exchange value but also a use value of a certain sort, there may be an interest—for example, in national security—for severely restricting access to it. But according to the traditional imperative of communalism, I am doubly obligated to share freely the results of my work, as a moral obligation pertaining to science's claim to be acting in the name of and for the sake of all; and as a technical obligation, since the sharing of knowledge with the community is the basis for all scientific work. How has this imperative been questioned or compromised in recent years as a result of commodification? I will mention a few examples to illustrate the situation.

In some instances it is scientists themselves who have become secretive in order to protect their valuable property. The fields of genetic research and molecular biology have recently emerged as having considerable commercial potential. According to one estimate the industrial market for genetic research—"biocommerce"—alone has been set at $40 billion.[34] These fields exemplify what may become a wider phenomenon insofar as other sciences come to offer knowledge that has market value.

Donald Kennedy, in investigating the commercialization of biomedical research at universities, discovered that some scientists have now refused to divulge detailed information about their research at scientific meetings because they consider it to be potentially marketable.[35] Scientists at the University of California, San Diego, and the nearby Salk Institute and Scripts Clinic and Research Foundation, became involved in a dispute about who had developed a new method for identifying proteins after it was discovered that one group had been negotiating with Johnson and Johnson about commercial application of the method. In the words of one of the scientists involved: "There used to be a good, healthy exchange of ideas and information among researchers at UCSD, the Salk Institute, and the Scripts Clinic. Now we are locking our doors."[36] In a lecture on the question of whether utility and quality can coexist, Kennedy observed that "Scientists who once shared prepublication information freely and exchanged cell lines without hesitation are now much more reluctant to do so. . . . The fragile network of informal communication that characterizes every especially active field is liable to rupture.''[37]

In some instances scientists themselves invoke the ethic of openness, only to find their claims challenged by those who have funded the work and claim the right of ownership to protect their investment. Scientific whistleblowers have had numerous conflicts with their employers because of efforts to reveal important findings pertaining to the common good. Thomas Mancuso conducted research on radiation effects on a contract for the Department of Energy. For ten years he discovered no significant threats to workers exposed at the Hanford plant, and his contract was regularly renewed. When it subsequently appeared that his newer findings suggested a more significant cancer risk, his contract was terminated; the Department of Energy tried to confiscate his Hanford data and denied him access to other data he had assembled.[38] Employed by a consulting firm hired by Consolidated Edison to do an environmental impact study, research biologist Morris Baslow concluded that his employer's study was faulty, because it had ignored data he had developed, and that plant discharge was damaging river wildlife. The firm disputed his findings and left them out of its final report. Baslow tried and failed to get his company to let him present his findings to the Environmental Protection Agency. He informed the EPA anyway, and was fired, taking his data with him. The firm claimed he had stolen their property.[39]

Extension of control over scientific work and its products occurs not only in the private sector. Scientists have long been accustomed to restrictions, for reasons of national security, on sharing information and results of research when it pertains to a variety of technical devices relating to military hardware. But in recent years the government imposition of control in the name of secrecy has extended beyond technical devices to scientific knowledge itself. In 1980 the MIT mathematician Leon Adelman applied for a grant from the National Science Foundation for work in computer mathematics, an area that has a bearing on cryptography. The NSF sent his grant to the National Security Agency for review because of its potential implications for military intelligence. Adelman received his grant but was disturbed to discover that his work could end up being classified, unpublishable and not available for public use.[40] According to Dorothy Nelkin, what is new and disturbing here—and this is not the only case—is the move to extend government control beyond areas directly funded by national security agencies and to institute control not only over things but ideas.[41]

These examples illustrate, first, a clash of interests: particular market interests in pursuing and attaining salable commodities or a governmental interest in controlling valuable information versus an interest in pursuing and attaining universal knowledge. Scientists seeking government funding may discover that some agency's perception of the national interest conflicts with the renunciation of secrecy and of withholding information central to the scientific interest in attaining and disseminating knowledge. What may be done in the best interest of producing and realizing the value of a certain commodity may not be in the best interest of furthering knowledge for its own sake. The California biologists discovered that their traditional interest in sharing information with fellow scientists for the common good of science conflicted with an economic interest to preserve for themselves the market value of something they had produced. The whistleblowing scientists discovered that those who fund research are likely to claim, on broadly recognized market principles, that they are the only ones who determine their own best interests, including what is to be done with the products they have paid for. That is, after all, the freedom of the market.

In addition, these examples illustrate a clash of ethics. Scientists have traditionally perceived a higher obligation to the universal end of truth. Consequently, they have committed themselves to the imperatives of disinterestedness (asking only for recognition and honor) and communalism (sharing what they produce) in order to attain that end. But the contemporary economic reality of the market is predicated not just upon different but upon antithetical, radically particularistic values. Its ethic is precisely an ethic of particularity rather than universality. The market exists as a sphere to *pursue* one's particular private interest, not to renounce it, and it serves that particular end not through free sharing but rather by regarding everything as private property that no one else has any legitimate claim to and that is only available to others for a price the owner may (or may not) agree to. What this clash suggests is that, ethically speaking, scientists may face an unresolvable dilemma, given the reality of the present economic system. Who in our world has any choice but to participate in the market in some fashion? And given the enormous costs of research, an individual desirous of pursuing scientific research has no choice but to accommodate themselves to the market. What I am suggesting is that if scientists are breaking the social contract upon which their claim to autonomy is based (by accommodating interests that are antithetical to the universal interest in truth and cooperating in the privatization of knowledge that had been regarded as belonging to everyone), they are not doing so willingly. Given the inescapability of the market and the pervasiveness of its ethic of self-seeking, can we blame the genetic researchers for wanting to profit from their discoveries? Can we blame those who invest in and fund research for insisting that the knowledge produced is their property, to do with as they see fit, even if that means altering or suppressing it? Alternatively, given scientific tradition, can we blame the whistleblowers who feel that an obligation to science's universal ends overrides their obligation to their employers?

The seriousness of what is at stake here goes beyond ethics to the practice of science itself. Can science avoid accommodating itself to the market, or to governmental interests? Given the enormous costs of training and research, will any science be done except that which the funders see as valuable for their own ends? Can science recapture its self-determining status? And now that scientific knowledge itself and not merely technology is a valuable commodity and the process of its production is brought under market controls and market principles, can science continue to maintain its claim—and its social responsibility—to serve universal ends? If it cannot—if science becomes thoroughly penetrated by the market—is it still deserving of social autonomy?

I think that the emerging subservience of science to the market, owing to its costs and the commercial value of its product, threatens the quality and integrity of science itself, in two ways. (In her essay "Professions, Institutions, and Moral Risk," Joan Callahan points to some other threats, and especially to the proliferation of fraud.) First, insofar as secrecy and proprietary ownership of knowledge become more common, science is threatened in the long run since its cumulative growth presupposes (or has in the past) the sharing of information. The less scientists or their employers are willing to communicate, the more difficult it is for any scientists to do their work. This very fact could function as a corrective on excessive secrecy.

Second, if scientists or their employers are no longer willing to share information for the purposes of peer review, because data or methods are (or may be) commercially valuable and not to be given away, then the quality—or the nature—of the product will be altered. Remember that it is peer review and peer review alone, according to defenders of scientific autonomy, which ensures the quality of scientific knowledge. Peer review is the sole effective guarantee of the objective, universal character of scientific knowledge.[42] It is the control on the subjective, and possibly self-seeking, interests of the individual scientist. If it is bypassed or avoided, if those in control of the process of producing scientific knowledge are not peers, but capitalists or bureaucrats, how can the claim that scientific—universal—knowledge is being offered be sustained? And if it cannot be sustained, then the claim that science deserves autonomy in virtue of this production is compromised.

There is an obvious reply to this and I will address it immediately. The rejoinder reminds us that science has been granted autonomy both because universal knowledge is intrinsically valuable and because it has utility. The reply says that we can substitute the latter as a control for the former and lose nothing. May it not be the case that science is still offering universal knowledge (and is still deserving of its social autonomy) even if the imperatives of openness and sharing are eliminated, because, even under market control, useful knowledge will still be produced? Won't the necessary utility of the knowledge be indicative of its universality? Now the traditional claim for scientific autonomy recognizes the utility of scientific knowledge, but holds that truth—as exclusively determined by the autonomous community of scientific peers—must be the basis for utility: scientists alone can determine what is the truth, and when they are allowed to do so utility will follow. So the traditional view is that if you compromise autonomy you will sacrifice utility. The reply I am sketching says something else, for it holds that science's autonomy from particular private interests—market interests—may be safely compromised without compromising science's claim to offer universal knowledge.

It may be that, as a result of the commodification of science, we are witnessing a transformation in the standards by which "scientific" knowledge is defined. Perhaps there is shift underway, in the direction of technological or utilitarian standards that do not require the communal procedures that necessitate sharing and the renunciation of secrecy. If this is so, then the proof of scientific knowledge would not be determined by judgment of the scientific community, but by its use, or more precisely by its marketability. In any case, the question at hand is whether utility as determined by the market provides the "independent, impartial criteria" that are the *universal* criteria needed to justify scientific autonomy from social regulation. I would suggest not. Notions of utility, with perhaps a few exceptions so general as to be unhelpful, are varying. They depend on different value judgments and perceptions of ends, and they are *appropriately* particular in a democratic society. While "utility," *otherwise unspecified*, may be in some sense a universal end, in practice it must always be defined in a particular, varying fashion (unless, of course, some particular group in society is in the position to impose its definition of utility on the rest of us.) Beyond this, the more specific problem with a market definition of utility, to put it quite baldly, is that it does not recognize a manifold variety of notions of what is useful, but only those notions of utility that can command ready cash. So a science subservient to direction by those concerned with market utility would be a science in the interest of a few, not of all. (Not to be forgotten in this regard is how susceptible to manipulation by the market are our notions of what is desirable and useful.)

If it is the case that science cannot escape market direction, and thus that it has sacrificed a right to social autonomy as a consequence of its no longer being independent of special particular interests, what is to be done? If science has a social responsibility to serve universal ends, can this be in any way assured? Given the importance of science to everyone in society, a counterbalance to the subservience of science to market interests would seem to be called for. If we cannot agree as a society on any single set of interests, science's aim of fulfilling a universal interest may best be accommodated by opening it up to a plurality of interests, including those not mediated by the market. In calling for such a democratization of science in the name of once again aligning science with a universal end, this view assumes that the recapture of science's autonomy from the market through a return to earlier circumstances or by governmental intervention is unlikely. The market system has led us forever beyond the former and has, at least temporarily, captured the latter.

Thus, ensuring that nonmarket interests have a voice in the scientific enterprise would require something other than simply more governmental regulation in the traditional format. We are all painfully aware of the cozy relationship governmentally managed regulators establish with those they are ostensibly watching. (For example, the Bush administration consistently pushed, on economic grounds, for a loosening of controls on the release of genetically novel organisms.[43]) Democratization would require the participation of outsiders not representing the interests of public or private big science, for the problem is just that those institutions are increasingly captive to certain special interests; scientific autonomy as traditionally understood has already been compromised. If we cannot expect that those whose task it is to represent the public interest will in fact do so, if something like a coherent notion of *the* public interest has become problematic, then what is needed is the creation of mechanisms that ensure the systematic representation of those interests that currently have no voice in the business of science. Additionally, the effectiveness of this democratization would require allowing nonscientists to play a role in science. This last compromise of the traditional ideal of scientific self-regulation is needed in order to counterbalance the already prevailing influence of nonscientists from industry or the government whose special interests are increasingly efficacious in science today (not to mention the increasingly commercial interests of the scientific community itself). Some things that might be done:

Increased pressure by public interest groups modeled on consumer activists (such as Science for the People) needs to be brought to bear on big industrial science (and on its partner, the government). The involvement of such countervailing special interests should concern not just obvious matters such as possible hazards of dangerous research, but the whole spectrum of research, including its direction. Concern for public safety may be a foot in the door, leading to the raising of other concerns. (The model of the Cambridge, Mass., City Council's intervention in genetic research at Harvard and MIT indicates that local involvement that includes nonscientists can work to the satisfaction of both parties.) Intervention might be approached on a market, exchange basis, rooted in the perception that, while business has a right to profit, scientific matters are of vital and legitimate public concern, not least of all because of the risks involved. More specifically, industrial science (as well as the government) should be pursuaded to set aside some percentage of its profits for projects that are not of immediate and obvious market value.

Universities need to take their traditional obligations as institutions that serve public interests much more seriously. Practically, it is in the university context that research "for its own sake" can best be undertaken. As I have argued, in the contemporary context, this does not mean renouncing outside funding and the influence and interests of those funders, but insisting that there be a balancing of interests, by way of a setting aside of a percentage of funds—again—for commercially nonviable research and for research that is more obviously directed to "small" interests. (For example, research directed specifically to what is called "sustainable" or "alternative" agriculture.[44])

The possible success of such democratization would rest finally, I think, on a change in the nature of the prevailing market ideology. As Lester Thurow has argued, what reigns now is the traditional competitive Friedmanesque view of individual entrepreneurs who are and who must remain opposed to any form of public involvement in their operations. Thurow contends that this model is outdated and that the U.S. economy is threatened by the greater success of cooperative models (in Japan and Germany) where capitalism is seen more as a cooperative group enterprise and where a public role in business operations is seen as good business.[45] Unless the market can be more generally democratized along such lines, the democratization of science also seems unlikely. Science as we have traditionally understood it may be the victim not of irrationality or indifference but rather of the rival claim to universal rationality presented by the market.

Notes

1. Science has "a leading place if not . . . the first rank in the scale of cultural values." Robert K. Merton, "The Normative Structure of Science" in Robert K. Merton, *The Sociology of Science: Theoretical and Empirical Investigations*, ed. Norman W. Storer (Chicago: University of Chicago Press, 1973), 268. Discussing a survey of 800 scientists, Dorothy Nelkin reports that "seventy-seven percent agreed that 'The pursuit of science is best organized when as much freedom as possible is granted to all scientists.' " The study also suggests that certain attitudes are characteristic of scientists: " 'A pure scientist must not deny himself a discovery by worrying about social consequences.' 'I would insist that no area of investigation be closed because someone feels that society is incapable of handling it.' Wide consensus on the importance of autonomy has meant significant federal patronage of science with minimal public control." Dorothy Nelkin, "Threats and Promises: Negotiating the Control of Research," in *Limits of Scientific Inquiry*, ed. Gerald Holton and Robert S. Morison (New York: W. W. Norton, 1978), 192. According to physicist Gerald Holton "calls for any explicit limits [to scientific research] go against long-standing traditions of academic and research freedoms as still understood by most scientists. They contradict the predominant philosophical base of science as an infinitely open system. . . ." Gerald Holton, "From the Endless Frontier to the Ideology of Limits," in *Limits of Scientific Inquiry*, ed. Holton and Morison, 229 (hereafter, the Holton and Morison collection is cited as *Limits of Inquiry*).

2. Robert L. Sinsheimer, "The Presumptions of Science," in *Limits of Inquiry*, 23.

3. "Society *invests in* the training, professional development, and general work of technical communities. It invests heavily: including research facilities and instruments, information banks, communication systems, and other aspects of infrastructure, as well as R&D grants and contracts, substantial public subsidy of one form or another goes to virtually every college, university,

medical center, field station and research facility in the United States. . . . The situation is similar in most other countries. For the most part the technical professions are left free to govern themselves, control admission to memberships, direct their own research, enforce quality of work, and advise on allocation of public and semipublic funds." William W. Lowrance, *Modern Science and Human Values* (Oxford: Oxford University Press, 1985), 81–82.

4. Lowrance sees science as having two sorts of social obligations. The first involves maintaining its integrity as a self-governing institution (and this importantly involves peer accountability and the sharing of information) and the second is service to society. Ibid., 82.

5. See Harvey Brooks, "The Problem of Research Priorities," in *Limits of Inquiry*, 177. For a detailed discussion of the history of scientific autonomy in post-World War II USA see Nelkin, "Threats and Promises."

6. "Probably the strongest reason for championing the hallowed ideal of scientific freedom is, quite pragmatically, that it gets scientific results." Lowrance, *Modern Science and Human Values*, 102. *Science, The Endless Frontier*, by Vannevar Bush (reprinted 1960, National Science Foundation, U.S. Government Printing Office), details how science has had its autonomy delegated to it by society in the post-World War II years; it articulates the contract. "It is likely indeed that scientists today enjoy greater freedom of inquiry than ever before in history, in terms of both public support through use of tax funds and reasonableness of government restriction." Peter Barton Hutt, "Public Criticism of Health Science Policy," in *Limits of Inquiry*, 157.

7. Francis Bacon was among the first of the moderns to envision modern science as combining the separate ends of theoretical and practical knowledge: "now these two directions—the one active, the other contemplative—are one and the same thing; and what in operation is most useful, that in knowledge is most true." *Novum Organum*, bk. 2, aphorism 4. According to historian of science Loren Graham, "The greatest value of science is not what it does for scientists, but what it does in both intellectual and material terms for society. . . ." Loren Graham, "Concerns About Science and Attempts to Regulate Inquiry," in *Limits of Inquiry*, 19. The physicist Gerald Holton holds that "the 'old credo' of science" has "immense power and usefulness" and has helped to "fashion two activities of great strength. The first is concerned with " 'pure' or 'basic' science rather than public need. It is the product of a largely autonomous self-governing system, not directed by the calculus of risk and benefits. If there are other affected interests, most often these are placed at a distance and the scientists are insulated from them. The hope for social utility as a by-product of one's discipline-oriented research may be in the background. But the ruling motto is that 'truth must set its own agenda.' " The "second mode of current excellence" involves applying "the basic scientific findings to a multitude of public needs. . . ." Holton, "From the Endless Frontier," 231.

8. ". . . the scientific and technical enterprise needs a certain measure of

internal autonomy in order to pursue the most pragmatic goals. This is true because the ends we can pursue are constrained by the possibilities presented to us by nature, and in the words of Charles Fried we cannot affirm 'truth as a constraint on the pursuit of the useful, while denying truth any power to set its own agenda.' " "Even in the most applied research activity, once the search is underway, utility is bracketed and reality must be the goal, lest the desired utility itself never be reached." Harvey Brooks, "The Problem of Research Priorities," in *Limits of Inquiry*, 177.

9. Bernard Barber, *Science and the Social Order* (New York: Collier Books, 1962), 41.

10. According to Don Price science is "the only institution for which tax funds are appropriated almost on faith, and under concordats which protect the autonomy . . . of the laboratory." Don Price, "The Scientific Establishment," *Science* 134 (August 18, 1961): 1099. The medical and legal professions might seem to be a counterexamples: like science they are of considerable social significance and are largely self-regulating. What distinguishes medicine and law from science is that they are still for the most part private enterprises undertaken by individual practioners for the sake of individual clients. According to William Lowrance, physicians are subjected to "elaborate societal and peer controls." Lowrance, *Modern Science and Human Values*, 61.

11. For a discussion of the "discomfort and irritation" of scientists when, in a public forum, laypersons demand that they identify their "political base" or "source of support," see Nelkin, "Threats and Promises," at 204.

12. *Dialogue on the Great World Systems*, in the Salisbury translation, ed. G. de Santillana (Chicago: University of Chicago Press, 1953), 63.

13. "For the most part, it is conceded that scientists cannot determine social goals, and politicians or the public should not determine scientific methods or tactics, nor influence conclusions. The problem is how to reach agreement on what constitutes ends and what constitutes means, where the line between strategy and tactics in science is to be drawn." Harvey Brooks, "The Problem of Research Priorities," 178.

This conventional distinction reflects two related features pertaining to science's accorded autonomy: Universal truth is not merely worthwhile as such but inherently value neutral in the following sense: those who pursue it do so in such a way that interests other than an interest in truth cannot enter into the results and, once attained, this truth (again as universal) is neutral as regards any possible application and as regards the particular direction such application might take. Insulated in these ways from interested value judgments in a way in which technology is not, autonomy from social regulation for science is seen as justified. Defenders of scientific autonomy traditionally make this distinction. See Nelkin, "Threats and Promises," 201; Holton "From the Endless Frontier," 231; Brooks, "The Problem of Research Priorities," 177.

14. Nelkin, "Threats and Promises," 193. "There is still a large category of

research where regulation of science should not be permitted. This autonomy of science should be defended not as a privilege for an elite, nor as an absolute right, but as a need of society itself." Graham, "Concerns about Science," 2.

15. Merton, "The Normative Structure of Science," 267–78.

16. Ibid., 270. This suggests that modern science has preserved a distinctive feature of premodern science: the notion that the pursuit of truth is morally beneficial to the pursuer, irrespective of any utility. See Hans Jonas, "The Practical Uses of Theory," in *Philosophy and Technology*, ed. Mitchum and Mackey (New York: The Free Press, 1983), 335–46.

17. Israel Scheffler, *Science and Subjectivity* (Indianapolis: Hackett Publishing Co., 1982), 2, 1.

18. Merton, "The Normative Structure of Science," 270.

19. Scheffler, *Science and Subjectivity*, 2, 1, 4. This vision of science as possessing a moral dimension because of its service to objective truth has distinctively Kantian overtones in that it locates the core of moral behavior in our rational ability to perceive and conform to the universal. At the heart of Merton's and Scheffler's sense that scientific activity is a kind of moral action is the notion that there is something independent of us, of the merely subjective, something universal and universally accessible, with which we need to accord our thoughts and actions, in order to correct or curb what, as merely subjective, may deviate from the norm of truth. Morality lies in just such accordance, and science, functioning impartially to provide access to this universal is thus inherently moral, even if the universal truths it aims for are not themselves moral laws (and even if these truths should, on occasion, not be useful). In fact, the moral character of scientific activity may well be enhanced in our age where there is considerable skepticism about the possibility of universal moral laws. See Max Weber, "Science as Vocation," in *From Max Weber: Essays in Sociology*, trans. and ed. Hans Gerth and C. Wright Mills (New York: Oxford University Press, 1946). The irony, of course, is that science appears to have attained this level of moral character precisely through the methodological provisions that restrict it from searching for moral universals.

20. According to Harvey Brooks, "[t]here appears to be ample empirical evidence from recent research by sociologists of science to indicate that . . . 'objective' criteria of scientific choice do exist. . . . " He thus "assume[s] that peer review does indeed select the 'best science' and that [there are] more or less universalistic criteria of scientific merit which any competent group of scientists will agree upon, at least in application to concrete proposals." Brooks, "The Problem of Research Priorities," 178.

21. Lowrance, *Modern Science and Human Values*, 74.

22. Ibid., 82.

23. Merton, "The Normative Structure of Science," 276.

24. Lowrance stresses the importance of following the community. See Lowrance, *Modern Science and Human Values*, 74.

25. Merton, "The Normative Structure of Science," 273.

26. Ibid., 275.

27. Ibid., 274.

28. Ibid.

29. Ibid., 275.

30. While this is a common defense of autonomy, one could take a completely pragmatic view and still defend scientific autonomy. I will argue below that this will not succeed.

31. See especially Hans Jonas, "Freedom of Scientific Inquiry and the Public Interest," *The Hastings Center Report* 6 (August 1976): 15–17; Sissela Bok, "Freedom and Risk" in *Limits of Inquiry*; and Ian Hacking, *Representing and Intervening* (Cambridge: Cambridge University Press, 1983).

32. Dorothy Nelkin, *Science as Intellectual Property* (New York: Macmillan, 1984), 2.

33. Richard Levin and Richard Lewontin, "The Commoditization of Science" in *The Dialectical Biologist* (Cambridge, Mass.: Harvard University Press, 1985), 203. Nelkin, *Science as Intellectual Property*, 61.

34. Nelkin, *Science as Intellectual Property*, 20.

35. Ibid., 25.

36. Ibid., 11.

37. Ibid., 12.

38. Ibid., 57–58.

39. Ibid., 58–60.

40. Ibid., 71–72.

41. Ibid., 72.

42. There is some question as to whether peer review alone, independently of the moral integrity of the participants, can yield its desired and promised results. See John Hardwig, "The Role of Trust in Knowledge," *The Journal of Philosophy* 88:12 (December 1991): 693–708.

43. Jack Kloppenburg, Jr., "Alternative Agriculture and the New BioTechnologies," *Science as Culture* 2:13 (1991), 492.

44. See Kloppenburg, "Alternative Agriculture," 482–506.

45. Lester Thurow, *Head to Head: The Coming Economic Battle Among Japan, Europe, and America* (New York: Morrow, 1992).

12

Professions, Institutions, and Moral Risk

Joan C. Callahan

Introduction

In 1982, *New York Times* journalists William Broad and Nicholas Wade published a book that offered a description of science from the perspective of scientific fraud.[1] In reporting on cases of fraud in science, Broad and Wade came to reject the conventional ideology of science as "the ultimate arbiter of truth," and they concluded that the actual practice of science "bears little resemblance to its conventional portrait."[2] Cheered by some and jeered by others, Broad and Wade's iconoclastic conclusion on science and its practitioners is gloomy and cynical, captured as it is in the book's title, *Betrayers of the Truth*. A number of recent developments in the scientific community, however, bolster Broad and Wade's claim that the conventional picture of how science is said to be practiced is one matter and how science is in fact practiced is often quite another matter.

In roughly the first two-thirds of what follows, I want to take a renewed look at the conventional ideology of science and at some of the many cases that argue against that ideology as an accurate description of scientific practice. Much of what I say will be consonant with Broad and Wade's troubling conclusion. But my emphasis will be different. That is, I am concerned to see how the institutions that house contemporary scientific practice cohere with the conventional ideology of science as a set of ideals regarding standards for scientific work and standards of virtue for practitioners of science. My conclusion on contemporary science will be that the institutions that house it subject it and its practitioners to grave moral risks. In roughly the final third of the paper, the "landscape" will change as I move from science to other professions, including my own. My concern here will be as much with a call for changes as with critique as I finish with the

suggestions that other professions are subject to moral risks comparable to those in science, and that professionals need to recognize that
there is an unavoidable political dimension to professional responsibility, which requires that each of us be aware of and work for changes in
what I shall submit are patriarchal presumptions embedded in our
practices and institutions, which add substantially and unnecessarily
to the moral risks in contemporary professions.

The Conventional Ideology of Professional Science

The conventional ideology of science holds that science is a public
activity, conducted by a community of scholars, whose search is for
the truth, whose methods involve disinterested and painstaking testing,
whose rationality is paradigmatic, and who openly exchange and
carefully study and verify one another's work. This is the popular
picture of the scientific enterprise and scientific methodology. It is a
picture of a noble enterprise, conducted by noble persons, with noble
goals, according to noble methods.

Despite all this nobility in the conventional portrait of science, we
have recently seen some stunning revelations of fraud in science, many
of them reported by Broad and Wade. For example:

—the case of Elias Alsabti, an Iraqi physician, who worked for a
number of prestigious U.S. institutions, including Temple University
and Jefferson Medical College in Philadelphia and M.D. Anderson
Hospital and Tumor Institute in Houston. Alsabti published some 60
papers, some alone and some with invented coauthors. It is now
believed that all of them may have been stolen from other authors.[3]

—the case of Mark Spector, a brilliant graduate student at Cornell,
whose kinase cascade theory of cancer causation was supported
by forged data. Belated checks on Spector's background revealed
additional fraud—he had earned neither the B.S. nor M.S. from the
University of Cincinnati, which he claimed on applying to Cornell.[4]

—the case of John Long, who received $759,000 in grant support
from NIH for his research at MIT on Hodgkins disease, but whose
test-tube cultures were in owl monkey cells.[5]

—the case of William Summerlin, a junior colleague of immunologist
Robert Good, who was found to have inked black patches on mice to
"demonstrate" the success of a skin transplant.[6]

—the case of Philip Felig, chief physician at Columbia-Presbyterian
Medical Center, who was forced to resign after failing to act swiftly

and decisively with a junior colleague and coauthor, Vijay Soman, who in reviewing another author's paper for a journal, blocked publication of the paper and went on to plagiarize the paper, publishing it as the work of Felig and Soman.[7]

—the current case of Nobel laureate David Baltimore, who adamantly refused to admit that Thereza Imanishi-Kari, a Tufts immunologist, used fraudulent data in an immunology paper they coauthored in 1986, and whose belated apology strikes many of America's top biomedical scientists as completely inadequate.[8]

—the current case of Robert Gallo, director of the NIH's National Cancer Institute's Laboratory of Tumor Cell Biology, and his longstanding dispute with Luc Montagnier of the Pasteur Institute, over who discovered the virus responsible for AIDS. Gallo finally conceded that the virus he identified (in work done in 1983 and 1984) was from a sample contaminated by a sample sent to him by Montagnier. An NIH investigation has found Gallo's report of the work full of falsifications of data and misrepresentations of method; but Gallo's junior colleague at the NCI, Mikulas Popovic, takes most of the heat.[9]

—the current case of University of Tennessee Space Institute professor of engineering Walter Frost, who is alleged to have allowed at least one student to copy Frost's own work to earn his master's degree under Frost's direction. The student, an employee of NASA's Marshall Space Flight Center, went on to direct a $55,000 NASA contract to a company owned by Frost, FWG Associates.[10]

The list goes on, but these examples from recent science should be sufficient to substantiate Broad and Wade's claim that scientific practice does not always live up to the conventional ideology. There is, of course, no telling from such examples how much fraud and duplicity goes on in contemporary science. But the examples do show that at least some scientists fall far short of the ideal. And that is worrisome in more ways than one.

Independent of considerations of the conventional ideology and considerations of virtue, fraud in science is costly. In the Felig-Soman case, it took the NIH researcher whose work was stolen by Soman well over a year to get Yale officials to investigate her charge of plagiarism. The whole affair was so distressing and time consuming that she left research for medical practice. Felig, who had been associated with Soman at Yale and who, it seems, did not intentionally participate in the fraud, still lost his position at Columbia because of his failure to deal with Soman in a timely and appropriate manner. Margot O'Toole, the Imanishi-Kari postdoctoral researcher who challenged the Baltimore/Imanishi-Kari paper, originally did so in 1986. It is now over a half decade later, and the case remains under inquiry, spawning a continual flow of news stories and letters in scientific journals. In one letter to the National Academy of Sciences, Harvard's John Cairns has said that ". . . the only question remaining is whether anyone will actually go to jail."[11] In cases of forged results, enormous amounts of time, money, and energy can be spent on investigations and by researchers who base their work on specious claims. And because so much research and investigation into charges of impropriety is paid for out of public funds, the taxpayer ends up paying handsomely for the cheater's lies. Fraud and duplicity are harmful, then, not only to the liars who are caught, but to innocent others as well.

As I have said, there is no telling from the examples I've sketched how much fraud there is in science. But, again, the fact remains that some brilliant scientists slip into fraudulent practices, and the question is why this is so.

Deranged Apples or Bad Barrels?

Cases like those sketched above led the federal government in 1981 to conduct a series of hearings on fraud in science. The U.S. House of Representatives Science and Technology Committee's Subcommittee on Oversight and Investigation, chaired by Albert Gore, was charged with conducting the hearings. Central to the hearings was the question of why scientists become involved in fraud. Typical of much of the testimony before the subcommittee was the testimony of Philip Handler, then president of the National Academy of Sciences. Said Handler:

> I find little satisfaction in testifying before a committee of the United States Congress on . . . "falsification of research data and institutional pressures on researchers due to the present scandals of falsification of research results." In my view, that problem has been grossly exaggerated in the full and fulsome treatment it has had in the press. . . . The matter of falsification of data, I contend, need not be a matter of general societal concern. It is, rather, a relatively small matter which is generated in and is normally effectively managed by that smaller segment of the larger society which is the scientific community. This occurs in a system that operates in a highly effective, democratic, self-correcting mode—the . . . "peer review system." . . . One can only judge the rare acts that have

come to light as psychopathic behavior originating in minds that made bad judgments—ethics aside—minds which in at least this one regard may be considered deranged. Happily, the vast bulk of the scientific community understands the circumstances well and has never transgressed—or resists temptation if you prefer. . . . [I]n the hot cauldron of the operation of peer review in the scientific world, such data cannot long survive undetected. And it is the culprit, not society, that is injured on the rare occasion in which this occurs.[12]

Handler's testimony captures the received description of the scientific enterprise as an enterprise that is objective, concerned only with truth, and rigorously self-correcting. Given his belief that this is how science is in fact conducted, his explanation of deviation from the ideological norms is the "bad apple" explanation, commonly accompanied by a pseudo-psychiatric diagnosis that serves, minimally, as a partial excuse for a culprit—he or she was deranged. Scientists who deviate from the norms set by the ideology are, on this account, not just bad apples—they are insane apples. But is this account of the causes of fraud in science really adequate?

Putting aside the conventional ideology and taking a hard look at the reality of scientific practice suggests that even though dramatic instances of major fraud, like Summerlin's inked patches on mice, might be relatively uncommon, other forms of fraud and duplicity might be far more common, and the major problem might well be more with the barrels than with the apples.

In a letter to the *New York Times*, Robert Ebert, former dean of Harvard Medical School, called upon scientific professionals to stop relying on the "human frailty and nothing more" explanation of fraud in science, and to begin looking at the role institutional factors might have on conducting science in our time.[13] Following Ebert's lead, what I'd like to suggest is that we need to take a long, hard look at how and where contemporary science is practiced, at how the institutions that house and support contemporary science create moral risks for scientists, by encouraging what I shall call "scientific malpractice," and, by implication, at how some of these risks might be minimized.

Scientific Malpractice

Fraud is a kind of scientific malpractice. As in medicine, I take malpractice to include not only deliberate engagement in bad practice, but also failures in practice of which practitioners should have been aware. The making of false or misleading statements in science can be sorted out the way we sort out such statements in other contexts. We distinguish between blameless statements of error (i.e., cases where a speaker had every reason to believe that what he or she said was true), and culpable statements of error. Culpable or blameworthy statements of error are themselves of several kinds.

In some cases of culpable misstatement the speaker believed that what he or she said was true, but the speaker should have known the doubtfulness of the claim. Among these are cases of bias, like the bias involved in the nineteenth-century investigations of human skull size that led researchers like Samuel Morton to use different measurement techniques for the testing of white, black, and Native American skull size. Morton's records and published papers suggest that he was not engaging in conscious fraud; but he should have been aware that his methods ensured that his observations would match his bias.[14] Other cases are akin to cases captured by the concept of criminal negligence, which allows that an agent is unaware that his or her action may lead to injury, but the agent's behavior unreasonably increases the probablity of injury. Examples here include Freud's too quick (and self-serving) conclusion that cocaine is not harmful to its users, as well as cases of scientists judging products to be safe when they should have realized that the grounds for that conclusion were inadequate. A number of examples in this class include the scientific endorsement of products that have had devastating effects on women—the initial version of "the Pill," the tranquilizer Thalidomide, the intrauterine Dalkon Shield, and, most recently, silicone breast implants.[15]

The most disturbing kind of culpable misstatement involves those claims where the speaker knows quite clearly that he or she is lying.

I am reluctant to label as fraud cases involving blameworthy but unwittingly biased distortion or those that I have framed under the negligence model. But such distortion and negligence do go on in science. Indeed, they are probably far more common than deliberate fraud, though they are much more difficult to detect. Broad and Wade, for example, suggest that self-deception resulting from researchers' expectations (or hopes) of what they will see (or can conclude) might be far more pervasive than we might even begin to realize, and that scientists' capacities for self-deception make them gullible and easily deceived by those they trust.[16]

Clear cases of deliberate fraud are those involving an intention to deceive, including the deliberate falsification of results. Included here are outright forgery or invention of results and "cooking" or selective reporting of results.[17] Failure to report negative results (cooking) is probably the most common form of scientific fraud in data reporting and the easiest form of fraud to fall into, since a researcher can easily rationalize such exclusions on the ground that negative results are the fault of some error falling within the margin of expected error. But the commonness and ease of cooking does not change the fact that it is fraud, involving, as it does, the deliberate manipulation of results.

Other cases border between these and the unwitting bias and negligence cases, yet also seem appropriately classified as cases of fraud. I have in mind here various other intentional manipulations of data, as well as different kinds of representation of the work of another as one's own. Understood in this way, fraud in science involves activities ranging from flagrant forgeries of people like Summerlin and the ruthless theft of work by people like Alsabti, to the more subtle falsifications involved in failing to report negative data, and the more subtle plagiarisms involved in failing to acknowledge sources and other credit taking for work and discoveries not one's own. Problematic for this last category is the common practice of senior researchers' taking credit for the work and discoveries of their students and apprentices, a practice to which I shall return shortly.

Once we realize that fraud in science is not limited to the so-called isolated dramatic cases like some of those sketched earlier, but that it includes far more subtle and common practices, Philip Handler's "deranged apple" explanation of fraud in science begins to look unconvincing, and Robert Ebert's suggestion that we turn our attention to the barrel seems a well-taken one.

What I want to suggest is that once we begin to look at the contemporary standards of success in scientific practice, the contemporary rewards for success in science, and the institutional structures that support the contemporary practice of science, we shall see that the research environment is a breeding ground for scientific malpractice in its several varieties.

Standards and the Fruits of Success in Science and the Academy: Publish or Perish

The conventional ideology paints a portrait of researchers disinterestedly committed to the truth. But in the day-to-day conduct of their activities, it is not so much this collection of ideals that motivates researchers, but rather more mundane considerations like competition with rivals; the need to keep funding coming in; the search for prestige, position, and recognition; the pressure to publish or perish in the university community and in the research community more broadly; and the pressure on students and apprentices to please and enhance the reputations of their professors or mentors. The most substantial rewards in science go to those who are first in discovery. Coupled with this in contemporary scientific practice, opportunities and rewards go to those with long lists of publications on their résumés. Despite the conventional ideology's emphasis on open communication among scientists and rigorous, painstaking peer review, these features of the reward structure foster secrecy in the scientific process and a relentless pressure to publish and publish first. As Broad and Wade point out, the pressure to gain publication credits has resulted in a proliferation of publications, which itself makes fraud in science difficult to detect and, in cases like some of those mentioned, makes possible dramatic instances of out-and-out stealing from others and fakery that may never be discovered.

Consider for a moment the publish-or-perish phenomenon and the proliferation of publications that have, in great part, resulted from publishing as a standard of success and condition of reward. When the Alsabti affair came to light, an article in the *British Medical Journal* speculated on the possibility of effectively preventing plagiarism in biomedical research alone:

> There are at least 8,000 medical journals in the world, and many of these receive thousands of papers a year. Checking credentials of authors would be a vast and embarrassing business. And checking to see if a paper has been published before (under a different name and probably with a different title) would be nigh on impossible. Editors would seem to have little choice but to trust to the integrity of their contributors and the astuteness of referees.[18]

Alsabti built up his publication record by lifting materials from a grant application and paper drafts of one of his bosses (Frederick Wheelock, a microbiologist at Jefferson) and by stealing whole papers from obscure European and Asian journals, simply changing the titles and appropriating authorship. He was not discovered (as the conventional ideology would have it) by a rigorous, capable, self-correcting peer review process. He was discovered making up data by two young researchers working with him in the lab. It is no secret that many scientific publications are never even once cited in the scientific literature succeeding them. As Broad and Wade point out,

. . . not one of Alsabti's articles had been cited by another scientist prior to his exposure as a grand purloiner. Alsabti stole insignificant research and thereby avoided detection. But the list of papers he compiled still gave him instant entree to the higher reaches of U.S. academia.[19]

Broad and Wade also point out that it is commonplace among scientific researchers to pad their résumés by publishing their results in the smallest possible segments, thereby generating several shorter publications instead of publishing a single longer publication.[20] Like the rush to publish insignificant work, this practice is not undertaken to forward science, but to secure and forward the careers of individual scientists. Indeed, publishing work this way obviously militates against the ideal of sharing information, since publishing work in the smallest possible segments involves holding back information as long as this will not jeopardize a researcher's priority in discovery.

The publish-or-perish phenomenon points away from bad apples to bad barrels. People who rush to publish insignificant research, who publish in the smallest possible segments, who claim more for their work than it can support are not deranged. But they are in a barrel that in many ways discourages practice of the kinds of virtues captured in the conventional ideology. The threat in the dictum "publish or perish" is a real one. And it is a real one not only for assistant professors of science who are seeking tenure in the university. It is also a real threat for senior researchers who must produce to keep the grant money coming in; and it is a real threat for students and postdoctoral researchers who are dependent on the continued success and favor of senior researchers if they are to complete their academic degrees and have continued opportunities to work. It is a problem not with individual scientists as such, but with the institutional arrangements that house science in contemporary society, and it is a problem not limited to the so-called hard sciences. It pervades the disciplines, pressing on assistant professors in the arts, humanities, and social sciences, as well, who will not be tenured unless they come up for review with publication records that enhance the reputations of their employing institutions and, even more, that suggest that their scholarship will continue to enhance those reputations.

It is no secret that university academics generally are not rewarded for fine teaching or for service to their departments, colleges, universities, or the public. We are rewarded for adding to the prestige of our institutions, and that means publishing. We can offer the familiar platitudes about teaching and research going hand-in-hand; but those of us who have come along the "tenure track" in universities know full well that teaching and research more often conflict—that every hour given to students tends to be an hour lost from the research. And so, we learn early in the professional game that our survival and scholarly reputations tend to stand in an adversarial relationship with our students. Some of the most able of us find as many ways as we can to escape teaching and the demands of service—sometimes for years at a time, on grant after grant, leaving our places at home to be filled with part-time instructors, who themselves are usually seeking tenure-track positions elsewhere, and who will not be helped along their ways by overextending themselves in teaching or in giving time to students or service, particularly in institutions that they expect will never house them again. And so it is that the pressure to publish in science and academia becomes so intimately tied to survival and self-promotion, which can be far removed from the ideals that are supposed to govern the work and from the disinterested virtues that are supposed to govern our characters as professionals.

Scientists and academics are engaged in *practices*: uniquely human activities with uniquely human rewards of engaging in those activities. As virtue ethicists have reminded us in recent years, some of the rewards of participating in a practice are external to that practice— they can be gained in ways other than participating in one particular practice. Security, prestige, money, position, influence—these are all rewards that can be gained by doing something other than science or other than engaging in some academic discipline within an institution of higher learning. Other rewards can only be gained by functioning well within a practice. The rewards of doing science as such can only be gained by avoiding compromise and doing science well. Scientists and academics alike need to ask some hard questions about whether the current arrangements and standards of institutions that support their practices encourage various forms of malpractice by, for example, so emphasizing results that the threat of moral compromise lurks just around every corner.

Related to all this is the problem in science publishing of senior researchers systematically signing junior researchers' work as coauthors. This custom, despite its common acceptance, raises several serious questions about ethics in scientific practice. One of these has to do with false claims, since far too often senior researchers have really had little or virtually nothing to do with a piece of scientific work. To be acknowledged as providing help or opportunity is one thing. To be cited as coauthor—and too often as the principal author—

when one has done no more than provide help or opportunity is quite another. Signing as a coauthor under such circumstances is a form of theft. For, like other forms of plagiarism, claiming coauthorship under conditions where one has had little or virtually nothing to do with the work or discovery is to represent another's work as one's own.

Broad and Wade recount one startling instance of such credit taking that occurred with the discovery of pulsars. The actual discovery was made by Jocelyn Bell, a graduate student of Antony Hewish of the Cambridge University Group of radio astronomers. Bell was working for her Ph.D. under Hewish's direction, and she was watching the skies for a very different phenomenon. After analyzing thousands of pages of recordings from a radio telescope, Bell noticed "a bit of scruff"—a signal that defied classification—and set out to find out whether it was repeated and if so, what it might be. She consulted with Hewish on the possible sources of pulses, but the history of the case unequivocally shows that the discovery belongs to Bell, who suspended her Ph.D. work to track down more pulses and work out an account of them. When the article announcing the discovery of pulsars appeared in *Nature*, Hewish appeared as the principal author, with Bell and two other members of the Cambridge group listed as coauthors. Hewish was subsequently awarded the Nobel Prize. The award outraged the eminent theoretical astronomer Fred Hoyle, who called the award a scandal. In a letter to *The Times* of London, Hoyle wrote:

> There has been a tendency to misunderstand the magnitude of Miss Bell's achievement because it sounds so simple—just to search and search through a great mass of [recordings]. The achievement came from a willingness to contemplate as a serious possibility a phenomenon that all past experience suggested was impossible.

Hewish, in turn, defended his receiving the award by writing to *The Times*, saying that Bell had been using his telescope, under his instructions, to make a sky survey that he had initiated. The explanation of the phenomena as pulsars was, said Hewish, developed under his direction. "Jocelyn," he said, "was a jolly good girl but she was just doing her job. She noticed this source was doing this thing. If she hadn't noticed it, it would have been negligent."[21] So much for appropriate credit to underling Jocelyn Bell.

Coauthorship as it is practiced is troubling in several ways. It is not uncommon for senior science researchers to list hundreds of coauthored works. Robert Good, for example, who was William Summerlin's lab chief at Sloan-Kettering, "coauthored" nearly 700 scientific reports in a five-year period by amassing an enormous number of researchers under his direction. Much to his later chagrin, Good had signed as coauthor much of Summerlin's work with its forged data. And it was not, by the way, a rigorous, self-correcting peer review system that discovered Summerlin's inked patches on mice. The forgery was discovered by a lab assistant to whom Summerlin returned the mice after showing them to the gullible Good.[22] Today, David Baltimore faces a similar embarrassment. And, again, it was not the peer review process that discovered the problem with data in the Baltimore/Imanishi-Kari paper, but a postdoctoral researcher working with Imanishi-Kari.

When Summerlin's frauds became public, Lewis Thomas, president of Sloan-Kettering, issued the following formal statement:

> I have concluded that the most rational explanation for Dr. Summerlin's recent performance is that he has been suffering from an emotional disturbance of such a nature that he has not been fully responsible for the actions he has taken nor the representations he has made. Accordingly, it has been agreed that the Center will provide Dr. Summerlin with a period of medical leave on full salary [$40,000], beginning now, for up to one year, to enable him to obtain the rest and professional care which his condition may require.[23]

The deranged apple again.

Summerlin's painting patches on mice does indeed sound like the action of a desperate man. But Summerlin himself offered a bad barrel account of the personal and professional nightmare:

> My error was not in knowingly promulgating false data, but rather in succumbing to extreme pressure placed on me by the Institute Director to publicize information. . . . Time after time, I was called upon to publicize experimental data and to prepare applications for grants from public and private sources. There came a time . . . when I had no new startling discovery, and was brutally told by Dr. Good that I was a failure in producing significant work. Thus, I was placed under extreme pressure to produce.[24]

Summerlin, of course, is not to be excused for his gross dishonesty. But his protest points to a very real fact about contemporary science; namely, that the pressure to produce and to publish is great, so great that people who might otherwise function virtuously may be sorely tempted to commit fraud, be it big fraud or little fraud. Competition for funding keeps senior researchers under pressure and they, in turn, must pressure their underlings to produce in order to keep their labs afloat. Much of contemporary science requires elaborate and expensive equipment, and junior researchers are utterly dependent on their seniors for opportunities to work. If they are not productive team members, churning out results and publications, junior scientists will quickly find themselves out of jobs. There are, in all these facts of contemporary scientific life, structures and customs that create moral hazards. And, again, many of them are not limited to the scientific disciplines.

As I put the finishing touches on this paper, I am reminded that it is not simply the case that individuals are invariably out to steal credit from their students and apprentices, and I am reminded how embedded, pervasive, and unquestioned the practice of coauthorship in science is. Not a week ago, a student with whom I am doing a tutorial had it suggested to her by her adviser that she should think about publishing the paper that she is writing under my direction. The adviser went on to tell her, however, that she would need to speak with me about it, because I would have to be listed as principal author, "since no journal would publish a paper by an undergraduate." In this case, if there is a cost of refusing to collude in what I consider to be a fraudulent convention, it, unfortunately, will not be my cost—it will be my student's missed opportunity.

In other, related cases, senior scholars are pressured to publish before thay have taken a piece through what they consider to be an acceptable process of rethinking and revision—for example, when a journal or book editor is anxious to have a scholar's prestige lend prestige and interest to his or her own work. That pressure is only increased when the editor is a junior scholar whom the senior scholar wants to support.

It is not, then, always self-serving motivation that leads individuals to participate in conventions that involve fraud or other forms of professional malpractice. Our insitutional conventions often have a way of taking on a life and force of their own, creating vexing and painful moral dilemmas for all of us.[25]

The Industry-Science-Academy Connection

The biotechnology boom has increasingly blurred the distinction between science as an enterprise and science as free enterprise. As it has become increasingly clear that there are new ways to make big dollars through science, private industry has come forward seeking the use, and often the exclusive use, of the skills of academic scientists. As federal funds for basic research continue to dwindle, as the friendships between academics and entrepreneurs grow warmer, and as academics themselves more frequently establish their own business ventures, the moral risks multiply. Consider, for example, just these few troubling issues:

Secrecy

I have already suggested that the reward structure of science and the publish-or-perish phenomenon work to vitiate the traditional ideal of science as a community of scholars working together in open communication, conducting rigorous, systematic peer review. As academicians become more deeply involved with the entrepreneurial enterprise, the tendency toward secrecy can only increase. It is not, for example, uncommon for companies supporting a research project to require that researchers shroud their work in secrecy and that publication of results be delayed until the company can secure an exclusive license from the university for use and/or a patent on (say) a new life form. As academics become more deeply involved with business, trade secrecy more thoroughly invades the scientific enterprise, and the openness and exchange held up by the conventional ideology, already assaulted by rewards and demands within scientific and academic circles, continues to wither away.

There are other problems with secrecy, as well. For example, experiments involving human and animal subjects conducted in public universities have been shrouded from public review in order to protect trade secrets. If university researchers will not protect a company's interests in maintaining its trade secrets, that company will go elsewhere, taking with it the funding that helps to contribute to the university in so-called indirect costs.[26] Heads of science departments who want their programs to thrive have little motivation to buck funding companies on the question of secrecy, and the same is true of higher-level university administrators.

The Shift from Basic to Applied Research

In January 1991, the newly elected president of the American Association for the Advancement of Science, Nobel laureate physicist

Leon Lederman, sent out what he called a "cry of alarm" on the status of American science. Lederman had surveyed scientists in fifty universities, and received nearly 250 responses, most of them from researchers who were demoralized and deeply concerned about their own futures and the future of their disciplines. Chief among their concerns was funding. According to Lederman, public funding in real dollars per researcher amounts to roughly one-half of what it was in 1968. Although Lederman's cry for twice the public funding currently available for scientific research took some serious criticism, it needs to be realized that as public monies grow increasingly scarce and as industry comes forward bringing more and more of the funding to the research arena, research increasingly shifts away from the basic to the applied areas, leading researchers to propose "safe" projects with clear and proximate payoffs for backing industries and companies.[27]

Exploitation

As academic researchers increasingly become involved in servicing the interests of industry and in acting themselves as entrepreneurs, additional questions of conflict of interest arise, not the least of which again have to do with junior researchers, who may easily be exploited for the gain of an adviser's employer or a company or interest owned by an adviser. As long as a decade ago, Stanford graduate students were publicly decrying their professors' increasing commitments of time and energy to industry, lessening commitments to teaching, and use of their students' work for such purposes as attracting venture capitalists to their companies. Lee Randolph Bean hit the nail on the head when he then suggested that the emerging imperative for young biomedical researchers was "patent or perish."[28]

The industry-university connection not only presents risks of abuse of junior researchers, it extends to others, as well. As I write this paper, I sit on a committee at my home institution that is charged to examine the connection between university medical school/hospital physicians and the pharmaceutical industry. The pharmaceutical industry spends enormous sums of money attempting to influence physician prescribing practices. Pharmaceutical company benefits to individual doctors range from small "reminder items" of ad-bearing pens and pads, through larger "gifts" of textbooks and meals and various forms of "hospitality," to lucrative honoraria and expense-paid trips to attractive locations for physicians and their spouses.[29] Physicians adamantly insist that these practices have no influence on how they prescribe pharmaceuticals.[30] If they are right, the pharmaceutical industry is throwing away billions of dollars, many of those dollars spent on targeting individual physicians for visits by company representatives. A profoundly disturbing article in the *Wall Street Journal* recently reported that, unknown to patients, a number of physicians and pharmacists are now opening patient records to companies gathering data on who prescribes what. These companies, in turn, supply physicians' prescribing information to pharmaceutical companies, who then know who needs to be targeted for support of or changes in prescribing practices.[31] The pharmaceutical industry is not a bumpkin.

But even if the pharmaceutical industry were throwing money away in providing all sorts of gratuitous benefits to physicians, that money is not really *its* money—it is money taken in from patients, included in the price of prescription drugs.[32] Hospitals and physicians' offices abound with company-imprinted pens and pads. Medical students grow up learning that pharmaceutical companies are delighted to buy the pop and pizza for lunchtime discussions and continuing education offerings, and that virtually every medical practitioner has every opportunity to give presentations at a pharmaceutical company's invitation in exchange for a $200–$5,000 honorarium, plus the benefits of first-class travel and accommodations.[33] And all of that is paid for by patients who can only get the medications they need on the say-so of physicians who hold a licensed monopoly on giving patients access to those medications. Such licensure makes physicians the marketing targets of pharmaceutical representatives and, as in any other marketing situation, sellers are often willing to use any ploy available to them to influence buyers. What is doubly troubling about this example, however, is that physicians who open themselves to the influence of pharmaceutical companies are the individuals who make the decisions on what drugs will be bought; but patients are the individuals who pay. And, again, they pay not only for the drugs that are ordered by their physicians, they pay as well for the variety of benefits that their physicians receive from the pharmaceutical companies seeking to influence their physicians' prescribing practices.

The discussion of academics and the example of physicians and pharmaceutical companies leads us beyond science to other professions, and the moral risks inherent in institutionalized contemporary professional practice more generally. I have already mentioned the publish-or-perish phenomenon, its ties to institutional reward structures, and the moral hazards it creates for academics as well as for nonacademic scientists. Other institutional factors create a variety of moral risks across the professions.

Professions, Institutions, and Moral Risk

Contemporary discussions of professional ethics in the service professions tend to focus on the professional/client relationship. There are certainly many crucial moral issues to be discussed in the professional/ client relationship, but these discussions often leave out other considerations that have to do with institutional design and the moral hazards institutions create for practitioners. The portrait of the lone professional providing services for individual clients becomes more and more misleading as attorneys, physicians, architects, engineers, psychologists, and others become increasingly bound by group practices and institutions that burden them with institution-protecting responsibilities and that hold out rewards that can easily pit the interests of clients against the ideals of the professions and against the interests of professionals themselves.

Consider again physicians, for whom the individualistic picture of practice has been among the most appropriate. Today, physicians are increasingly involved in corporate practices, where they function either as specialists taking care of some narrow set of client needs, or as providers sharing primary care responsibilities with others in group practices, or as corporate employees in health maintenance organizations (HMOs), or as house providers in trauma centers, extended care facilities, and hospitals, or as technical experts whose specializations (e.g., pathology, radiology) are practiced exclusively in institutional settings. Even those physicians who have solo private practices have recently found themselves much more beholding to the hospitals that grant them practice privileges. For example, diagnostically related groups (DRGs) now limit the amount that insurance carriers will reimburse institutions and providers for treatments and services rendered, and if physicians too often run up bills that won't be reimbursed or if they too frequently handle their patients in ways that result in lost profits for their employing institutions or the hospitals permitting them to practice, they might well lose their jobs or have their practicing privileges revoked.[34] Add to this that physicians increasingly have been forced to serve as gatekeepers, making decisions on when and how goods and services will be distributed on the basis of institutional requirements rather than client needs.[35] Primary care physicians in

HMOs decide whether a patient will or will not see a specialist. Emergency room physicians in for-profit hospitals are pressed to turn the indigent away and to limit services according to internal budget guidelines. As Peter Appleby remarks,

> Such dilemmas are now so common that medical professionals joke defensively about performing "wallet biopsies" on incoming patients in order to determine their eligibility for care.[36]

And, again, if physicians don't do this well, their jobs and/or practicing privileges may be at stake.

Nursing, on the other hand, has always been essentially affected by institutional "housing." The vast majority of nurses work in institutions and nearly all of those who do not work in institutions work for some employer or agency other than a direct-contracting patient. Among the many institutional factors affecting nurses is the distribution of authority and power indigenous to health care provision. Nurses have always been, and continue to be, subordinate to physicians in virtually every aspect of health care provision. There is a good deal of literature on how this thoroughgoing subordination has prevented individual nurses from fulfilling their moral obligations to protect the fundamental moral entitlements of patients,[37] yet physicians continue to maintain dominance in all aspects of health care provision, even in areas where that dominance cannot be justified on the basis of training that is peculiar to physicians. Thus, even in cases involving judgments that have a moral rather than a strictly medical content, physicians continue to lay claim to ultimate authority, even though their medical training provides them with no particular moral expertise,[38] and even though nurses tend to be in a position to know better their patients and their patients' value structures.

The question of the distribution of institutionally recognized authority and power between physicians and nurses in health care provision raises a deeper question about institutional design more generally. That is, it scarcely needs to be pointed out that medicine has been a male-dominated profession and that nursing has been a female-dominated one. Although the distribution of power and authority in health care provision probably cannot be explained entirely in terms of gender differences in medicine and nursing, gender differences clearly play a central role here, and I want to finish with some observations on what I take to be gender-associated forms embedded in the institutions that house science and professional practice more generally, how these forms issue in moral risks for the professions and their practitioners and, with these observations, some suggestions on the unavoidably political dimensions of contemporary professional practice.

Professions, Patriarchy, and Politics

Although feminism is not a monolithic theory and feminists disagree among themselves on many, many issues, there are common threads that link all feminist views. Among these threads in what I call "postliberal" feminist views is the understanding of patriarchy and patriarchal thinking as preoccupied with dominance and competition to the exclusion of cooperation.[39] The criteria for success and rewards embedded in the institutions that house science, which were discussed earlier, clearly reflect a preoccupation with competition. This preoccupation with competition militates against the conventional ideology of science as an open, cooperative enterprise; it also militates against some of the professional virtues that the conventional ideology of science implies. To rephrase Broad and Wade: Our rhetoric about science embraces the ideal of cooperation, community, and helping relationships to which postliberal feminisms subscribe; but the reality of our science embraces competition, individualism, and dominance. It is patriarchal in just those ways.[40]

If we look carefully at the institutions that house and support professional practice today we shall find (virtually invariably) that they are structured by men, that their standards for success and reward in one way or another embed dominance and competition as fundamental values, and that those standards often presume as the norm and best suit the realities of characteristically male lives.[41]

Consider again academia. Some years ago, when I was a beginning assistant professor, I went to a meeting on promotion and tenure. The project was to have senior women faculty advise junior women faculty about things to keep in mind as we traversed the time from initial appointment to tenure review. It was a lively and interesting evening, chock full of anecdotes, case histories, and practical advice. But many of the anecdotes and case histories were deeply troubling. And some of the advice, indeed much of the advice, was deeply troubling. It was troubling to the junior women faculty at the meeting, and it was troubling in itself.

There was advice to keep away from long research projects, and to concentrate our efforts on producing as many quality publications as we could from our research in the early years. Reminiscent of the plight of Anita Hill, there was advice to find men in our fields to mentor us—men who were well connected, preferably men with international professional reputations, who could bring us into the proper professional circles. There was advice to avoid too many commitments to department, college, university, or public service, so as not to detract from our research time. And there was *lots* of advice to avoid taking on tasks that we, as women, were likely to be asked to take on (such as directing undergraduate studies or freshman writing programs) that would involve us in too many hours of work with students. I don't think I'm being inappropriately cynical in thinking that much of that advice was sound then, and that much of that advice is equally sound today. And it is sound, I think, because it is responsive to a number of real, if embarrassing, features of the contemporary research university.[42]

Some years ago, a group of sociologists published a book that generated a tremendous amount of public discussion on the state of American culture. The book is *Habits of the Heart*,[43] and its authors rightly point out that contemporary research university faculty are under greater and greater pressure to produce pragmatically—that is, to perform studies and to produce technologies with immediate applications and to develop in students career-oriented skills. And they rightly point out some troubling similarities between the contemporary research university and the modern business corporation. But they do not notice that the expectations of the contemporary university and the contemporary corporation are typically demands made by men and most easily met by men—men who are free to concentrate on their professional lives, often (indeed, usually) with women in the background to manage their households and serve as primary care providers for their children.[44]

Men, too, have been the generators of liberalism and the individualistic ontology of persons that the authors of *Habits of the Heart* so stridently criticize. It is no coincidence, I think, that men, who are so often most free to function relatively unimpaired by the requirements of households, children, and community are also the primary creators and administrators of contemporary institutions with those forms of life that encourage an emphasis on extreme individualism, productivity, and competition among persons rather than an emphasis on community, nurturing, and connectedness among persons—an emphasis that is common—indeed, generally necessary—in characteristically female lives.[45]

That many of the features of institutions that house and support the professions are features common to characteristically male lives is important to notice because it opens us to realizing that what are taken to be fully objective norms are often informed by a definite perspective that is not universally shared. Indeed, the norms that inform our contemporary cultural, social, political, and economic institutions all reflect the perspective not only of male lives, but primarily of the lives of privileged white males. To illustrate: a woman judge was recently asked to remove herself from a sex-discrimination case. The implication: male judges are sexless. Similarly, a black judge was asked to remove himself from a racial discrimination case. The implication: white judges are raceless.[46] Such examples reveal that the unstated norm for judges is white and male, and then the perspective of the white male gets taken for perspectiveless objectivity—to borrow Nagel's phrase, as "the view from nowhere."[47] It is much the same with our other institutions, with the realities and values they presume as norms,[48] and with the structuring of professional practices that are housed by them.

It is, then, not at all clear that the institutional norms that currently mold professional practice are in any way what they might be or what they ought to be. Customs like thirty-six-hour shifts for interns and residents in hospitals hang on for the incomprehensible reason of tradition, despite the fact that placing the care of often critically ill patients in the hands of exhausted neophytes subjects those patients to potentially lethal danger. The customary subordination of nurses to physicians in virtually all aspects of health care provision has hampered nurses in protecting the rights and promoting the interests of their patients. Pressures on scientists and university faculty to publish or perish (or patent or perish) have led to cynicism and astonishing breakdowns in good practice and in virtue. Much of all this, I want to suggest, is a function of the presumptions of the perspective of privileged white male lives and of dominance and competition presumed as basic values in the very foundations of our societal institutions; I also want to suggest that such an institutional climate serves neither women *nor* men well.

Conclusion

John Hardwig has recently written an interesting and illuminating paper in which he argues that we cannot rely on the mechanisms of "strategic trust" in science (such as peer review and replication of results) to assure us of the veracity of the claims of scientists.[49] We need, he argues, to have "moral trust" in our scientists. Although Professor Hardwig finds this an epistemologically odd conclusion— that scientific knowledge must rest, ultimately, on the moral character of scientists—I suppose I find that conclusion less odd than he does. We come to have justified beliefs in various domains in quite various ways. If we are to have justified beliefs in the scientific domain, we need to secure as far as possible the reliability of the testimony of scientists. I think it is clear that peer review and the replication of results simply cannot fully ensure that reliability. And I think it is unquestionable, as Professor Hardwig emphasizes in his paper in this volume, that we must "trust experts. And we must trust them *as persons. . . .*"[50] But it is equally clear, I think, that the existing institutional arrangements that house and support "the experts" can easily compromise various forms of reliability in science and across the professions, even when professionals themselves genuinely want to be worthy of trust. Just as it isn't enough to look only to individuals fully to understand all moral failures in professional practice, it is not enough to look only to individuals to ensure consistent virtue in professional practice. We need, as well, to look carefully at the institutional arrangements, from the most general to the most particular, that surround contemporary professional practice and we need to ask how we might re-form those arrangements to ensure that they do as much as possible to foster, rather than impair, the moral trustworthiness of professional practitioners. Where our institutions need re-forming (be they social, political, legal, religious, educational, corporate, or basic economic institutions), professionals need to step forward in the name of their professional obligations to help make those reforms. And this is just to say that there is a political dimension to professional ethics that simply cannot be avoided.

Thus, for example, it will not do for social workers simply to decry the fact that they are often in the terrible position of being able to provide only short-term intervention for someone in desperate need of long-term help. Social workers must all do what they can to influence the political decisions that leave them so compromised. Nor will it do for individual nurses to accept the status quo, which continues to compromise them. Every nurse needs to attend to the distribution of power in health care provision, and help as she or he can with putting nursing in a position where its practitioners are subject to less in the way of moral risk. Nor will it do for academics to fall into disillusionment and yield to burnout after years of accepting without question the criteria for success and reward in the academy. We *all* need to engage in a process that subjects those criteria to careful and sensitive scrutiny.

Finally, and most important, it will not do for those who have the most power in forming and controlling our practices and institutions to go on failing to question the unstated norms that our practices and institutions embed. The professions will only be able to fulfill their social responsibilities reliably when the institutions that house and support them are good barrels that scrupulously attempt to preclude imposing unnecessary moral risks on the professions and their practitioners.[51]

Notes

1. William Broad and Nicholas Wade, *Betrayers of the Truth* (New York: Simon and Schuster, 1982).

2. Broad and Wade, pp. 7–8.

3. Broad and Wade, pp. 38–59.

4. Broad and Wade, pp. 63–73.

5. Broad and Wade, pp. 89–93; and Patricia Woolf, "Fraud in Science: How Much, How Serious?" *Hastings Center Report* 11:5 (1981), pp. 9–14.

6. Broad and Wade, pp. 153–57.

7. Broad and Wade, pp. 161–80.

8. See, for example, *Science* 253 (5 July 1991), pp. 24–25.

9. See, for example, Ellis Rubinstein, "The Gallo Factor: Questions Remain," *Science* 253 (16 August 1991), p. 732; and "Investigation: AIDS Article Falsified Data: Scientists Admonished for Disregarding Ethics," *Lexington Herald Leader*, 9 February 1992, p. A8.

10. See, for example, Debra E. Blum, "Inquiries at U. of Tennessee Focus on Charges That Degrees Were Traded for Federal Grants," *Chronicle of Higher Education*, 24 July 1991, p. A1.

11. David P. Hamilton, "Baltimore Case—Brief," *Science* 253 (5 July 1991), pp. 24–25.

12. *Fraud in Biomedical Research: Hearings before the Subcommittee on Investigations and Oversight of the Committee on Science and Technology, U.S. House of Representatives, Ninety-Seventh Congress, March 31–April 1, 1981.* Washington, D.C.: U.S. Government Printing Office, Publication Number 77-661, 1981, cited in Woolf, p. 10.

13. Robert Ebert, letter to the Editor, *New York Times*, 9 June 1980, cited in Woolf, p. 10. See also Broad and Wade, Chapter 5.

14. See, for example, Gerald Dworkin, "Fraud and Science," in *Research*

Ethics, ed. Kare Berg and Knut Erik Trany (New York: Alan R. Liss, 1983), p. 70.

15. Thanks to Joel Feinberg for suggesting the negligence model and the example of Freud. Although Thalidomide did not harm the women for whom it was prescribed, it had devastating effects on their fetuses. The drug came onto the market and was prescribed for thousands of women on the basis of a direct extrapolation from studies of its effects on rats and mice to its presumed effects on humans. Testing drugs for potential teratogenic effects on human fetuses was made mandatory after the Thalidomide disaster. For discussions of the history of "the Pill," Thalidomide, and the infamous Dalkon Shield, see James W. Knight and Joan C. Callahan, *Preventing Birth: Contemporary Methods and Related Moral Controversies* (Salt Lake City: University of Utah Press, 1989).

16. See Broad and Wade's discussion of self-deception and gullibility in Chapter 6.

17. The term "cooking" comes from an 1830 treatise by Samuel Babbage, *Reflections on the Decline of Science in England* (New York: Augustus M. Kelley, 1970). See Broad and Wade, pp. 29–30.

18. "Must Plagiarism Thrive?" *British Medical Journal*, 5 July 1980, pp. 41–42, cited in Broad and Wade, p. 50.

19. Broad and Wade, p. 53.

20. Broad and Wade, Chapter 3.

21. See Broad and Wade, pp. 143–48.

22. Broad and Wade, p. 155.

23. Cited in Broad and Wade, p. 157.

24. Cited in Broad and Wade, p. 157. Dr. Good denied that he told Summerlin that he was a failure.

25. Cf. Thomas Nagel's point regarding moral luck in one's circumstances in "Moral Luck," *Mortal Questions* (New York: Cambridge University Press, 1979), pp. 24–38.

26. The use of indirect costs has recently emerged as yet another area of professional malpractice. In 1991, Stanford University President Donald Kennedy was forced to resign after it was found that he charged the government for part of the costs of antiques, a yacht, sheets, and flowers. See, for example, Leon Jaroff, "Crisis in the Labs," *Time*, 26 August 1991, pp. 45–51. That inappropriate use of funds collected to cover indirect costs of research is not limited to the occasional "bad apple" is made clear in an audit of U.S. research universities being conducted by auditors from three federal agencies for the Energy and Commerce Committee's Subcommittee on Oversight and Investigations. See Goldie Blumenstyk, "Auditors Say Research Universities Charged U.S. $350 Million Too Much for Indirect Costs," *Chronicle of Higher Education* 38:22 (5 February 1992), p. A25.

27. See, for example, Jaroff, "Crisis in the Labs."

28. Lee Randolph Bean, "Entrepreneurial Science and the University," *Hastings Center Report* 12:5 (1982), pp. 5–9.

29. The pharmaceutical industry is (conservatively) estimated to spend $5 billion a year on promotion. On "hospitality," the meeting planner for the American College of Rheumatology estimates that the cost of turning down pharmaceutical company money for evening dinners and receptions at its 1991 convention was somewhere around $200,000. See "Pushing Drugs to Doctors," *Consumer Reports*, February 1992, pp. 87–94.

30. *Consumer Reports*, however, discusses a series of studies that found that physicians seem clearly to be influenced by drug manufacturers who sponsor continuing education offerings (pp. 91–92). Such sponsoring, along with other practices, such as company-sponsored publication of "supplements" to professional journals that adapt the appearance of the journals they supplement, have led the FDA to start looking at drawing clear boundaries between scientific and promotional activities. See *Consumer Reports*, pp. 90–93.

31. Michael W. Miller, "How Drug Companies Get Medical Records of Individual Patients," *Wall Street Journal*, 27 February 1992, p. A1. Miller reports that it is estimated that "nearly ½ [of] the 1.6 billion prescriptions filled each year in the U.S. today pass along this chain" (p. A1). Miller also reports that the incentive that encouraged more than 1,600 physicians to sign up with Physician Computer Network (PCN) over the past three years has been PCN's offer to lease a first-rate computer system and software for about one-third of the going cost. PCN is the first company gathering information by tapping directly into physicians' computers and copying patients' records (p. A1).

32. This point was made eloquently by Robert Noble, M.D., in his testimony before our Medical Center committee on 13 June 1991. *Consumer Reports* points out that the high prices of prescription drugs place a special burden on the elderly, who consume 34 percent of these drugs (p. 88). The same report cites American Association of Retired Persons' surveys finding that four out of ten Americans over sixty-five have no prescription drug insurance whatever, and that one in seven elderly Americans have not taken a prescribed medication because it was too expensive (p. 88).

33. Noble testimony; and *Consumer Reports*, p. 90.

34. See, for example, Larry Reibstein with Mary Hager, "Physician, Cut Thy Costs," *Newsweek*, 23 December 1991, p. 41.

35. See, for example, Peter Appleby's discussion in *Ethical Issues In the Professions*, ed. Peter Windt et al. (Englewood Cliffs, N.J.: Prentice-Hall, 1989), pp. 226–27.

36. Appleby, p. 236.

37. See, for example, James Muyskens, *Moral Problems in Nursing: A Philosophical Investigation* (Totowa, N.J.: Rowman and Littlefield, 1982); and E. Joy Kroeger-Mappes, "Ethical Dilemmas for Nurses: Physicians' Orders versus Patients' Rights," in Thomas A. Mappes and Jane S. Zembaty, eds., *Biomedical Ethics*, 2nd ed. (New York: McGraw-Hill, 1986), pp. 127–34.

38. See, for example, Roland R. Yarling, "Ethical Analysis of a Nursing Problem: The Scope of Nursing Practice in Disclosing the Truth to Terminal Patients," *Supervisor Nurse* Part I (May 1978), p. 49, cited in Martin Benjamin and Joy Curtis, *Ethics in Nursing*, 2nd ed. (New York: Oxford University Press, 1986), p. 12, as well as Benjamin's and Curtis's discussion of this point in Chapter 1.

39. I take postliberal feminisms to be those views that reject the central ontology and moral and political philosophies associated with liberalism; namely, the radical individualist ontology of persons presumed in liberalism, and moral/political philosophies that construe the basic moral positions of persons adversarily. Thus, feminist positions that I characterize as postliberal are those that depart from liberal feminism (in part) by conceptualizing persons as always embedded in a network of relationships and that reject the liberal's preoccupation with moral rights in favor of a morality that stresses cooperation and relationship rather than competition and adversity between persons. Despite this ontological agreement with communitarianism, however, I don't take postliberal feminisms to be reducible to communitarianism. See Joan C. Callahan and Patricia G. Smith, "Liberalism, Communitarianism, and Feminism," in *Liberalism and Community*, ed. Noel Reynolds, Cornelius Murphy, and Robert Moffat (Lewiston, New York: Edwin Mellen Press, in press).

40. In contrasting views that I label "postliberal feminist" with those I call "patriarchal" I do not mean to take any essentialist views regarding men and women (see Callahan and Smith, "Liberalism, Communitarianism, and Feminism"). Despite what some feminists are inclined to contend, I believe that men can be feminist and that women can be patriarchal in their views. For an illuminating discussion of the concept of patriarchy, as well as patriarchy's ties to technology and capitalism, see Barbara Katz Rothman, *Recreating Motherhood: Ideology and Technology in a Patriarchal Society* (New York: Norton, 1989). The theoretical perspective I adopt here is fully compatible with what is sometimes called "positional feminism"; that is, the view that rejects a commitment to essentialism, but allows that, in fact, women as a class have a gendered identity that leads to certain characteristically "women's needs" in the present world. On this kind of view, see, for example, Linda Alcoff, "Cultural Feminism versus Post-Structuralism: The Identity Crisis in Feminist Theory," *Signs* 13/3 (1988), reprinted in *Feminist Theory in Practice and Process*, ed. Micheline R. Maison et al. (Chicago: University of Chicago Press, 1989), pp. 295–326. Such a view can also recognize that men have a gendered identity that commonly leads to their lives having certain features. More on this in the text and notes that follow.

41. Again, no claims about essentialism are presumed here. The point is just that men's lives commonly have certain characteristics, women's lives commonly have certain characteristics, these common characteristics are not the same for men and women, and that they are not makes for some important

differences. This point is compatible with essentialism, nominalism, and positionalism (see Note 40) on the matter of explaining these differences. I mean to stay agnostic on this issue for the purposes of this paper. (See also Notes 42 and 44.) For a discussion of difference that focuses on how the science professions exclude women and why what might be called the "ways of life" in these professions might lack appeal for many women, see Stephen G. Brush, "Women in Science and Engineering," *American Scientist* 79 (September-October 1991), pp. 404–19. For a number of views on sexual difference, see Deborah L. Rhode (ed.), *Theoretical Perspectives on Sexual Difference* (New Haven: Yale University Press, 1990). For a discussion of difference more generally, see Martha Minow, *Making All the Difference: Inclusion, Exclusion, and American Law* (Ithaca: Cornell University Press, 1990).

42. Joe Pitt rightly points out to me that men in the academy often give much of the same advice to their junior male colleagues. But part of my point here is that women are more often pressured to take on tasks that will not help them gain tenure under existing standards, and that men are, historically and still usually, in a better position to meet the criteria for tenure commonly applied in the university (see the next paragraph in the text). These criteria ignore the fact that far many more women than men are (even in the 1990s) primary caretakers for young children during the early years of their professional lives and, because of this, their most productive research years often come later—at about the time when some men begin to slow down or become more interested in teaching or administration than in publishing. Even progressive thinkers in the university who want to support a system that recognizes a variety of professional profiles for senior faculty still tend to want to retain the emphasis on publishing for the untenured professor, which, again, presumes the picture of a relatively unbounded individual—a picture that, in fact, excludes many more women than men in their early years as academics.

43. Robert N. Bellah et al., *Habits of the Heart: Individualism and Commitment in American Life* (Berkeley: University of California Press, 1985).

44. This is an example of what I mean by a feature common to "characteristically male lives"—men commonly have wives who bear primary responsibility for households and child care; women commonly don't.

45. For just one discussion of how the features of characteristically male lives press away from nurturing, community, and connectedness, see Annette Baier, "Trust and Antitrust," *Ethics* 96:2 (1986), pp. 231–60.

46. See Minow, pp. 60–61.

47. Thomas Nagel, *The View From Nowhere* (New York: Oxford University Press, 1986).

48. For just one fuller discussion of how our institutions and practices in general reflect the lives (i.e., embed the perspective) of the most powerful (viz., able-bodied and otherwise "normal" white males), see Callahan and Smith, "Liberalism, Communitarianism, and Feminism."

49. John Hardwig, "The Role of Trust in Knowledge," *Journal of Philosophy* 88:12 (December 1991), pp. 693–708.

50. John Hardwig, "Toward an Ethics of Expertise," this volume, p. 89.

51. Thanks to Jennifer Crossen, Joel Feinberg, Joy Kroeger-Mappes, Larry May, Joe Pitt, Bruce Russell, Ferdy Schoeman, and Dan Wueste for helpful comments on an earlier draft of this paper.

13

Overlooking the Merits of the Individual Case: An Unpromising Approach to the Right to Die

Joel Feinberg

I.

There are many standard situations in life in which authorities are expected to make decisions based on the merits of the individual cases they are evaluating. In most of these situations we expect the decision makers rigorously to exclude consideration of any grounds other than the merits of the case before them. We are not accustomed, for example, to having referees at athletic contests declare that even though the victory in the 100-meter dash would be awarded to Angelo if the referee considered the case entirely on its merits, he proposes instead to appeal to other relevant criteria independent of the merits of the case, and judge "all things considered" that Mario has won the race. And it would be unusual candor at the very least for an employer to award an important position to Paolo while conceding that the case for appointing Gianna based strictly on her fittingness for the job has greater merit. Nevertheless, the deliberate overruling of strictly internal considerations for the sake of normally irrelevant external ones is a common practice in many legal and moral arguments. The controversy over the legalization of voluntary euthanasia is a good example.

In his influential 1958 article[1] the legal scholar Yale Kamisar seems to concede that when judged entirely on their merits there are instances of mercy killings by doctors or others that have full moral justification. I think Professor Kamisar would agree that in cases of the kind he has in mind, the patient has a *moral right* to end his life, or lacking the ability for self-remedy, to have it ended for him by those who are willing and in a better position to do so. Kamisar even gives us a general account of the qualifying characteristics of the mercy killings he has in mind: The patient must in fact be "(1) presently incurable,

(2) beyond the aid of any respite which may come along in his life expectancy, suffering (3) intolerable and (4) unmitigable pain and of a (5) fixed and (6) rational desire to die."[2]

Nevertheless, Kamisar opposes the legalization of euthanasia, resolutely arguing against proposals to transform the moral right to die into a legal right to die by giving it legal recognition and enforcement. The reasons for his opposition have nothing further to do with the merits of the cases he considers, but with the dangerous social consequences of giving any acts of killing legal certification. It would be better, he claims, to leave the law of homicide unchanged; bring murder charges against the family members, friends, and doctors who violate it; and then leave the fate of the mercy killers in the hands of sympathetic prosecutors, judges, and juries who will either refuse to indict, or else grant acquittals, suspended sentences, or reprieves, out of their recognition of the moral innocence of the criminal act. In that way, the "law on the books" will continue to testify to the community's profound and universal respect for human life, and serve to deter those who would kill for any reason, while "the law in action" would enable the bolder mercy killers to go unpunished for the crimes they undoubtedly committed, though from the highest and purest motives.

And what are the considerations powerful enough to outweigh the merits of individual cases of morally justified euthanasia? Kamisar lists them for us: weighed against the moral quality of some individual cases considered solely on their merits are the inevitable occurrences of mistakes and abuses in *other* cases. In effect, then, what Kamisar tells the suffering patient whose moral right to die is beyond question is: "If we change the law to permit *your* worthy case, then we will be legalizing other less worthy cases—patients who have been misdiagnosed, patients who might otherwise recover, patients who don't really want to accelerate their deaths despite earlier death requests made hypothetically, patients who are being manipulated by family members who see their life savings dwindle as the medical costs rise, and other instances of 'mistake' and 'abuse.' " What the blanket prohibition of homicide tells the responsible patient whose moral right to die is undoubted is that *he* may not do something that would be harmless or beneficial on balance because *others* cannot be trusted to do the same thing without causing grievous harm (unnecessary death).

Much the same kind of argument, it might be noted, was made in support of a blanket prohibition of alcoholic beverages in the United States in the 1920s. It is not an implausible argument on its face. Compulsive consumers of alcoholic beverages cause an enormous amount of harm to themselves and to others, including (among many other examples) over 50 percent of the fatalities in motor car accidents. Many millions of us, on the other hand, are unaddicted social drinkers who imbibe for occasional relaxation and pleasure, and never to excess. We are responsible in the way we drink wine (say) with dinner, and we might well insist on our moral right to drink as we please. But the very law that permits that innocent activity in our case permits the not-so-innocent drinking of others who are certain to cause widespread death, mutilation, and heartbreak. Is it really asking too much of us to forgo our nightly highballs so that others might be prevented from wreaking their havoc on the highways and their destruction of families elsewhere? Perhaps it is an unfair sacrifice to force on us, the argument concludes, but on balance, more harm by far is prevented by a blanket prohibition than by blanket permission, and if error in this difficult calculation is inevitable, it is better that we err on the safe side.

If there is a crucial disanalogy between this argument for the prohibition of wine and spirits and the argument of Professor Kamisar for the continued prohibition of voluntary euthanasia, it is that the alcohol example is addressed to persons like us who are reluctant to give up some innocent pleasures, whereas the euthanasia argument is addressed to those, like Matthew Donnelly and the parents of Nancy Beth Cruzan, who are bent on escaping intolerable pain, in Donnelly's case, or pointless psychological suffering in the Cruzan case, and who might well wonder what it is in their horrible circumstances that can be described as erring on "the safe side."

Matthew Donnelly's experiences in his final days were "sadly typical" of a class of cancer victims, and seem to match closely the sort of case Kamisar had in mind when with admirable candor, he conceded that some patients might have a moral right to die. As James Rachels describes it,

> Skin cancer had riddled [his] tortured body. . . . A physicist, he had done research for the past thirty years on the use of X-rays. He had lost part of his jaw, his upper lip, his nose, and his left hand. Growths had been removed from his right arm and two fingers from his right hand. He was left blind, slowly deteriorating, and in agony of body and soul. The pain was constant; at its worst, he could be seen lying in bed with teeth clenched and beads of perspiration standing out on his forehead. Nothing could be done except continued surgery and analgesia. The physicians estimated that he had about a year to live.[3]

The "law on the books" commanded Donnelly not merely to sacrifice some harmless pleasures so that less responsible persons might not abuse theirs, as in the alcoholic prohibition example. Rather, it commanded him to forgo his clear moral claim to a release from a full year's intolerable suffering. The argument that would overturn the merits of the individual case in the euthanasia example is to that extent at least, much weaker than its counterpart in the alcohol prohibition example. We have more reason, I think, to ban drinking wine with dinner than we do for prohibiting euthanasia in cases like that of Matthew Donnelly.[4]

The urgency of Donnelly's pain was missing in the case of Nancy Beth Cruzan who was permanently incapable of experiencing pain—or anything else, for that matter. While I was writing this lecture,[5] young Miss Cruzan lay, at state expense, in a Missouri state hospital. As a consequence of a car accident, she had suffered virtual destruction of her cerebral cortex, leaving her irreversibly in a "persistent vegetative state," without cognitive function, permanently comatose, which is to say forever without consciousness. It is impossible for me to understand how from her point of view this condition could possibly be preferable to death. Indeed, it is impossible to understand how, from the perspective of the person involved, this condition is distinguishable from death itself. Common sense would maintain that Miss Cruzan was dead from the time her coma became irreversible. Legally, however, this judgment of common sense had no bearing on Miss Cruzan's status. Despite the fact that her "cerebral cortical atrophy [was] irreversible, permanent, progressive, and ongoing,"[6] the brain stem continued to function, permitting various motor reflexes, maintaining body temperature, heartbeat and breathing. She was unable to swallow food or water, so her body was kept going by a surgically implanted gastrostomy feeding and hydrating tube. Her parents, after six years of constant visits to the bedside of their unconscious daughter's body, sought a court order directing withdrawal of the feeding and watering tube. The Supreme Court of Missouri declined to issue this order. The parents then appealed to the U.S. Supreme Court, and their case became something of a cause célèbre in 1990.

If we assume that Nancy Cruzan, when alive, preferred that her body not be kept alive if she were ever to be in such circumstances, then the merit of her parents' case is clear. All of the judges agreed that American constitutional law gives every competent adult the right to refuse medical treatment, and that the feeding and hydrating techniques that were keeping Nancy Cruzan's body alive did constitute medical treatment. The issues became cloudy only when the court considered the factual question of what Nancy's preferences actually were or would have been as to the continuance of this medical treatment. What little evidence was available to the court, the verbal testimony of a close teenage friend, suggested that Nancy had a deep aversion to her body being kept alive in a persistent vegetative state. Thus, if the standard of evidence was that which is normally used in noncriminal cases, namely a "preponderance of the evidence," the court should have decided that the available evidence of Nancy's *not* wanting continuance being greater than the evidence that she would have preferred continuance, her consent to the feeding-hydrating tube could not be inferred. In other words, we had no evidence that she wanted to be kept alive, but *some* evidence, weak though it was, that she would prefer death. But the U.S. Supreme Court, backing up the Missouri Supreme Court, argued that a higher standard of evidence is required in cases where the state's "interest in the protection and preservation of human life" is brought into play. The situation in the Cruzan case, as the U.S. Supreme Court saw it, involved a conflict between the state's "interest in preserving human life" and Nancy Cruzan's constitutional right to have her preference for discontinuance of medical treatment in such circumstances honored.

The main problem, of course, was that there is only scanty evidence of what Nancy's preference actually was. So, given the state interest in preserving life (as we shall see, a very strange notion indeed as interpreted in this case), the state has the right to require especially convincing evidence of the preference for death. And so Missouri required not just a preponderance of the evidence, or a probability barely greater than half, but rather that "evidence of the incompetent's wishes as to the withdrawal of treatment be *proved by clear and convincing evidence.*"[7] The main issue before the U.S. Supreme Court was whether the Missouri Supreme Court had a right to substitute this higher standard of evidence, and the highest court ruled that it did have that right.

What the Court did, in effect, was to go beyond the probable facts that constituted the merits of the Cruzan case to an external value judgment that would determine, from the outside as it were, what the facts of the case were. That value judgment is the same as that underlying Kamisar's argument in euthanasia cases involving conscious suffering patients, namely that the Court's (skewed) allocation of the risk of error in our inferences to Nancy's preference is justified because it is more important *not* to terminate life support for someone who would wish it continued than to honor the wishes of someone (like Matthew Donnelly) who would not wish it continued. Like

Professor Kamisar, the majority of the Supreme Court is determined that if it must err, it err on the "safe side." But the comparative value judgment that they bring in from the outside to give shape to the facts of the case distorts those facts and, as I shall argue, misrepresents the case's actual merits.

II.

Before we return to the subject of euthanasia, it will be useful to consider one of the patterns of argument in other contexts that purports, often quite plausibly, to justify deciding cases on grounds other than what we can call their "internal merits." Consider for example the argument from abusable discretion. Suppose a legislature must decide what kind of nighttime traffic signal, if any, to install at an intersection that has been the site of many nocturnal accidents. The least expensive solution would be to leave drivers free to decide whether lighting and traffic conditions require a complete stop, or only a slowdown and careful perusal of the traffic in both directions. The two rival proposals are that the ordinary three-color alternating stoplight continue to operate all night long and the counterproposal that from midnight until 6:00 in the morning the three-color alternating signal be converted into a yellow blinker, which is only a cautionary warning signal not requiring a stop. Imagine that studies of accident rates at similar intersections elsewhere show that there are twenty deaths a year at intersections that have all-night yellow blinkers, and only ten deaths at the intersections that have ordinary three-color alternations day and night. The argument for the all-night operation of the standard three-color light, then, is that it will probably cut in half the death rate from accidents at that corner. The argument on the other side is that 99 percent of the drivers can be trusted to exercise careful discretion at this and other intersections, especially at night when traffic is very sparse and there are no obstructions to vision. It is not fair to this vast majority, so the argument goes, to inconvenience then by requiring them to stop, in total indifference to the merits of their own cases, just in order to deprive the tiny minority of untrustworthy drivers of a discretion they might abuse.

The riddle of abusable discretion does not arise where it is practical to design a system of licensing that will in fact judge each case on its merits, as, for example, one that licenses only exceptionally vulnerable and clearly capable and trustworthy persons to carry handguns. But a system that awards to some drivers a special license to go through red lights when they believe it is safe to do so would indeed be excessively difficult to administer. And when such special licenses are impossible, a form of ethical argument is often heard that strikes some people as highly paradoxical. A statute requiring the all-night operation of a normal stoplight is indeed justified, a motorist might admit, simply because it will save two or three human lives a year. "But," the motorist might continue, "I am a skilled and responsible driver quite capable of deciding on my own when conditions at that intersection require a stop. So I will feel quite justified on bright moonlit nights when no cars can be seen for a kilometer in either direction, in cautiously proceeding through a red light." And what if a traffic policeman gives him a ticket? "He too will be quite justified in giving me a ticket for my fully justified infraction of a fully justified statute." Only the justification of the driver's disobedience refers to the internal merits of his case. For the other two justifications, one political and one legal, this driver's case is not judged on its intrinsic merits. The decision to enact the statute was based on statistical studies of the behavior of *other* drivers (facts "external" to *this* driver's own conduct and disposition), and the wording of a statute that makes no allowance for the "internal" characteristics of this driver's situation that give his behavior its own justification. So much for judging each case on its merits!

An argument of similar form was frequently used by moderate drinkers in defense of their violations of the 1920s alcohol prohibition law, a law they often conceded to be supported by good reasons. The prohibitory law appeared to have a morally legitimate aim; namely, reduction of the great harms caused by drunkards. But for people who had enjoyed their moderate drinking habits for decades and knew that they could be trusted to drink wine for dinner, or a highball at a party, without harmful consequences to others, it was natural to proceed in violation of a law they thought legitimate (for others) and to do so with clear consciences. This created a "market of innocents" and a business incentive for gangsters to sell in that market, with all the violent crime that led to the discrediting, and eventually to the downfall, of Prohibition.

A law that grants terminal patients, their loved ones, or their physicians the legal authority to terminate lives thereby confers discretion on those parties to decide their cases on the merits. If the situation is analogous to that in the traffic signal example, there will be some rare cases in which that discretion is abused. But the analogy is highly tenuous. What would count as "abuse" in the euthanasia case? What would be analogous to drunken or reckless driving in the other case? Again there is a danger of begging a central question in one kind of reply. One might say that the abuser of discretion is precisely he who uses it to choose death and not life, this being the kind of moral abuse that consists in giving priority to unworthy values like freedom from pain and personal autonomy. Whether in fact those values or the respect for human life are the most worthy ones is of course precisely the question at issue.

It is natural at this point to mention *the defective analogy to capital punishment*. There is an argument against the death penalty that is sometimes used as a model for arguing against the legalization of euthanasia. The arguments are superficially parallel in form: they both urge that the merits of the individual case be overlooked in order to prevent a greater evil, consisting of the inevitable occasional mistake. The resemblance of the two arguments, however, is only superficial. The crucial differences can best be appreciated by laying the two arguments side to side and comparing them.

The Argument Against Permitting the Death Penalty

If we use the death penalty as our punishment for murder, then an occasional innocent person (maybe one in a thousand) by mistake or abuse[8] will be executed, and execution of course is irrevocable. This consequence is so evil that we are justified in overlooking the merits and demerits of individual cases, overlooking, that is to say, most prisoners' desert of death for what they have done. That would be to give these convicted murderers an *undeserved benefit*, a reprieve from the death penalty they deserve, but it is worth doing all the same, since they will still suffer life imprisonment with all its hardships (which they must deserve if they deserve the even greater evil of death), and they will not be turned loose to prey on other victims. (The loss in marginal deterrence would be very slight.) So the overall cost would not be great for securing a gain that is of supreme moral importance; namely, the prevention of an occasional serious and unjust mistake, the execution of an innocent person.

The Parallel Argument Against Honoring Death Requests from Suffering Terminal Patients

If we legalize voluntary euthanasia, then an occasional salvageable, or not truly consenting patient (maybe as many as one in a hundred) will by mistake or abuse be killed or allowed to die. This consequence is so evil that we are justified in overlooking the merits of individual cases and turning down *all* death requests regardless of their merits, that is regardless of the requestor's desert of a cessation of suffering and shortening of the death process, both of which he takes to be benefits. This would be to confer not an undeserved benefit, but an *undeserved harm*; namely, the continuance of suffering and the extending of the death process. It is worth doing this, however, because *the cost is not great* [sic] to the terminal patients and their families;[9] and a great gain, the prevention of unnecessary killings, would be achieved.

In one respect the argument against euthanasia may actually be stronger than the argument against the death penalty. If the presumed incidence of unnecessary deaths in euthanasia cases would be ten times as great as in capital punishment cases, as we supposed in our formulation of the arguments above, then the anti-euthanasia argument is strengthened proportionately. But that surmise is entirely arbitrary, lacking the necessary empirical support. Moreover, we must remember that prisoners who were entirely innocent of murder but falsely convicted anyway though they had nothing whatever to do with the crime are only a tiny percentage of those who do not deserve to be executed. There are those who did the deed they were accused of, but did it by mistake or accident, those who should have been convicted of manslaughter instead of murder, those who killed because they panicked in the face of threats from the victim though the imminence of harm required by the self-defense justification was missing, or who mistakenly believed they were being attacked with a knife during a scuffle. Perhaps all of these prisoners mistakenly convicted of murder are in fact guilty of *something*, and deserve some punishment or other. But it would be a tragic and unjust mistake to inflict the penalty on them that is reserved for murder, the most serious crime of all, when in fact, though not in law, they are guilty of a lesser crime than that. When we add prisoners in this category to the presumably much rarer totally innocent bystanders who were arrested, prosecuted, and convicted by mistake, then the incidence of prisoners executed by mistake, it seems reasonable to suppose, would be at least as great as the number of patients mistakenly permitted to have the euthanasia they request.

But the most important point of disanalogy between the two arguments is the one which renders the argument against capital punishment much stronger than the parallel argument against euthanasia.

Rejecting the death penalty on grounds external to the merits of the individual case confers an undeserved benefit on those who deserve to die for the sake of the suspected but unknown minority that do not deserve to die. It confers this windfall blessing at very small cost to any other interests. Rejecting euthanasia, on the other hand, confers *undeserved harm* on a majority of those terminal patients who request their own deaths. It thereby achieves a benefit to the small numbers of those whose requests are not genuine and those for whose disease a new cure will at the last minute be discovered (surely not a significant number), and those whose disease was curable all along. The argument must maintain, however, that this gain is achieved only at *small cost*, presumably the cost of frustrating the desires of suffering terminal patients to die—a value judgment so callous as to be utterly perverse. How, Matthew Donnelly might have asked, could a whole year of hopeless pain, intense and unremitting, be a "small cost"?

In summary, we have found in everyday reasoning that there are some prohibitory rules that are defended with argument even though their defenders acknowledge that their applications in some individual cases are harmful. Deliberately overlooking these bad results in some individual cases is said to be a price worth paying to secure the greater benefits of the absolute prohibition. Some of these everyday arguments can be quite rational and convincing. It *can* be a rational social policy to withhold from trustworthy individuals discretion to make their own decisions on the ground that the less trustworthy individuals who would also be given that discretion by the same general rule might abuse it with socially harmful results. This form of argument can be rational to the extent that techniques to separate those who can be trusted with discretion from those who cannot, say by licensing procedures, are difficult and impractical.

The important point for our present purposes is that even though they all can be convincing in some everyday contexts, none of these forms of argument are plausible models for the categorical restriction of voluntary euthanasia. The least implausible model is that presupposed in Professor Kamisar's forceful argument for absolute prohibition. There may be no moral defect, Kamisar admits, in a given terminal patient's death request, when considered on the merits alone, and no reason internal to his case, for denying him the discretion to decide on his own whether his own life should continue. But if we grant discretion generally to all patients in similar circumstances, then some mistakes and abuses are bound to occur, and that would be an evil greater than the evil of denying the majority of patients the discretion their personal autonomy seems to require. So goes the argument from abusable discretion as applied to voluntary euthanasia. What separates the supporters from the critics of this argument is not a disagreement over the requirements of logic or over the empirical facts. It is a disagreement in value judgments—assessments of comparative costs or evils. Is it a greater evil that ten terminal patients suffering intolerable anguish be required to extend their hopeless existence against their clearly documented will than that one patient through medical mistake or the coercive influence of impatient relatives dies prematurely? The controversy over legalized voluntary euthanasia hinges on questions of this form.

III.

There is a comparative value judgment embedded in the Anglo-American criminal law, and traced by at least one writer to an Italian proverb,[10] which had wide currency in the eighteenth century, and has been treated almost as a truism in western nations ever since. In the pithy formulation of Sir William Blackstone, the maxim says that "It is better that ten guilty persons escape than that one innocent party suffer."[11] This use of numbers, of course, is a mere rhetorical device designed to make its message memorable. We cannot say with any degree of confidence that punishing the innocent is not only more unjust but exactly ten times more unjust than acquitting the guilty or that we are made to feel exactly ten times worse by the one kind of injustice than by the other. In fact, "we possess neither moral intuitions nor moral theories which could establish such a specific ratio."[12] The core message in the famous slogan then is simply that it tends to be more unjust (even) to punish the innocent than to acquit the guilty. This maxim of justice should probably be treated like other moral precepts, as deliberately but usefully vague.

Still there are two ways in which numbers might get involved when this ethical maxim is actually invoked in a real-life context. The first of these is well illustrated in the following series of examples:

> "One of two identical twins is witnessed committing cold-blooded murder. It is impossible for anyone but the twins to tell themselves apart, and each claims that he was elsewhere when the murder was committed. You must choose between executing both or acquitting both." Since you would choose the latter (wouldn't you?) you regard it as worse to punish

an innocent person than to let a guilty one escape punishment. The
example giver might then increase the size of the suspect family. "Two of
three identical triplets are witnessed committing cold-blooded murder
(etc.). You must choose between executing all three or acquitting all
three. Since you would still choose the latter (wouldn't you?), this implies
even more strongly that you regard it as worse to punish an innocent
person than to let a guilty one escape punishment."[13]

In principle, we could increase the size of the murderous group to ten
or more, although we should soon have to find some nongenetic
explanation for the indistinguishable features of the suspects.

Part of what these hypothetical examples show is that our so-called
"intuitions," which are so strong in the simple case of the identical
twins, tend to weaken as the group of indistinguishable murder suspects grows larger. Part of the reason this is so, no doubt, is that we
can no longer keep out of consideration the rights of unknown potential
victims of this group of murderous rogues, and that weakens the focus
of the example. No longer are we dealing with a comparison of two
abstractions—ten acquittals of guilty persons versus one conviction of
an innocent person. Now we have to add into our judgments a larger
indeterminate number of potential innocent victims, and that so com-
plicates the task for our intuitions that they can no longer give clear
verdicts about the simple abstract moral problem with which we began.
But we do learn something else of a useful nature from these examples,
namely that occasions for the making of comparative numerical judgments between evils (types of injustice) can and do arise, within limits,
in ordinary life.

The second way in which numbers may become involved in our
judgments of comparative evils occurs at the level of policy creation.
When we want to decide which is the worse evil, the enforced depriva-
tion of a moderate "social drinker's" glass of wine with dinner or
the continuance of the drunkard's heavy and dangerous drinking
opportunities, for the purpose of legislating wisely in this area of drug
abuse, then we need to have some accurate even though approximate
sense of the relative numbers in the two groups. Once we get the
numbers, our original question now assumes the more complex traditional formulation: which is the worse evil, X million unrestrained
drunkards or the prohibition of the harmless drinking of Y million
"social drinkers"?

We have done enough, however, to set the stage for a consideration
of the "abusable discretion" argument against legalized voluntary

euthanasia. The question before us has at least two parts, one involving numbers and one involving values (or evils). Which is the greater evil, we might ask, a rule that permits authorities to end the lives each year of X thousand suffering or comatose terminal patients at the cost of Y number of fatal mistakes; *or* a rule that categorically forbids the X thousand instances of voluntary euthanasia, thus preventing the Y number of mistaken killings? The evil caused by the first (permissive) rule is suffered by the Y number of patients who because of diagnostic error, unanticipated development of new cures, or psychological pressures die needlessly or against their real wills. The evil caused by the second (prohibitory) rule is at the expense of terminal patients who are suffering pain, severe discomfort, and the anguish of hopelessness, and those who are irreversibly comatose but whose voluntary preferences for death in these circumstances are known or inferable, and their friends and close relations. The prohibitory rule secures its benefits at the cost of pointless, emotionally wrenching and expensive maintenance of cortically dead bodies, and the continuance in pain and suffering of X thousand terminal patients. Is it possible to defend some rough rule of thumb like the Blackstone formula that is used in the quite different context of guilt and punishment? Can we even hope to agree that X lives delivered from irreversible coma or intolerable pain is a greater good than the prevention of Y deaths through mistakes? Or, put negatively, that Y lives pointlessly ended is a greater evil than X lives pointlessly preserved in coma or pain?

The numbers do make a difference. Those who have had the universal nightmare, perhaps inspired in some cases by Edgar Allan Poe,[14] of being buried alive in their caskets can imagine few greater horrors. And who can doubt that in the long history of human burial customs this must actually have happened a few times? Maybe it still happens, say in one out of every fifty million burials, not because of the demonic madness of enemies but through the inevitability of careless mistakes. Even those of us who would rank accidental live burial at the top of a list of macabre evils would require worse odds than one chance in fifty million for a justification of a statute forbidding burials, or even requiring long delays and reexaminations of the deceased. Incontrovertibly evil though it is, accidental premature burial is too rare and speculative a harm to have much weight in our policy decisions. If we thought its frequency were greater, say one in one million, we might consider tightening up our standards of care, even at the cost of considerable inconvenience and greater expense to many people, but surely not at the cost of extreme pain and suffering to many people, as in the voluntary euthanasia example.

Professor Kamisar in his famous article apparently estimates that the number of victims of mistaken and unnecessary killing, if voluntary euthanasia were legalized, would be quite substantial, but his arguments for this estimate of numbers are not convincing, perhaps because he thinks that even small numbers of mistakes and abuses would be sufficient to discredit the euthanasia proposal, given the nature of the evil in those instances when compared with evils to those whose requests to die are turned down when euthanasia is kept illegal. In Blackstonian terms, I think that Kamisar believes that one life needlessly ended is a worse evil than ten lives needlessly and painfully extended.

Why does Kamisar think that under a system of voluntary euthanasia there would inevitably be, in his word, "appreciable"[15] mistake and abuse? Mistakes, he thinks, would arise primarily from mistaken diagnoses and prognoses, and the chance of last-minute medical discoveries. Exactly how frequently doctors diagnose curable illnesses to be fatal ones, and thus withhold treatments that would have been lifesaving, I cannot say. But any sensible scheme of euthanasia would require multiple medical consultations and other necessary ways of making sure, and despite the inevitability of some mistakes there are many more cases, like those of Matthew Donnelly and Nancy Beth Cruzan, that are perfectly clear. Why isn't the incorrect judgment in clearly incurable cases that those cases might be misdiagnosed, so far as we can know, just as morally telling a mistake as the rarer misdiagnoses given so much emphasis by Kamisar?

As for last-minute medical discoveries, surely they cannot be the source of "appreciable" numbers of unnecessary killings. There is always a substantial delay between the discovery of a new medicine or a new surgical technique and its availability, and I suppose that awareness of the new possibility during that interval might in some cases revive hope and lead to postponement of mercy killing. In those cases the patient (or her guardian or proxy) and the physicians might keep the flickering hope alive as long as possible. In that way a sensible euthanasia scheme could accommodate the possibility of last-minute discoveries. But equally certainly there are other cases that are incorrigibly hopeless, or such that the slenderness of the chance of a last-minute discovery may not be worth the continued pain involved in the waiting. And in other cases there can be no chance whatever of a last-minute cure, since the last minute has already come and gone. Once a cerebral cortex has been destroyed, for example, there can be nothing, short of a literal miracle, that can restore the existence of the comatose person. One can quibble about numbers and probabilities, and even concede that the number of otherwise terminal patients who turn out to be salvageable because of last-minute discoveries is more than "tiny." The essential point from the moral point of view is that suspension of mercy killing for the vast majority of those who need and want it would be at least as serious a mistake as killing those who might have been saved, for all we can know, by a last-minute discovery. Glanville Williams puts the point well: "Because of this risk for this tiny fraction of the total number of patients, patients who are dying in pain must be left to do so, year after year, against their entreaty to have it ended."[16]

Our traditional criminal law, Kamisar notes, does permit intentional killing in some circumstances, when it appears necessary; for example, to the defense of a threatened person or of third parties. And of course, mistakes in judging this "necessity" in individual cases are inevitable. Reasonable mistakes in self-defense or defense of others, Kamisar explains, "are the inevitable by-products of efforts to save one or more human lives."[17] But can we not, in a perfectly parallel way, consider reasonable mistakes in a legalized voluntary euthanasia scheme to be "the inevitable by-products" of efforts to deliver human beings, at their own requests, from intolerable suffering, or from elaborate and expensive prolongations of a body's functioning in the permanent absence of any person to animate that body? Kamisar's answer is revealing: only the saving of human lives, he thinks, is a value great enough to justify the taking of a human life. "The need the euthanasiast advances . . . is a good deal less compelling. It is only to ease pain."[18]

This view of the matter, which would have astonished Matthew Donnelly and the parents of Nancy Cruzan, is readily expressible in a Blackstonian formula without any numbers in its comparative judgment. In respect to guilt and innocence, Voltaire writes of "the great principle that it is better to run the risk of sparing the guilty than to condemn the innocent."[19] Here there is no mention of numbers, no comparison of ten guilty men with one innocent person, as in Blackstone's more rhetorical formula. Perhaps Voltaire intends (or should have intended) a *ceteris paribus* clause—numbers and other possibly relevant matters being equal—to disconnect and isolate the point he was making, while acknowledging that in real-life applications, matters are much more complex than his "great principle" would otherwise suggest, that numbers do count, and so do such externalities as the risk of further harm caused by the guilty who are "spared." Using Voltaire's maxim as a model for imitation, we can attribute to Kamisar the view that it is better to run the risk that a patient, or her relatives and loved ones, will be made to suffer needlessly than to run the risk that a patient who requests euthanasia is not truly "terminal" or that his consent is not truly voluntary. Numbers aside, the maxim now says, when we compare one instance of needlessly taken life with one instance of harmfully extended life, considered in this abstract way, other things being equal, the former is always and necessarily a greater evil than the latter. That is, it is always a greater evil, other things being equal, to let someone die by mistake than to keep a person alive by mistake. This non-numerical formulation of Kamisar's view makes it into a more modest and therefore a more plausible claim. Nevertheless, in the concluding section of this paper, after some efforts at clarification, I shall find reasons for rejecting it.

IV.

It should be clear then that two kinds of mistakes are possible in the voluntary euthanasia situation, that both have their costs and projected frequencies. One creates the danger that curable patients will needlessly be killed or killed without their real consent; the other creates the danger that incurable terminal patients will have their sufferings pointlessly prolonged. It is the task of rule makers to adopt the policy that will prevent the more serious mistakes, both in number and degree of evil, even at the cost of incurring inevitably the kind of mistake that exposes a smaller number to evils of lesser degree.

It will be my conclusion that one cannot say that one of the two kinds of mistake is in itself, isolated from other factors, always more serious than the other, and that *ceteris paribus* (degree of risk, numbers of affected people in each class, etc., being equal) that one kind of value, life, always is a weightier consideration than the other— cessation of suffering. Ordinarily we cannot get a pure *ceteris paribus* case, for there are always many variables in the euthanasia situation. In real life we compare real people who are always concrete and particular, and not mere abstract subjects for certain properties that interest us, and anyway, no two have exactly the same properties. When we compare Matthew Donnelly or Nancy Beth Cruzan, say, with another specific person who *can* be saved, though knowing it not, he demands euthanasia *now*, we must consider properties other than the minimal characteristics that define the classes we are comparing. We must consider how severe the suffering is; thus how great an evil it is in itself; how old the patients are; how complex, expensive, and likely to succeed any future discovered treatment would have to be; and so on.

Suppose we consider Donnelly who, let us imagine, is being asked to forgo euthanasia because the rule permitting it will also enable a second patient to forgo the soon-to-be-discovered, last-minute treatment that can cure him. In a concrete example like this, we would have a hard time ignoring such traits as the comparative ages, the life expectancies with and without treatment, the degree of vigorous activity that in the best outcome will be possible. We do not in this case deal with people as if they were personifications of abstractions like Suffering and Potential Salvageability. The degrees of comparative value and evil in our options will always be more complicated than that, since every patient must have some specific age, physical condition, and general prospect. Can we in good conscience impose another year of unremitting pain on Donnelly in order to protect a general rule that would permit a seventy-year-old Alzheimer's disease patient to be ready for a last-minute cure, when he will have a two-year life expectancy and an enfeebled bodily condition even if the possible last-minute "cure" eventuates?

My thesis is that in the abstract, or as close as we can get to it, it is misleading to judge either kind of consideration to be always more serious than the other *ceteris paribus*, or that one type of mistake is always and necessarily more serious, *ceteris paribus*, than the other. Kamisar, on the other hand, implies that there is a categorical difference between the two types of mistakes, so that the one category in its entirety must always have priority. Considered "in themselves," in abstraction, *ceteris paribus*, he seems to say, we should always prefer the value in one category (life) over that in the other (surcease of hopeless suffering). On my view, in contrast, if we are forced to play the "whole category" game at all, we would have to conclude that the two categories of mistake are of equal seriousness.

It would be better, however, if we avoided this kind of judgment altogether. We might be tempted to say that the two kinds of mistakes *can* be compared in the abstract and that they are always of equal seriousness. But that is the wrong point, a conclusion as paradoxical as Kamisar's. It is *not* that the comparison between the two value categories can be made and always results in a tie. Rather the comparison cannot be made at all. The disagreement between Kamisar and me, as I have been reconstructing it, is not that he says "*ceteris paribus*, death is always worse" and I say "*ceteris paribus*, the two evils are always equal," but rather that he says the former, and I deny what he affirms. I assert nothing parallel to his affirmation, but simply deny that any such sweeping judgment can be made, either that death *or* suffering is always worse than the other "in itself, other things being equal."

In fact, "other things" (if we should ever reach such agreement about which "other things" are relevant) hardly ever are equal, and even if *mirabile dictu* they were equal in a given case, the resultant value judgment would make no sense. To say that other things being equal death is a worse evil than suffering (or vice versa) is not to say something like: "Other things being equal an intense pain is a worse evil than a moderate one." In respect to intensity, duration, extent, and so on, pains are the sorts of things that can meaningfully be compared. But death and suffering lack relevant dimensions in which comparisons are possible. Units of time (days, hours) may be applied to both, but the relevant temporal measure for death is not the duration of the death itself, which of course is infinite, but rather how many days one might have been expected to live had a preventable death not occurred when it did. That is not the same temporal dimension in which we measure the duration of sufferings (how long do they last from start to finish?). In this and other relevant respects, then, death and suffering are simple incommensurables. It is easy enough to speak of "death in the abstract" or "suffering in the abstract," but real people don't live in the abstract.

Suppose we must compare the mistakenly permitted death of an eighty-five-year-old who is thereby deprived of an additional six months of sickly life with the mistakenly prolonged suffering of Matthew Donnelly. Here it would seem that the suffering in one person is a worse evil than death in the other, or so at any rate we might judge if we were *forced* to judge. In contrast, the mistakenly permitted death of a twenty-year-old deprived of fifty years of vigorous life is probably a worse evil than the mistaken prolongation of the suffering for one day of another person. What if an enemy of mercy killing declared that the young person deprived of fifty years of life suffered a worse evil than any amount or degree of "mere" suffering in anyone? It is unlikely, I think, that he would maintain confidence in that judgment in the face of the hypothetical example of a person forced against her will to remain alive through fifty years of intense suffering. Identifying the one evil as belonging in the "death" category and the other in the "suffering" category only introduces the problem; it by no means settles it.

I am satisfied to let the Donnelly and Cruzan cases speak for themselves as examples of values that *can*, in a fully concrete context, outweigh life. That will enable me in the space that is left to deflate the value of "life preservation" as interpreted by various opponents of legalized voluntary euthanasia, especially the present U.S. Supreme Court. In this concluding section then, I shall concentrate, as it happens, on the recent pronouncements of that Court about the value of life in the case of Nancy Beth Cruzan.

Why is it that the enemies of voluntary euthanasia attribute so great a value to "life as such" that it is supposed to outweigh even the evil of suffering whenever they conflict? Justice Rehnquist, in his majority opinion in the Cruzan case, admits that U.S. constitutional law[20] grants a right to all competent adults to refuse medical treatment if they wish. But this private "interest" in liberty must be balanced, Rehnquist declares, against relevant state interests. Chief among the latter is the state's interest in "the protection and preservation of human life." I am not sure how to explain this sense of "interest," but it would not be far off the mark to substitute for it "legitimate governmental concern." Sometimes the state interest in the protection and preservation of human life overrides the liberty interest of an individual in making his own decisions whether or not to accept a given medical treatment. Rehnquist's example of this is a Massachusetts case in 1905 in which the court favored the state's interest in preventing epidemic disease over an individual's liberty interest in declining an unwanted smallpox vaccination.[21] So even though "The forcible injection of medication into a nonconsenting person's body represents a substantial interference with that person's liberty,"[22] the state must give due weight to its function as protector of human life, even to the point sometimes of nullifying a citizen's constitutional right to liberty.

It is easy enough to understand why a court would legally compel a vaccination to help prevent the spread of a lethal disease, but how does this example serve to explain the state's interest in keeping Nancy Cruzan's mutilated body alive long after Nancy's person has vanished forever from it? Preservation of the functioning body of a departed person does no one any good. Not Nancy, because she never knew the difference, being permanently and irreversibly unconscious. Not the state of Missouri, which paid costs of approximately $100,000 a year. Not Nancy's parents, for whom the unnatural preservation of the body of their beloved daughter was a ghoulish torture.

There remains of course the interest of Nancy as she was before she suffered her accident. Let us suppose for a moment that it was her firm and informed preference to be let die in case she should ever be rendered irreversibly comatose in an accident. This in fact was what she did prefer, according to the testimony of her friend and former roommate. If that is true, then keeping Nancy's body going while she is comatose is not in the interest of Nancy as she was before her accident. I think we can speak of interests surviving the death of the person whose interests they were, as a kind of useful fiction. If I have an interest while alive that my estate go to my wife after I die, but then after I die my widow is cheated out of her inheritance by a conspiracy between my lawyer and my accountant, not only my widow's interest but the interest of my own in her security, which I was promoting before I died, is also set back. In deciding how to redistribute whichever of my widow's assets come to hand, the authorities might say such a thing as: "it is the testator's interests alone that should determine what is to be done." And this might be said quite intelligibly even though I, the testator, am now dead. In any event, on the assumption that Nancy Cruzan preferred before her accident that nutrition and hydration be withheld if she should ever become irreversibly comatose, it follows that it is not in her interest (not in the interest she had when she was capable of having any interests) that her body be kept alive at this time.

Now consider the other possibility, that Nancy did *not* have an informed preference for the discontinuance of medical sustenance after the onset of permanent coma. On this assumption either she was indifferent, never having even considered the matter perhaps, or she had a firm and informed preference that her living body be sustained. If she was indifferent, then it cannot be the case that her pre-accident interest would be set back by discontinuing her support. But if she preferred continuance, then it would appear that discontinuance would violate her pre-accident interest. But what kind of interest could it be that would be based on such a preference? It could not be an interest in having *her life* continued, for *ex hypothesi* nothing that happens will ever make any differences to her. If she were asked whether she would prefer death or permanent unconsciousness, she could not possibly express a rational choice, because from her own subjective point of view, there is not one iota of difference between death and permanent unconsciousness. From the perspective of the person whose life is at issue there is only a choice between permanent unconsciousness on the one hand and permanent unconsciousness on the other. On either alternative, there is no possibility of strivings, aversions, projects, goals, attachments, plans, actions, perceptions—the necessary components of a *human* life, as opposed to the "life," if we may use the word in that way, of a mere biological organism.

There remains a further possibility. A person in Nancy's position might conceivably think of her body as her own property and accordingly dictate what is to be done with it after she ceases to be. She might make a provision in her will that if she should become irreversibly comatose, her body should be kept alive so that it could be a useful test of the safety of new medications, thus sparing some poor animal that sacrificial role, or so that it could be an organ bank for keeping spare bodily parts in good working order until they can be transplanted, and the like. We can even imagine a time in the distant future when the state would claim to have an interest in that sort of resource, and overrule the claim that a body is the private property of the person who died to be disposed of as she pleases, so that the state could seize all "living corpses" for medical purposes. For the present, however, it makes sense to say that a person has an interest and a right in the disposition of her future vital remains, even though the organism that was once her body is still alive. But it doesn't follow from a person's donation of her living body to a recipient that the recipient has a duty to accept it or use it according to its previous owner's desires. The state of Missouri, stuck with the heavy financial costs, might well say, if only the law permitted it—"Thanks, but no thanks." The situation, it seems to me, is much like a person willing his 1953 Chevrolet to the state to be preserved in a well-lit automotive show room in perpetuity. After all, the car was the testator's property to dispose of as he wished. But even if he had also willed an adequate amount of money to cover costs, the state could feel justified in turning it down as not worth the bother. Indeed, when one realizes what an irreversible vegetative state is, one wonders why it would ever be the interest of the state to preserve a body in that condition, unless it be through lingering doubts about the medical diagnoses. At any rate, no state interest remotely analogous to the interest in preventing epidemics can be imagined for keeping an unoccupied body alive.

Two types of mistakes might be made in the treatment of patients in a persistent vegetative state like Nancy Cruzan; one of them very infrequent, the other very insignificant whenever it does occur. The infrequent mistake would be misdiagnosis—the expectation that the coma is irreversible when in fact it is not. In this age of high-tech x-ray instruments, however, a cerebral cortex can be known to be both functionally incapacitated and progressively deteriorating, so that only a negligently superficial examination could lead to the mistaken prognosis. Physicians, being human, are of course fallible, and there will always be the possibility of error, but mistakes of this kind will not occur in significant numbers.

The other kind of mistake would be one of misattribution to the patient of a preference about the disposition of her living body. If she wants discontinuance of nutrition and care and doesn't get it, then that is a serious error, if not for her interests, for the interests of her parents, close relations, and friends, not to mention the bill-paying taxpayers. If, however, she prefers to have her body preserved in the manner of transferred property, just as if it were some handsome machine or art object, at the state's expense, and this genuine preference is misinterpreted or otherwise not honored, then *that* mistake is not a serious one. In short the risk of mistaken killing in cases of this kind is not in itself a very grave danger, partly because the purely medical mistake that could lead to the killing would not be made in significant numbers, and the mistaken attribution to the patient of a prior preference for death would not in itself be a very great evil.

The majority of the U.S. Supreme Court, however, found the danger of a mistaken withdrawal of life-sustaining treatment from Miss Cruzan a more serious evil than the danger of a mistake in the opposite direction, mainly because death is irrevocable and mistaken killings are therefore uncorrectable. The official summary of the Court's decision encapsulates the argument exactly:

> The clear and convincing evidence standard . . . serves as a social judgment about how the risk of error should be distributed between the litigants. Missouri may place the increased risk of erroneous decision on those seeking to terminate life-saving treatment. An erroneous decision not to terminate results in the maintenance of the *status quo* with at least the potential that a wrong decision will eventually be corrected or its impact mitigated by an event such as an advance in medical science or the patient's unexpected death. However, an erroneous decision to withdraw such treatment is not subject to correction.[23]

To this argument from the irrevocability of mistaken decisions to kill, Justice Brennan in his dissenting opinion makes the clear and obvious rejoinder: "From the point of view of the patient, an erroneous decision *in either* direction is irrevocable."[24] She is nonexistent in either case, but her remains are on display permanently in the one case, but decently removed from view on the other.

> An erroneous decision to terminate artificial nutrition and hydration, to be sure, will lead to failure of that last remnant of physiological life, the brain-stem, and result in complete brain death. An erroneous decision not to terminate the life-support however, robs a patient of the very qualities protected by the right to avoid unwanted medical treatment. His own degraded existence is perpetuated; his family's suffering is protracted; the memory he leaves behind becomes more and more distorted.[25]

Justice Brennan correctly points out that there is no state interest in the preservation of merely biological life without consciousness, and hence that there can be no more a legitimate governmental function to maintain such "life" than there is to preserve some giant plant or vegetable. A life "completely abstracted from the interest of the person living that life"[26] can have no special value the state is committed to protect—nothing like the public health that can be threatened by an epidemic disease.

Of course Matthew Donnelly in *his* last days was in no way like a vegetable. Vegetables do not suffer pain and despair. But given the incurability of his condition, Donnelly's life was even less worth preserving, against his manifest will, than Nancy Cruzan's against the presumed preference she might have had before her accident. There is no point at all in keeping Nancy Cruzan's body alive, but no more possibility of harm to Nancy in doing so. The case for granting Donnelly his passionately requested relief, however, is stronger than that. We owe deliverance to the likes of Donnelly and we cruelly wrong him by withholding it from him. Letting him suffer unnecessarily for a full year is not to err on the "safe side." In life's difficult closing games there is often no safe side to err on; delay and inaction can be as serious a mistake as hasty or premature action. In that case we had better do whatever we can to let suffering patients determine their own course.

V.

In summary, we have seen that most of the arguments against the legalization of voluntary euthanasia (or in favor of creating legal impediments to it) are indirect arguments. They don't argue that individual cases judged internally, that is on their own merits, do not warrant euthanasia. Indeed, some of these arguments candidly concede that judged on the merits, many individual cases do deserve euthanasia. Rather, these arguments favor deliberately overlooking the merits of individual cases, and cite extraneous considerations in favor of a blanket prohibition. The most plausible of these arguments is the argument from abusable discretion, which maintains that if legally competent individuals are granted the discretion to decide on their own whether in certain circumstances to continue or to terminate life-sustaining treatment, the inevitability of honest mistakes and not-so-honest abuses will create evils that outweigh the evils of sustaining the comatose and the pain-wracked against their presumed wills. Convincing as the argument from abusable discretion may be in some context (e.g., traffic control) it fails in its application to the euthanasia situation, because it cannot be shown that the likely number of mistakenly killed individuals would constitute a greater evil than the likely number of mistakenly sustained individuals. The philosophical problem of voluntary euthanasia is in large part a matter of comparing real risks. The enemy of voluntary euthanasia errs in minimizing the evils of human suffering and overrating the value of merely biological life in the absence of a human person, or in the presence of a human person whose sufferings are too severe for him to have a human life, even though his heart beats on.

Notes

"Overlooking the Merits of the Individual Case: An Unpromising Approach to the Right to Die," was published in *Ratio Juris* 4 (July 1991): 131–51. Professor Feinberg presented this paper in a revised form as the C. Calhoun Lemon Lecture in Philosophy on November 22, 1991. Blackwell Publishers has graciously granted permission to reprint. (Ed.)

1. Yale Kamisar, "Euthanasia Legislation: Some Non-Religious Objections," in *Euthanasia and the Right to Death*, ed. A. B. Downing (London: Peter Owen, 1969).
2. Ibid., 87.
3. James Rachels, *The End of Life* (Oxford: Oxford University Press, 1986), 32.
4. Rachels writes that "Mr. Donnelly begged his brother to shoot him and he did." Ibid.
5. Ten days after I gave the original version of this lecture, new testimony

about Miss Cruzan's preferences was presented to a Missouri Court, which then was able to assess the *new* evidence as "clear and compelling." The Court then approved the request that the feeding apparatus be removed, and Miss Cruzan died a few days later.

6. *Nancy Beth Cruzan, By Her Parents and Co-Guardian, Lester L. Cruzan et ux, Petitioners v. Director, Missouri Department of Health*, 110 S.Ct. 2841 (1990).

7. *Cruzan By Cruzan v. Harmon* 760 S.W. 2d, 408 (Mo banc 1488) at 415 (1988).

8. See Charles L. Black, Jr., *Capital Punishment: The Inevitability of Caprice and Mistake* (New York: W. W. Norton, 1974).

9. See Kamisar, "Euthanasia Legislation," p. 104.

10. B. Stevenson, ed., *The Macmillan Book of Proverbs* (New York: Macmillan, 1948), p. 1249. Jeffrey Reiman and Ernest van den Haag paraphrase the *Macmillan Book* account thus: "Thomas Fielding, *Proverbs of All Nations*, p. 59 (1824), citing an Italian proverb which is also a maxim of English law, [Fielding] says it originated in Italy, and that Dr. Paley was against it, while Blackstone and Romilly approved of it." The Reiman–Van den Haag discussion, "On the Common Saying that it is Better that Ten Guilty Persons Escape than that One Innocent Suffer" is found in *Social Philosophy and Policy*, vol. 7, no. 2, Spring 1990, pp. 226–48.

11. William Blackstone, *Commentaries on the Laws of England*, 21st ed. (1765), (London: Sweet, Maxwell, Stevens & Norton, 1844), book 4, chapter 27, p. 358.

12. Reiman and Van den Haag, "On the Common Saying," p. 227.

13. Ibid., p. 228.

14. See for example, Poe's short stories "The Black Cat," "A Cask of Amontillado," and especially "The Fall of the House of Usher" in E. A. Poe, *Selected Writings*, ed. D. Galloway (Harmondsworth: Penguin Books). See also Michael Crichton, *The Great Train Robbery* (New York: Alfred A. Knopf, 1975), pp. 191–94, from which I quote:

> During the nineteenth century both in England and in the United States, there arose a peculiar preoccupation with the idea of premature burial . . . for the Victorians, premature burial was a genuine palpable fear.
>
> Nor was this widespread fear a simply neurotic obsession . . . there was plenty of evidence . . . [that] premature burials did occur, and that such ghastly happenings were [often] only prevented by some fortuitous event . . . Victorians dealt with their uncertainty in two ways. The first was to delay interment for several days—a week was not uncommon—and await the unmistakable olfactory evidence . . .
>
> The second method was technological; the Victorians contrived an elaborate series of warning and signaling devices to enable the dead person to make known his resuscitation. A wealthy individual might be buried with a length of iron pipe connecting his casket to the ground

above, and a trusted family servant would be required to remain at the cemetery, day and night, for a month or more, on the chance that the deceased would suddenly awake and begin to call for help. Persons buried above ground in family vaults were often placed in patented, spring-loaded caskets, with a complex maze of wires attached to arms and legs, so that the slightest movement of the body would throw open the lid . . .

Most signaling devices were costly, and available only to the wealthy classes. Poor people adopted the simpler tactic of burying relatives with some implement—a crowbar or a shovel—on the vague assumption that if they revived, they could dig themselves out of their predicament.

15. Kamisar, "Euthanasia Legislation," p. 105.

16. Glanville Williams, "Euthanasia Legislation: A Rejoinder to the Non-Religious Objections," in Downing, *Euthanasia and the Right to Death*, p. 142.

17. Kamisar, "Euthanasia Legislation," p. 104.

18. Ibid.

19. François Marie Arouet de Voltaire, "Zadig or Fate," in *Candide and Other Stories* (London: Dent & Sons, 1962), as quoted by Reiman and Van den Haag, "On the Common Saying," p. 226.

20. The primary source is the "Due Process" clause of the Fourteenth Amendment: ". . . nor shall any state deprive any person of life, liberty, or property, without due process of law. . . ." The key word in the application of this clause to medical treatment is "liberty."

21. Rehnquist cites *Jacobson v. Massachusetts*, 197 U.S. 11, 24–30 (1905).

22. Quoted by Rehnquist from *Washington v. Harper*, 110 S.Ct. 1028 (1990).

23. *Cruzan v. Director, Missouri Department of Health*, 110 S.Ct. 2841 (1990), at 2844.

24. Ibid., at 2873.

25. Ibid.

26. Ibid., at 2870.

Selected Bibliography

Abbott, Andrew. *The System of Professions*. Chicago: University of Chicago Press, 1988.

Abrahamson, Mark, ed. *The Professional in the Organization*. Chicago: Rand McNally & Company, 1967.

Bayles, Michael. *Professional Ethics*. Belmont, Calif. Wadsworth, 1981.

Boland, Richard J. "Organizational Control, Organizational Power, and Professional Responsibility." *Business and Professional Ethics Journal* 2:1 (1982): 15–25.

Bowman, James S., Frederick A. Ellison, and Paula Lockhart. *Professional Dissent: An Annotated Bibliography and Resource Guide*. New York: Garfield, 1984.

Bradley, F. H. "My Station and Its Duties." In *Ethical Studies* (1876). Oxford: Oxford University Press, 1970.

Braude, L. "Professional Autonomy and the Role of the Layman." *Social Forces* 39 (1961): 297–301.

Bucher, Rue, and Anselm Strauss. "Professions in Process." *American Journal of Sociology* 66 (1961).

Callahan, Joan C., ed. *Ethical Issues in Professional Life*. New York: Oxford University Press, 1988.

Callahan, Joan C., and James W. Knight. *Preventing Birth: Contemporary Methods and Related Moral Controversies*. Salt Lake City: University of Utah Press, 1989.

Camenisch, Paul. *Grounding Professional Ethics in a Pluralistic Society*. New York: Haven, 1983.

Carr-Saundres, A. P., and P. A. Wilson. *The Professions*. Oxford: Oxford University Press, 1933.

Chalk, Rosemary, Mark S. Frankel, and Sallie B. Chafer. *Professional Ethics Activities in the Scientific and Engineering Societies*. Washington, D.C.: American Association for the Advancement of Science, 1980.

Childress, James F. "Citizen and Physician: Harmonious or Conflicting Responsibilities?" *Journal of Medicine and Philosophy* 2:4 (1977): 401–9.

Cogan, Morris L. "Toward a Definition of Profession." *Harvard Educational Review* 23 (Winter 1953): 33–50.

Cullen, John B. *The Structure of Professionalism: A Quantitative Analysis.* New York: Petrocelli, 1978.

Cumont, Matthew P. "The Changing Face of Professionalism." *Social Policy* 1 (1970): 26–31.

Curran, William J., and Ward Casscells, "The Ethics of Medical Participation in Capital Punishment by Intravenous Injection." *New England Journal of Medicine* 302 (1980): 226–30.

De George, Richard T. "Ethical Obligations of Engineers in Large Organizations: The Pinto Case." *Business and Professional Ethics Journal* 1:1 (1981): 1–14.

Dingwall, Robert, and Philip Lewis, eds. *The Sociology of the Professions.* New York: St Martin's, 1983.

Downie, R. S. "Responsibility and Social Roles." In *Individual and Collective Responsibility*, ed. Peter A. French, 65–80. Cambridge, Mass.: Schenkman, 1972.

Emmet, Dorothy. *Rules, Roles and Relations.* New York: St. Martin's Press, 1966; Boston: Beacon Press, 1975.

Feldstein, Donald. "Do We Need Professions in Our Society? Professionalization versus Consumerism." *Social Work* 16 (1971): 5–11.

Ferren, John M. "The Corporate Lawyer's Obligation to the Public Interest." *Business Lawyer* 33 (1978): 1253–89.

Freedman, Monroe H. *Lawyers' Ethics in an Adversary System.* Indianapolis: Bobbs Merrill, 1975.

———. "Personal Responsibility in a Professional System." *Catholic University Law Review* 27 (1975): 191–206.

Fuller, Lon L. "The Philosophy of Codes of Ethics." *Electrical Engineering* 74 (1955): 916–18.

Gewirth, Alan. "Professional Ethics: The Separatist Thesis." *Ethics* 96:2 (1986): 282–300.

Goldman, Alan H. *The Moral Foundations of Professional Ethics.* Totowa, N.J.: Rowman and Littlefield, 1980.

Goode, William J. "Community Within a Community: The Professions." *American Sociological Review* 22 (1960): 194–200.

Hampshire, Stuart. *Morality and Conflict.* Cambridge, Mass.: Harvard University Press, 1983.

————, ed. *Public and Private Morality*. New York: Cambridge University Press, 1978.

Hardwig, John. "Robin Hoods and Good Samaritans—The Role of *Patients* in Health Care Distribution." *Theoretical Medicine* 8 (1987): 47–59.

Hershman, M. "The Murky Divide—Professionalism and Professional Responsibility—Business Judgement and Legal Advice—What is a Business Lawyer?" *Business Lawyer* 31 (1975): 457–63.

Howard, W. Kenneth. "Must Public Hands Be Dirty?" *Journal of Value Inquiry* 11:1 (1977): 29–40.

Jones, W. T. "Public Roles, Private Roles, and Differential Assessments of Role Performance." *Ethics* 94:4 (1984): 602–20.

Jonsen, Albert R., and Andrew L. Jameton. "Social and Political Responsibility of Physicians." *Journal of Medicine and Philosophy* 2:4 (1977): 376–400.

Kipnis, Kenneth. "Engineers Who Kill: Professional Ethics and the Paramountcy of Public Safety." *Business and Professional Ethics Journal* 1:1 (1981): 77–91.

————. "Goldman on Professional Ethics." *Westminster Institute Review* 1:1 (1981): 8–10.

————. "Professional Responsibility and the Responsibility of Professions." In *Profits and Professions: Essays in Business and Professional Ethics*, ed. Wade L. Robison, Michael S. Pritchard, and Joseph S. Ellin, 9–22. Clifton, N.J.: Humana Press, 1983.

Ladd, John. "Philosophical Remarks on Professional Responsibility in Organizations." In *Designing for Safety: Engineering Ethics in Organizational Contexts*, ed. Albert Flores, 191–203. Troy, N.Y.: Rensselaer Polytechnic Institute, 1982.

Larson, Magali S. *The Rise of Professionalism: A Sociological Analysis*. Berkeley: University of California Press, 1977.

Luban, David. *Lawyers and Justice: An Ethical Study*. Princeton: Princeton University Press, 1988.

————. "Smith Against the Ethicists." *Law and Philosophy* 10 (1991): 91–107. (See Smith, 1990, 1991.)

————, ed. *The Good Lawyer: Lawyers' Roles and Lawyers' Ethics*. Totowa, N.J.: Rowman and Allanheld, 1984.

Lynn, Kenneth S., and the Editors of *Daedalus*, eds. *The Professions in America*. Boston: Houghton Mifflin, 1965.

May, Larry. "Professional Actions and Professional Liabilities." *Business and Professsional Ethics Journal* 2:1 (1982): 1–14.

May, Larry, and Martin Curd. *Professional Responsibility for Harmful Actions*. Dubuque, Iowa: Kendall/Hunt Publishing, 1984.

Nagel, Thomas. "Ruthlessness in Public Life." In Hampshire (1978): 75–91.

Near, Janet P., and Marcia P. Micete. "Organizational Disobedience: The Case of Whistleblowing." *Journal of Business Ethics* 4:1 (1985): 1–16.

Nelkin, Dorothy. "Whistleblowing and Social Responsibility in Science." In *Research Ethics: Progress in Clinical and Biological Research*, vol. 128, ed. Kare Berg and Knut Erik Tranøy, 351–57. New York: Alan R. Liss, 1983.

Parsons, Talcott. "Professions and Social Structure." *Social Forces* 17 (1939): 457–67.

———. "Professions." In *International Encyclopedia of the Social Sciences*, 2nd ed., ed. Daniel L. Sills, 536–47. New York: Macmillan and the Free Press, 1968.

Patterson, L. Ray. *Legal Ethics: The Law of Professional Responsibility*. New York: Matthew Bender, 1982.

Perrucci, Robert, and Joel Gustl. *Profession Without Community: Engineers in America*. New York: Random House, 1969.

Pirsig, Maynard E., and Kenneth F. Kirwin, eds. *Professional Responsibility: Cases and Materials*, 3rd ed. St Paul, Minn.: West, 1976, Supplement, 1981.

Postema, Gerald. "Moral Responsibility in Professional Ethics." *New York University Law Review* 55 (1980): 63–89.

———. "Self-Image, Integrity, and Professional Responsibility." In Luban (1984): 286–314.

Pound, Roscoe. "What is a Profession?: The Rise of the Legal Profession in Antiquity," *Notre Dame Lawyer* 19 (1944): 203–28.

Presidential Commission on the Space Shuttle Challenger Accident. *Report to the President on the Space Shuttle Accident*. Washington, D.C.: U.S. Government Printing Office, 1986.

Primak, Joel, and Frank von Hippel. *Advice and Dissent: Scientists in the Political Arena*. New York: New American Library, 1976.

Simon, William H. "The Ideology of Advocacy: Procedural Justice and Professional Ethics." *Wisconsin Law Review* 1978 (1978): 30–144.

Smith, M. B. E. "Should Lawyers Listen to Philosophers About Legal Ethics?" *Law and Philosophy* 9 (1990): 67–93.

———. "Reply to David Luban." *Law and Philosophy* 10 (1991): 427–32.

Swazey, Judith P., and Stephen R. Sher, eds. *Whistleblowing in Biomedical Research*. Washington, D.C.: U.S. Government Printing Office, 1981.

Thompson, Dennis. "Ascribing Responsibility to Advisers in Government." *Ethics* 93:3 (1983): 546–60.

U.S. Merit Systems Protection Board. *Whistleblowing and the Federal Employee*. Washington, D.C.: U.S. Government Printing Office, 1981.

Veatch, Robert M. "Professional Medical Ethics: The Grounding of Its Principles." *Journal of Medicine and Philosophy* 4:1 (1979): 1–19.

Walzer, Michael. "Political Action: The Problem of Dirty Hands." *Philosophy and Public Affairs* 2:2 (1973): 160–80.

Wasserstrom, Richard. "Lawyers as Professionals: Some Moral Issues." *Human Rights* 5 (1975): 1–24.

———. "Roles and Morality." In Luban (1984): 25–37.

Weber, Max. "Politics as Vocation" (1919). In *From Max Weber: Essays in Sociology*, ed. and trans. Hans Gerth and C. Wright Mills, 77–128. New York: Oxford University Press, 1946.

———. "Science as Vocation" (1919). In *From Max Weber: Essays in Sociology*, ed. and trans. Hans Gerth and C. Wright Mills, 129–56. New York: Oxford University Press, 1946.

Westin, Alan, ed. *Whistleblowing: Loyalty and Dissent in the Corporation.* New York: McGraw-Hill, 1981.

Wilensky, Harold L. "The Professionalization of Everyone?" *American Journal of Sociology* 70 (1964): 137–58.

Williams, Bernard. "Professional Morality and Its Dispositions." In Luban (1984): 259–69.

Winston, Kenneth I. "A Civic Vocation." *Harvard Public Policy Review.* 6:1 (1989).

Index

303

About the Contributors

ROBERT J. BAUM is Professor of Philosophy at the University of Florida. He is the editor of *Business and Professional Ethics Journal*. His publications include "Engineering and Ethics," which appeared in *Hastings Center Report* and *Professional Engineer* in 1977.

JOAN C. CALLAHAN is Associate Professor of Philosophy at the University of Kentucky. She is coauthor of *Preventing Birth: Contemporary Methods and Related Moral Problems*, and editor of *Ethical Issues in Professional Life* and *Menopause: A Midlife Passage*.

KATHLEEN MARIE DIXON is Associate Professor of Philosophy at Bowling Green State University (Ohio). Her work has appeared in several collections as well as journals such as *The Journal Of Family Practice* and *Medical Humanities Review*.

JOEL FEINBERG is Regents Professor of Philosophy and Law at the University of Arizona. He is the author of *Doing and Deserving*; *Social Philosophy*; *Rights, Justice, and the Bounds of Liberty*; and *The Moral Limits of the Criminal Law*. His most recent book is *Freedom and Fulfillment*.

JOHN HARDWIG is Professor of Philosophy and Chair of the Department of Philosophy and Humanities at East Tennessee State University. His work has been published in a variety of journals including *The Journal of Philosophy*, *Ethics*, *Hastings Center Reports*, and *Journal of Clinical Ethics*.

DAVID N. JAMES is Associate Professor of Philosophy at Old Dominion University. His work has appeared in journals such as *Bioethics*, *Business and Professional Ethics Journal*, *Kinesis*, and *Journal of Social Philosophy*.

WILLIAM MAKER is Associate Professor of Philosophy at Clemson

323

324 About the Contributors

University. He is the editor of *Hegel on Economics and Freedom* and author of *Philosophy Without Foundations: Rethinking Hegel*, which is scheduled for publication in 1994.

LARRY MAY is Professor of Philosophy at Washington University in St. Louis. He is author of *The Morality of Groups* and *Sharing Responsibility*, and coeditor of *Collective Responsibility* and *Rethinking Masculinity: Philosophical Explorations in Light of Feminism*.

SERENA STIER is Associate Professor of Law at the Albany Law School. She has published articles in various law reviews including *Northwestern University Law Review*, *Ohio State Law Review*, *Iowa Law Review*, and *Journal of Legal Education*.

ROBERT WACHBROIT is Research Scholar at the Institute for Philosophy and Public Policy at the University of Maryland. He has published articles in a variety of journals including *Philosophy of Science*, *The Philosophical Review*, *The Yale Law Journal*, and *Maryland Medical Journal*.

KENNETH I. WINSTON is Professor of Philosophy at Wheaton College (Massachusetts). He is the editor of *The Principles of Social Order: Selected Essays of Lon L. Fuller*, and coeditor of *Gender and Public Policy* and *The Responsible Judge: Readings in Judicial Ethics*.

DANIEL E. WUESTE is Associate Professor of Philosophy at Clemson University. He was the director of the Conference on Professional Ethics and Social Responsibility at Clemson University, November 1991. He has published articles in *The Canadian Journal of Law and Jurisprudence*, *Cornell Law Review*, *Harvard Journal of Law and Public Policy*, and *The Southern Journal of Philosophy*.